THE PROFOUNDLY MENTALLY RETARDED

Charles C. Cleland

The University of Texas at Austin

PRENTICE-HALL, INC., ENGLEWOOD CLIFFS, NEW JERSEY 07632

Library of Congress Cataloging in Publication Data

CLELAND, CHARLES CARR.
The profoundly mentally retarded.

Bibliography: p.
Includes index.
1. Mentally handicapped. 2. Mentally handicapped—Care and treatment. 3. Mentally handicapped—Rehabilitation. I. Title.
HV3004.C52 362.3 79-1258
ISBN 0-13-729566-9

Printed in the United States of America

10 9 8 7 6 5 4 3 2 1

PRENTICE-HALL INTERNATIONAL, INC., London
PRENTICE-HALL OF AUSTRALIA PTY. LIMITED, Sydney
PRENTICE-HALL OF CANADA, LTD., Toronto
PRENTICE-HALL OF INDIA PRIVATE LIMITED, New Delhi
PRENTICE-HALL OF JAPAN, INC., Tokyo
PRENTICE-HALL OF SOUTHEAST ASIA PTE. LTD., Singapore
WHITEHALL BOOKS LIMITED, Wellington, New Zealand

c. 1

301-00031-6

Contents

Foreword

In some respects, the history of the care and treatment of handicapped persons in the United States is the history of court decisions, decisions based upon legal actions brought by parents of their handicapped children. And now the States have been mandated to provide free public education for all children, regardless of physical or mental handicap.

Public Law 94-142, "Education of All Handicapped Children Act," decrees that public schooling shall be open to any person between the ages of 3 and 21 years, regardless of severity of physical or mental defect. The intent of this legislation seems to be to expand, improve, and diversify special education opportunities for all handicapped children, including the profoundly mentally retarded. The point often missed, however, is that the various educational programs are to be constructed on the basis of children's <u>needs</u>. Moreover, most of these children must have individually tailored programs--programs designed to provide specific educational services, appropriate evaluation procedures, and annual goals, among other requirements.

How well equipped are we to write such educational programs for the profoundly mentally retarded? Is our knowledge of this handicapping condition such that we can easily fashion individually tailored programs for each profoundly retarded individual? The fact of the matter is that not only is the knowledge base scarce, but it is widely scattered throughout the professional and scientific literature. In no single source can one find critical reviews of the profound mental retardation literature and helpful and practical educational/training strategies to use with this group. The education of the profoundly mentally retarded represents a quantum leap from any child heretofore taught in the public schools of this country. Yet, by 1980, individualized educational plans must be in operation for all those who request them!

Recently, mental retardation experts have lamented the fact that professionals in the area were not interested in the lower intelligence levels and had to be taught--by the courts, by parents, and in some cases by the retarded themselves--that they should be interested in this lowest level of intelligence.

One professional did not wait to be told that he should be interested in the profoundly mentally retarded. Since the early 1960s, long before it was fashionable to be interested in these neglected human beings, Dr. Charles Carr Cleland was passionately interested in the profoundly mentally retarded. Over 15 years ago, he was lecturing on the profoundly mentally retarded in his courses at The University of Texas at Austin. In 1961 he carried out research on the profoundly retarded as a separate nosological group (publishing the results in 1962). In 1965, he began teaching a graduate seminar on the profoundly mentally retarded, the first such course offered anywhere in this country! With the emergence of the ethological approach of Lorenz, Von Frisch, and Tinbergen in this country, Professor Cleland saw in this paradigm an application for the wholistic study of the profoundly retarded.

As clearly expounded by Edward Zigler in his Foreword to Cleland's earlier book, <u>Mental Retardation: A Developmental Approach</u>, the ethological approach involves making careful and complete observations of organisms in their own natural habitats. One of the basic premises of ethology is that most behavior patterns exhibited promote survival of both the species and the member of the species exhibiting these behaviors. Some of the more atypical behaviors of the profoundly mentally retarded, behaviors that most observers view as pathological, may be the only way they can express some of their human needs. Employing the ethological paradigm, Professor Cleland has been able to show how this approach explains so much of the atypical behaviors of the profoundly retarded--behaviors that are adaptive within their physical and mental limitations.

In this, his latest book, Professor Cleland presents innovative and creative approaches to the care and education of that most misunderstood and under-researched human group--individuals who have intelligence quotients below 20, and who, at adulthood, attain a mental age of 3 years or less. Professor Cleland's suggestions are innovative yet practical, his proposed programs creative yet workable, his writing style speculative (and sometimes controversial) yet highly positive in approach. All of these characteristics combine to produce a most interesting book to read, and an extremely valuable one for promoting stimulating discussion in the classroom--and needed research in the laboratory and in the natural settings in which these individuals live out their all-too-short lives.

This textbook should prove to be of inestimable value to houseparents, nurses, teachers, administrators, recreational workers, and other persons working in institutional settings, as well as to special educators, psychologists, social workers, and other professionals involved with the profoundly mentally retarded outside of institutional settings.

JON D. SWARTZ

Brown Visiting Professor of Education and Psychology and Director of Testing and Guidance
Southwestern University
Georgetown, Texas

Preface

This text aims to bring together much of the scarce but growing literature on the profoundly mentally retarded--the smallest and most neglected subgroup within the mentally retarded. The intended audience includes all those currently working with the profoundly retarded and those preparing to do so. Social workers, special educators, school psychologists, physicians, dieticians, nurses, administrators, and recreation workers, in school or residential settings may find, in this brief text, ways to improve services to the profoundly retarded. For teachers or principals in public schools facing the challenge of P.L. 94-142, but lacking any substantial experiential or knowledge base relative to the profoundly retarded, this text may assist them in the implementation and design of programs. Throughout the book, I have attempted to convey an "attitude of mind" toward the profoundly retarded--specifically, one of optimism rather than despair.

Since our knowledge base is impoverished where the profoundly retarded are concerned, I have included both speculation and controversial content to stimulate discussion and generate research. This material is included since profound retardation, by definition, means "unfathomable" and, in large measure, we are ignorant of their wants, hopes, and fears. However, ignorance can be a powerful driving force and Hackerman (1974) has suggested that we inventory our ignorance. Thus, another objective of this text is to map some of the parameters of our ignorance relative to the profoundly retarded and to review some of the knowledge that does exist.

Since at least half of the profoundly retarded are institutionalized, a lion's share of the research consists of studies of the institutionalized profoundly retarded. This inescapable bias is reflected throughout the text. Another bias, purposeful on the author's part, is a heavy emphasis on the emotional or affective life of these nonverbal people. Every effort has been expended to chart a lifestyle for the profoundly retarded that is reflective of Maslow's need hierarchy, with emphasis on the higher order needs.

Finally, the principal objective of this brief text is to generate interest on the reader's part in this most neglected subgroup of retardates. As the reader will become aware, no single person or academic discipline possesses the sophistication or wisdom to fathom those we term unfathomable.

As an instructor using this book, you should know that profound mental retardation and PMR have been used interchangeably. Also, you may find the appendices helpful in tailoring exams and in generating class discussion.

I am indebted to my wife for her patience and encouragement, to Drs. Harry Powell and Victor Hinojosa for their willingness to listen to my questions, and to numerous attendants who work with the profoundly retarded. Thanks are also due Ann Shaughness for the typing of the manuscript and to Ted Jursek and Serena Hoffman of Prentice-Hall for their editorial and production assistance.

CHARLES CARR CLELAND

University of Texas at Austin

1

Introduction

In beginning the study of profound mental retardation, a few sobering quotations from some of the leading authorities of the twentieth century will serve to dramatize the challenge that lies ahead. Presenting the pessimistic views that have been so pervasive where profound retardation is concerned will allow us the remainder of the text to address more optimistic issues. Listen to what some who "have been there" have to say:

> They have eyes but they see not; ears, but they hear not; they have no intelligence and no consciousness of pleasure or pain; in fact, their mental state is one of entire negation. (Tredgold, 1937)

> They would be equally helpless and ill-adapted in a society of savants and in a society of savages. (Kanner, 1942)

> Those of profoundly deficient mentality are quite literally incapable of providing us with accounts of their past circumstances, their present predicaments, and their hopes and fears for the future. (MacAndrew, 1973)

> Left to his own resources, even in a grocery store, the

> profoundly retarded person dies within a matter of days of starvation if he does not meet with accidental death before that. (Bowman, 1968)

> Samuel, with an IQ of about 10, is so severely deficient that any other information about him becomes relatively meaningless; it matters comparatively little how stimulating his environment, for example, although of course the attitudes of those about him and the quality of his medical care affect his behavior to some extent. (Robinson & Robinson, 1965)

> They create symbols only rarely if at all, they sustain little culture, develop few rules of their own, evidence relatively little exploratory curiosity, and their interaction with one another is both minimal and peculiarly 'ahistorical.' (MacAndrew & Edgerton, 1964b)

At this point you may well ask, "Is the author of this text insensitive to the words of others, or does he merely have a peculiar penchant for wasting time?" The answer is neither. I am intrigued and challenged by the profoundly retarded and convinced that there is now enough empirical and clinical literature on this rare human group to bring together purposefully. I hope that readers of this brief text will also become sensitized to the challenge of the profoundly retarded. Until very recently, this group has not attracted much attention.

Where do we stand now in terms of alleviating the neglect these individuals have so long endured? During the past decade, a revolution occurred in care for the retarded. New concepts of care were introduced and changes in terminology were adopted in response to the emphases on de-labeling, normalization, deinstitutionalization, and humanization. "Idiot," long employed in the field, became "profound mental retardation," and other terms that had taken on a pejorative connotation were deleted from the lexicon of mental retardation. While this alteration of terminology had a salutory effect on many retarded individuals and their parents, the effect has been largely cosmetic for the profoundly retarded. Rights of the retarded have been extended. Many have championed the virtues of the retarded, and numerous advocates have spoken eloquently of the need to humanize, normalize, and mainstream. However, although some advances have occurred, the status of the profoundly retarded is still pretty much as MacAndrew described it in 1973: "when we descend from the celestial reaches of official rhetoric to an examination of everyday ward activities, we find that the ward remains essentially custodial in nature" (MacAndrew, 1973).

DISTINCTION BETWEEN PROFOUNDLY AND SEVERELY RETARDED

What is profound mental retardation, and in what ways does it differ from severe retardation? Usually, on standardized, individually administered intelligence tests or adaptive behavior scales the profoundly retarded will fall over 5 standard deviations below the norm, or in terms of intelligence quotients, below 19. The standard deviation on the Stanford-Binet and Cattell Scales is 16, and 15 on the Wechsler Scales. In profound retardation, there will rarely be any intelligible speech even at adulthood except for a few individuals who may say "mama" or "da-da." The profoundly retarded more frequently than severely retarded will manifest sensory, skeletal and other physical abnormalities. Often, sensory defects, skeletal anomalies, or other disabilities co-exist in profoundly retarded persons (Cleland & Clark, 1966; O'Grady & Talkington, 1976). Therefore, total life support is essential to their survival, and up to 40% of the profoundly retarded are either bedfast or semi-ambulatory (O'Grady & Talkington, 1976). From a standpoint of test administration, the profoundly retarded are incapable of responding, and the experienced clinical psychologist, neurologist or pediatrician can ordinarily recognize this level of retardation without tests (Grossman, 1977). Kennedy, almost 40 years ago, indicated "In this category it is, with care and knowledge, impossible to be mistaken in either diagnosis or prognosis" (1942). Today, the prognosis for the profoundly retarded is a bit more uncertain, for reasons given in later chapters.

In contrast to the profoundly retarded, the severely retarded by adolescence will manifest some useful speech in most instances. Most severely retarded will attain adult mental ages of around years 3½-4 whereas profoundly retarded mental age attainment will ordinarily cluster at about 2 or 2½ years. Intelligence quotients in severe retardation range between 20 to 35 and most experienced clinicians and researchers acknowledge that the distinction between profound and severe retardation is of value in research, grouping or placement, and in program planning. The severely retarded less often have multihandicaps and their life span is longer (Cleland & Patton, 1965).

Among certain research and professional workers in the field of mental retardation, there is a tendency to lump the profound and severe levels of retardation together for purposes of research or placement (O'Grady & Talkington, 1976). This is an indefensible practice and most who are experienced with both categories adhere to Grossman's (1977) distinction of profound _and_ severe. Individual differences are manifest at every level of intelligence, and even in the narrow IQ band of 0-19 some profoundly retarded are more capable than others (Cleland, Rago & Mukherjee, 1978). The specification of four levels of mental retardation has proven useful and humane as well. In the past, institutions often housed together residents having an IQ range from a hypothetical 1 to 50. Needless to say, those we currently term profoundly retarded were often bullied and mistreated by the higher level retardates. For those workers who tend to group profound and severe together with the implication that "below IQ 35 what difference does it make?" this writer would respond, "A great deal."

Other dangers inhere in grouping these two levels together for research purposes unless a valid reason exists, such as comparing the two groups on motor performance or learning tasks. There is the danger that parents of profoundly retarded may be led to believe that their profoundly retarded child should be accomplishing at the rate of the severely retarded. Failure to clearly distinguish between the two levels can thus, inadvertently, lead parents to unrealistic expectations.

For these reasons, studies reviewed throughout this text will be restricted to those that give full information on the subject's descriptive characteristics. Some authors merely state, "The subject(s) was profoundly retarded" and give no IQs, SQs, or other essential data. Without more detailed subject information, other investigators cannot replicate a study (Cleland & Rago, 1978). Many studies have recently appeared that include profound retardation in the article's title when, on closer reading, the subjects are mostly _or all_ severely retarded. In the chapters ahead, we will come to a fuller appreciation of why precision is so important if we are to advance the welfare of the profoundly retarded.

OCCURRENCE AND LOCATION OF THE PROFOUNDLY RETARDED

The profoundly retarded, like geniuses, are rare in number. In 1964, MacAndrew and Edgerton estimated that only about 100,000 of the total United States' population were profoundly retarded. Extrapolating from this estimate to allow for population growth, a reasonable current estimate might range between 130,000 to 150,000--still an insignificant fraction of our population. Figured another way, and based on Mercer's (1973) 1% model, the current estimated number in the United States would be only 110,000. However, Bowman (1968) points out that sulphonamides discovered in 1937, penicillin in the early forties, and other potent antibiotics are now saving the very fragile, who in earlier times would have perished. Thus, the prevalence rate of profounds, which includes both new and old cases, would in all likelihood reach a total of 130,000 or 150,000.

MacAndrew and Edgerton (1964b) also revealed where the profoundly retarded are located--half their number live in institutions. It is also known that of all levels of the retarded who are institutionalized, the profoundly retarded are institutionalized earliest, are least often visited or receive furloughs, and die at the earliest age (Cleland, 1978).

Because of the rarity of the profoundly retarded, little is known about the estimated 50% who are not institutionalized. If the noninstitutionalized persons live in their own homes, one could speculate on their circumstances. If the profoundly retarded person were a couple's first child, it would be somewhat reasonable to hypothesize that such a child would likely become an only child. This is not to say that such is, in fact, the case but only to suggest that the enormous and easily detectable defect(s) would discourage many from further attempts to have children. A further speculation may well be that the only child who is profoundly retarded and lives at home could be, rather naturally, peer deprived. This too is predicated on the fact that such a grossly retarded child would, at any age, have difficulty attracting neighborhood companions, and in addition, parents would tend to be more shielding or guarding where retardation is of profound level. Again, one could speculate that the profoundly retarded child living at home would be more apt to be semiambulatory or bedfast. This is based on the knowledge that ambulatory profoundly retarded would likely overwhelm parental vigilance, because they can be destructive of self or objects, albeit not necessarily with malicious intent. Another speculation might be that his or her parents are separated or divorced, and the likelihood would be that mother, not father, is caring for the child. Finally, it would be anticipated that mother, father or both would be characterized by a zealous dedication to the child.

> Mrs. Jones, a 66-year-old divorcee, lives in a small, four-room home with her 25-year-old son, Bill--a bedfast, profoundly retarded person. Bill, who was born when Mrs. Jones was 41, is totally helpless and has never been capable of any intelligible speech. Bill's father and mother divorced three years subsequent to his birth, but the father continues to send enough money for the support of his ex-wife and child.
>
> Mrs. Dexter, a social worker with the State Welfare Department, was recently sent to visit on the request of Mrs. Jones. Mrs. Jones' health had become progressively worse and she was worried about Bill's future should she become dependent herself. Institutionalization was ultimately decided upon as the only recourse. Mrs. Dexter noted in her visitation report, "It's amazing! Mrs. Jones has literally been on 24-hour duty for 25 years. Her entire life has gone to Bill."
>
> About three months after Mrs. Dexter's visit, Bill was admitted to the __________ State School. Exactly two months after admission, Bill succumbed and about a month after burying Bill, Mrs. Jones died.

In Bowman's (1968) words, "the existence of the profoundly retarded youngster is one of the greatest human tragedies, and perhaps the severest blow that could be dealt to a parent." The above case is true and aside from illustrating human tragedy, it shows how change of environment is so poorly endured by the profoundly retarded.

The foregoing speculations about the noninstitutionalized portion of the profoundly retarded are <u>only speculations</u>--the bulk of our limited knowledge about the profounds derives from research on institutionalized samples. It is evident that research on the noninstitutionalized is needed.

Knobloch and Lilienfeld (1956) introduced the concept of a continuum of reproductive failure. Simply put, at one extreme of reproductive failure something goes badly awry in either the germinal, embryonic, or fetal stage of prenatal life and death occurs. A somewhat less extreme failure, in that they are occasionally born alive, is the gross maldevelopment of anencephalic children (literally, having no brain). Such medical monstrosities as anencephaly and cyclops (having one median eye, or two eyes fused into one [Dorland, 1951]) are usually stillborn though not always. At a lesser level of insult, the child may be viable but of profound mental defect and, where all goes well in development, we find a normal, viable child. Thus, when viewed against Knobloch and Lilienfeld's continuum of reproductive failure and where the insult occurred during prenatal life, the profoundly retarded are those who "barely made it." If some trauma such as anoxia, birth injury, or encephalitis renders a child profoundly retarded, he will still remain a fragile human and have a shorter than average life expectancy.

Well over 200 causes of mental retardation have been identified, and of the four levels of retardation (mild, moderate, severe and profound), it is unlikely that any other level would have as varied an etiological representation as the profoundly retarded. In a recent unpublished study by Cleland, Manaster and Case, over 10,000 institutionalized profoundly retarded cases were analyzed. This data, as of 1977, reflected that 74.39% were diagnosed as organics, 20.9% were of unknown etiology, 3.06 due to presumed psychosocial deprivation (formerly called familial or "garden variety"), and 1.65 classified as "other." It was interesting to note, although hardly surprising, that the unknown etiology was employed less frequently at the profound level and largest (by almost 10%) at the mild level of retardation. More specifically, of 787 cases of profound retardation taken from one institution, 225 were due to presumed psychosocial disadvantage, 125 cases were due to chromosomal abnormality, 175 were of unknown cause, and the remaining cases scattered widely over the various etiologies, for example, due to infections and intoxications, gross brain disease (postnatal), and so forth. The most interesting feature of these various institutions' data was seen in the diagnostic variations. For example, one large institution gave 7.25% of their profoundly retarded an etiology of "due to presumed psychosocial deprivation" (cultural-familial); five large institutions recorded 0% in that diagnostic classification. Speaking only of the profoundly retarded, one institution recorded that 60.63% of all cases were of unknown etiology! In the classification "organic" etiology, for the profoundly retarded only, the range of percentages was from a low of 22.9 to a healthy 99.03! Truly the assignment of a specific diagnostic or etiological classification is a complex undertaking and, since autopsies are only rarely performed on institutionalized retardates (or noninstitutionalized retardates either), it seems apparent that the classification "other" (formerly unknown) will remain widely used.

For readers unfamiliar with or desirous of gaining greater knowledge of the wide variety of etiologies in mental retardation, Grossman (1977) is the established authority.

DEATH AND LONGEVITY IN PROFOUND RETARDATION

It has already been mentioned that the profoundly retarded are among the most fragile of all humans. In one study involving 32,691 cases, it was learned that the average age of death was about 38 (Cleland & Patton, 1965). As is true of the larger U.S. society, female PMRs outlive males. While medical advances, improved diets and dental care have undoubtedly lengthened the life span of the profoundly retarded relative to those who were institutionalized a 100 years ago, they are still the shortest-lived of any intellectual level. In Miller's (1975) study of mortality trends in PMRs, he indicated, "Attaining an age over 40 is no mean accomplishment for a member of this group whereas IQ over 20 is predictive of a much improved life span" (p. 2). There is no evidence that contradicts Miller's assertion that PMRs have an abbreviated life span relative to other intellectual levels. Of greater interest perhaps is "What causes their death?" Table 1-1 below provides answers to this question. As can be seen, these mortality figures differ in major ways from the mortality statistics for the United States as a whole. Notable, for example, is the absence of cancer as a cause of death in the profoundly retarded (a clue for cancer researchers?). Another interesting aspect of Table 1-1 is that food aspiration accounted for 41 of the total 660 deaths or fully 3½%! This is much higher than for the population at large (Cleland, Powell & Talkington, 1971). More recently, Robert Chaney, a California physician, has studied respiratory disorders in a large sample of profoundly

Table 1-1

Fourteen Major Causes of Death

Cause	N	Male	Female	$\bar{M}$ Death Age	Range	Percent
Pneumonia	241	165	76	17.30	1-62	36.5
Myocarditis	59	38	21	25.07	2-62	8.9
Cardiac Failure	59	42	17	20.52	1-57	8.9
Tuberculosis	56	34	22	26.20	12-55	8.4
Epilepsy	29	18	11	14.85	4-30	4.4
Influenza	24	15	9	15.41	7-50	3.6
Food Aspiration	23	18	5	18.73	6-33	3.5
Dysentery (Shigella)	18	12	6	16.78	3-51	2.6
Coronary Occlusion	17	12	5	25.52	7-68	2.5
Accidental Deaths	11	7	4	28.45	15-51	1.6
Septicemia	10	5	5	16.70	3-29	1.5
Intracranial Pressure	8	4	4	9.75	1-31	1.2
Secondary Anemia	7	7	0	17.85	7-36	1.0
Asphyxiation	7	5	2	18.28	7-35	1.0
TOTALS	660	382	278	20.33	1-68	85.6

retarded and concluded that predisposing factors such as large tongues (in Cretins), epilepsy, being bedfast help account for the very large number who succumb due to respiratory disorders (Chaney, 1978).

Although, as Grossman (1977) indicates, the skilled clinical psychologist, pediatrician, or neurologist can ordinarily recognize profound retardation without the use of tests, there are exceptions. The major mimic of profound mental retardation would likely be severe early childhood autism (ECA), although those having congenital deafness or congenital aphasia may also occasionally be misdiagnosed as PMR. In Table 1-2, it is easy to note symptom overlap between PMR, SMR and early childhood autism.

Table 1-2

Comparative Chart of Symptom Overlap Among Profound Mental Retardation, Severe Mental Retardation, and Autism

Characteristic or Symptom	PMR	SMR	Autistics
String-Twirling	*	*	*
Pica	**	*	*
Whirling	*	*	*
Sleep Disorders	*	*	*
Mutism	**	*	*
Self-Biting	**	*	*
Echolalia (if words present)	*	*	*
Echophraxia	*	*	*
Fecal Smearing	**	*	*
Public Masturbation	**	*	*
Puberty Delayed	***	**	*
Many Enjoy Travel (quieting to them)	*	*	*
Tool-Use (Doll; Cleland-Rago)	*	*	*
Left-Handed (> than normals)	**	*	*
Head-Banging	*	*	*
Rocking	*	*	*
Flapping Hands	*		*
Toe-Walking	*		*
Self-Recognition (often lacking)	**	*	*
Found in All Cultures	*	*	*
Frequently Instititionalized	**	*	*
Rumination	**	*	*
Seizures Common	***	**	**
Gaze Aversion	*	*	**
Abnormal EEGs (oft-noted)	**	*	*
Hyperactivity (oft-noted)	*	*	*

Table 1-2 (cont.)

Characteristic or Symptom	PMR	SMR	Austistics
Scant Attention Paid Others	**	*	**
Enuresis	***	*	*
Encopresis	***	*	*
Hand-Regard	*		*
Pain Thresholds Appear High	**	*	*
Reliance on Proximal Senses (Rimland)	*	?	*

*** = Frequent
** = Not Uncommon
* = Occurrence Not Pronounced

Since most tests of intelligence ordinarily employed are of questionable value when the subject is nonverbal, a differential diagnosis between similar-appearing conditions will depend on other considerations. A positive diagnosis of either PMR or ECA will entail dedicated observation in natural and clinical settings and an extremely detailed history of the child's behavior from birth on. That diagnostic errors do occur is occasionally revealed in the conduct of research.

SPEECH: THE UNEXPECTED

On rare occasions, employees and researchers working with the profoundly retarded encounter cognitive dissonance when a profoundly retarded person speaks an intelligible sentence. Obviously, the major explanation would be a misdiagnosis since sentences from the profoundly retarded are not considered possible. Let's examine one example of this unexpected behavior and then entertain a little speculation about why the <u>speaker</u> became mute.

> In a study of simulated aggression toward profoundly retarded adults, notations were made of avoidance responses or in ethological terms, appeasement gestures, of these adults having mental ages below three (Cleland, Altman & Swartz, 1971). The author, serving as the experimenter, elicited appeasement gestures (smiling, etc.) and aggression--being struck in the eye by one subject. Near the end of the subject run, the experimenter encountered one

of the final subjects and simulated aggression was instituted (running rapidly toward subject). Clearly and distinctly, when the experimenter was within two feet of the subject, the subject said, "They won't hurt you, honey." The school director and several houseparents, who were observing, were shocked in disbelief. The subject who was 26 years old and had been institutionalized for over 9 years had never been known to utter a single word and his level of intellectual functioning was listed on entry and all subsequent intellectual re-evaluations as "profoundly mentally retarded." His sentence length and word order clearly indicated him to be well out of the profound level of retardation--in effect, he "confessed" to being an imposter. The immediate increase in interest and attention showered on this resident by houseparents was truly dramatic and the subject, incorrectly admitted, was later placed in a more appropriate training facility. Emotional problems, of very early origins, apparently obscured his true intellectual level and potential. But how?

One clue to this question arises by reference to Erikson's (1963) "Eight Ages of Man." The first developmental emotional hurdle encountered, according to Erikson, is Trust vs. Mistrust. Gradually, the infant through ministrations of maternal care such as feeding, soft vocalizations, and various comforts provided to him builds up an expectation of mother's predictability and certainty. This is the infant's first demonstration of social trust. In the prevention of <u>physical</u> problems, good medical care involves a variety of laboratory tests (blood, urine, etc.) and innoculations to prevent certain contagious diseases. Let us speculate as to why our subject became mute. Suppose as an infant he possessed good or even superior intellectual potential and had meaningfully employed words as early as nine months (some children do), and had a mother who was somewhat cold and rejecting. Thus, social mistrust was somewhat ascendant over basic trust. It is tempting to speculate that on his first visit for immunizations our subject, immediately prior to the pain of the shot, heard mother say, "They won't hurt you, honey." Conceivably, "They won't hurt you, honey" plus the almost instantaneous pain established, beyond doubt, mistrust at a very basic level. Our infant's subsequent withdrawal from human contact seems to uphold this line of reasoning.

Erikson suggests as much when he states, "In psychopathology the absence of basic trust can best be studied in infantile schizophrenia" (p. 248). In the case under consideration, although a definitive diagnosis was not given on admission, there seems little doubt that a serious emotional problem was at least partly responsible for the intellectual handicap and long years of mutism. That a state of high arousal, years after becoming mute, was necessary to reinstate speech has been noted even among talking birds. Lorenz, the pioneer ethologist and Nobel Laureate, describes a crow that learned a complete sentence on hearing it only once. The occasion entailed a great fright and pain to the bird. The sentence, "Got'em in t'bloomin' trap!" was remembered, Lorenz indicated, because the crow heard it at a moment of great excitement--immediately after being caught (Lorenz, 1952). If true of birds who speak, it would appear even more plausible of humans. While my interpretation is speculative, the incident was real. The subject had been in several institutions for the retarded and in no records had speech ever been noted. To coin a Thorndikian phrase, ideas or words can be "stamped-in or out" and once <u>out</u>, it seems in certain instances that only a similarly high level of arousal will again occasion the expression of a long dormant response. The following figure graphically illustrates the foregoing case.

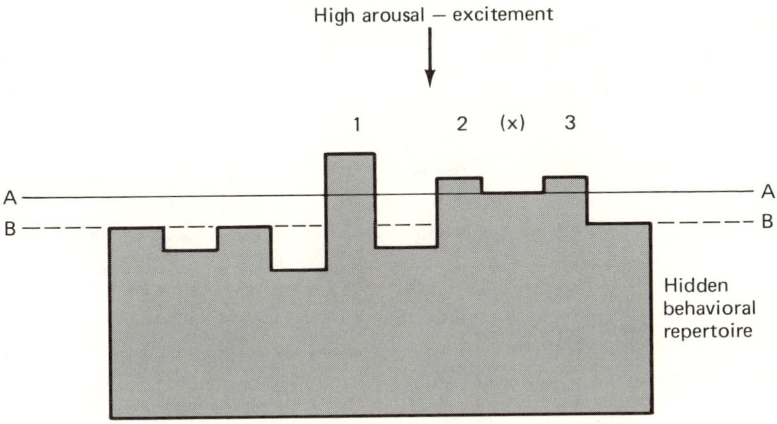

A = Previous prearousal level showing what behaviors are *usually* seen
B = Level subsequent to high arousal revealing other behaviors
(x) = Speech revealed as existing in hidden behavior

Figure 1. Arousal template.

What this example illustrates is that possibly even an innoculation can cause some individuals prolonged withdrawal, and preparation and care must be exercised by parent and physician alike. It also demonstrates how interdependent intellectual functioning can be on social or emotional events. Every child, especially the very young, needs emotional support to insure the first developmental hurdle will be met with a very basic social trust. As Erikson indicates, it is not the quantity of love or food but the quality of the relationship with the mother.

The foregoing case illustrates that under high arousal, an imposter in the PMR ranks "confessed" that his true diagnosis was something other than PMR. Are there other oblique approaches to differential diagnosis?

> A novel study by Rosenhan (1973) revealed that in the context of a psychiatric residential facility, normal people posing as patients were not detected as sane by the hospital staff. One reason cited by Rosenhan for the failure of staff to identify these pseudopatients was that "once labeled schizophrenic, the pseudopatient was stuck with that label" (p. 252). Furthermore, failure to identify imposters was neither attributable to the quality of the hospitals nor to insufficient time for observing the pseudopatients' behavior. "Finally, it cannot be said that the failure to recognize the pseudopatients' sanity was due to the fact that they were not behaving sanely" (p. 252). The really intriguing aspect of Rosenhan's study is that it contains the germ of an idea to improve our diagnostic tools. How?
>
> Rosenhan's own words suggest a novel approach to differential diagnosis. For example, a severely autistic child may exhibit many symptoms of the profoundly retarded, and institutionalization in the wrong place occurs. Years later, under strong arousal, he may verbally reveal the diagnostic error--in a sense, "confess" that he is not truly profoundly retarded (Cleland, Altman & Swartz, 1971). In his study, Rosenhan (1973) writes:
>
>> It was quite common for the real patients to "detect" the pseudopatients' sanity. During the first three hospitalizations, when accurate counts were kept, 35 of a total of 118 patients...voiced their suspicions, some vigorously. "You're not crazy. You're a journalist, or a professor (referring to the continual note-taking). You're checking up on the hospital...." The fact that the patients often recognized normality when staff did not raises important questions. (p. 252)

One important question not addressed by Rosenhan, but one that crossed the author's mind was, "Could schizophrenics be experimentally employed as diagnosticians?" In the profoundly retarded (nonverbal) wards of State schools for the mentally retarded, one occasionally and accidentally discovers an autistic "imposter" in retarded clothing (Cleland, Altman & Swartz, 1971). Some patients do get erroneously labeled and may spend years in the wrong company. Recognition of patients' apparent diagnostic acuity suggests that patients might be employed as diagnostic aides.

If we descend to monkeys in the phyletic order, a related diagnostic phenomenon is noted in Pratt and Sackett's (1967) study involving a sociometric test with monkeys. Three groups of infant monkeys were subjected to three different rearing conditions. One group was provided full contact and interaction, another received only visual and auditory contact, while a third group was reared in total isolation. Using an ingenious sociometric apparatus, the authors determined that peer preferences were directed toward monkeys similarly reared from infancy; that is, "like seeks like." From their results, it was clear that socially abnormal monkeys preferred other abnormals, and socially normal monkeys chose not to approach abnormals.

Perhaps the old cliche, "It takes one to know one," contains a grain of truth. As a test, one could select only those mental patients who have demonstrated a keen knack of spotting imposters, that is, "normals." Next, these "diagnosticians" could be transported to a school for the mentally retarded. A visit to a ward housing the profoundly retarded would be arranged and these instructions given: "Pick out a child (or adult) you'd most like to take back to the hospital." In the event several _known_ autistic children were "planted," one would predict from Rosenhan's and Pratt and Sackett's work a preference for the autistic children as opposed to the organically profoundly retarded. Should the experimental use of patients in diagnostic work be supported, some might be so employed on a paid basis and perhaps hastened on their way to recovery. Conceivably such an arrangement could be of mutual benefit to both types of patients.

Regarding the experimental approach to differential diagnosis, a further hint appears in Deane and Ansbacher's (1962) finding of therapy enhancement as a function of attendant-patient commonality of background. The logistics, ethics, and potential gain from such an oblique approach to diagnosis require study. Getting the job done, however, may be accelerated if we inventory our ignorance as Hackerman (1974) suggests.

A fanciful and needless speculation--schizophrenic diagnosticians? Perhaps, but since there is still room for diagnostic refinement, let's entertain some other untried approaches. A clue is afforded by examination of Table 2-1 in Chapter 2. Sleep and bio-rhythms have scarcely been addressed as research topics in mental retardation, yet we spend about a third of life in a sleep state. Although highly improbable, altered states of awareness afford one possible situation where, say, a PMR could "confess" to being an imposter, if indeed he was. When either a profoundly retarded or a severely autistic person requires surgery and a general anesthetic is given, we have another chance to learn if these nonverbals have any hidden speech. When normal individuals are under anesthesia and are in the recovery room, occasionally some become quite loquacious and some will even sing. Ordinarily, surgeons or anesthesiologists will be too preoccupied to play psychologist or psychiatrist, even though informed that their patient is mute. However, when surgery is necessary, it would appear advisable to have a parent or attendant in the recovery room with a tape recorder to pick up any sounds made by the patient. The observer should also be alert to any other behaviors that are revealing of something not previously exhibited. This suggestion has the aim of giving us yet another window to the person's mental life.

It is also known that some people talk, often quite distinctly, during sleep (Kleitman, 1972). Although it is highly improbable that those classified as profoundly retarded will have any speech of recognizable quality, observations supplemented by concealed tape recorders should be made to determine with greater assurance that indeed there is no speech. The institutionalized profoundly retarded (and those living at home also) are under almost constant surveillance during waking hours (MacAndrew, 1973). This is not the case during the hours of sleep as everyone knows but, as sleep researchers also know, behavior does occur during rest. Thus, to be truly certain that a person does not speak would require that it is true for 24 hours daily--not just in an awake state.

Over a number of years, I have questioned numerous houseparents with one question, "When do the profoundly retarded seem to babble or try harder to communicate more?" Usually, after some reflection, they would answer, "When they're sick." While this is scarcely very convincing "evidence," sickness does tend to bestow more dependence on others to "help me!"

Avoiding misdiagnosis is an important consideration when we are confronting nonverbal individuals. The suggestions offered are untried and are merely designed to engage readers' thinking on indirect approaches to differential diagnosis. Readers desiring a fuller discussion of traditional diagnostic and assessment procedures should consult standard psychiatric or psychological works on mental retardation.

SUMMARY

Thus far, we have learned what a number of authorities consensually agree upon as the prognosis for the profoundly retarded. Something of their nature has been described and it was indicated they pose a challenge of a high order indeed. Their rarity in number (approximately 130,000-150,000 in the U.S.) and their location (half or more in institutions) was indicated. It was also suggested that a more heterogeneous etiological array is likely among the profoundly retarded than at any other level of mental retardation, and death comes relatively soon for these fragile people.

The most important point of this initial chapter, at least in my view, is that the profoundly retarded are different from the severely retarded. It is hoped that the remainder of this brief text will convince the skeptic of this. The difference between the two levels, however, can be understood more readily than by reading this book. A visit to an institution having both profound and severely retarded should be more impressive and convincing. As Confucius put it, "A picture is worth a thousand words."

2

Beyond Deficit Needs—Up to Emotions

Recently, an experienced professional in mental retardation stopped by the office for a brown-bag lunch and "gabfest." During the discussion, my friend, Mr. Leath, became quite serious and asked, "If you think back to the level of sophistication of caring for PMRs 15 years ago and compare it with what you see today, do you see much difference?" I started to respond but was interrupted with "I mean aside from nicer buildings and lots more houseparents do you see much difference in programs, etc." I was forced to confess that "basically, things aren't much different." Ellis (1963) gave one reason for this "snail's pace" of progress with the profoundly retarded: "As the child's behavior capacity deviates from normal, the methods used with normal children become increasingly less appropriate." Another reason that could be advanced is that the grossly deviant behaviors observed in the profoundly retarded of any life age so overwhelm our social and cultural overlearnings that we are blinded to whatever their strange behaviors are trying to tell us. In this respect, we are going against a built-in headwind. Consider the following case and remember, it is one thing to read about bizarre behavior but quite another order of magnitude to actually see the behavior.

What Did Professor _________ Recommend?

R. G. is an adolescent, ambulatory male whose social age was 1.4 years and whose social quotient was 11 when last tested on the Vineland Social Maturity Scale (Doll, 1953b). He was referred to Professor _________ because his self-abusive behavior had reached the point where the school's director said, "I'm at my wits end, and my staff members can't solve R. G.'s problem, and we are ready to throw in the towel!"

Professor _________ had had many challenging cases from the profoundly retarded ranks but R. G. was somewhat of a novelty in self-abuse. Essentially, although he displayed some head-banging, the main problems were his intractable habit of sticking objects into his penis and pulling out his toenails. Insertion of matchsticks, buttons and even a mattress spring into his penis was presenting a major medical problem and infection that had developed was, due to repeated re-injury, worsening.

In his attempts to nail down the possible underylying motivation for such behavior, Professor _________ elicited the following information from R. G.'s most experienced houseparent. First, on direct questioning, Professor _________ learned that the frequency of self-injurious behavior increased when R. G. was provided 1 to 1 attention. Somewhat ironically, the Professor also teased out that R. G.'s frequency of self-abusive behavior was quite high during the hours of 11:00 p.m. to 7:00 a.m. Inquiry regarding houseparent turnover revealed a "revolving door" situation--extremely heavy turnover. R. G., of course, cannot verbalize his wants or needs to his caretakers and only grunts or squeals.

On the basis of this limited information, write out an individualized plan of solving R. G.'s problems that would include some of the proposals Professor _________ made to the school's authorities.

The foregoing case clearly illustrates how divergent from normal behavior the profoundly retarded can be.

Omissions in the research literature can sometimes illustrate quite dramatically how we inadvertently overlook certain potentially important research topics. For example, numerous mental retardation authorities have indicated the retarded are more anxious and subject to more frustrations than are normal individuals. Most studies on anxiety in the retarded have been conducted with the mildly retarded--those usually having as their etiology "MR due to presumed psychosocial disadvantage." If the mildly retarded are, in fact, more anxious than normals, then we could surmise the profoundly retarded would be even more so. Emotional stress or chronic anxiety could augment the likelihood of the retarded developing some psychosomatic disorder. Yet, when we scan the textbooks on mental retardation or the research literature, there is an almost total absence of any reference to psychosomatic disorders in the retarded and none, to my knowledge, on the profoundly retarded. Asthma, obesity, peptic ulcers, anorexia nervosa are thought by many to have psychic or stress-related origins. Selye (1946) discusses how the organism relates to a wide array of stressors of acute or chronic nature by activating physiological defense mechanisms. If too acute or prolonged, actual structural changes can occur. As you are already aware, the profoundly retarded are fragile people and have no immunity from stress, frustrations, or anxiety. From this brief discussion of psychosomatic disorders and the curious lack of research on the subject with the profoundly retarded, one might conclude that professionals think the PMRs are "too cognitively out of it" to acquire a psychosomatic disorder. Readers interested in stress-related illnesses in the retarded can find further reading on the subject in Cleland, Sluyter and Rago (1977).

Another omission relates to sex, and it is true that sex has gotten in our way. Reference here is to the fact that our social-cultural taboos have, until about 20 years ago, kept institutionalized PMRs from having both mother and father surrogates. Male PMRs, once postpubertal, were deposited into a monastic existence. Because of their now visibly developed primary and often secondary sexual characteristics and the fact they often spurned wearing clothes, female houseparents were "spared this terrible sight." Both professionals and attendants reinforced this, avoiding putting a female attendant in with "grown" men who would exhibit themselves. For, if a female attendant whose "boys" had become "men" wanted to remain with her boys, others would think and often say "loose woman--female voyeur!" For male attendants (father surrogates) it was, and still is, common institutional practice that they never work on a female ward regardless of the PMRs' age. The only man with carte blanche to be on female wards is the physician.

The author, nearly three decades ago, was an institutional psychometrist. When the person to be tested was PMR and female, it was often required that I take test materials to the ward rather than the usual practice of having the resident brought to the psychology office. At that period of time, patient helpers of mild level worked on all PMR wards. Aside from the usual bed making, cleaning chores, etc., the attendants used helpers as "spotters" to let them know who and what was approaching the ward. As I would approach a female ward, the spotter helper-patient or a low-ranking employee would scream out, "Man coming to door" or, if the ward door was unlocked (a rarity) and I entered to wait in the vestibule, "MAN ON THE WARD!"

Although institutionalized retarded persons would appear to need both mother and father surrogates for sex-role models and other reasons, it is curious that in ERA days, male attendants are seldom seen to be employed on female wards.

At another level, namely research on the PMR, it is of interest that most of the research has been conducted by males. Also, most has been done with institutionalized subjects and mostly, they are males. This points up the need in PMR research to give additional attention to female samples. This is so because until fairly recently, women PhDs and MDs were reasonably rare. And, because of taboos "guarding" the security of the female wards, researchers studied those easiest to get to--males. The great bulk of literature on the profoundly retarded then has focused on males and on institutionalized samples. Needed are more studies focusing on both sexes and with a balance between institutionalized and noninstitutionalized samples. Finally, providing the institutionalized PMR, male or female, with both mother and father surrogates would appear to foster normal child-rearing practices and to offer fundamental help in establishing of sex-role identity in PMRs.

What do researchers choose to study when the PMR is their focal interest? In Berkson and Landesman-Dwyer's (1977) review article on "Behavioral Research on Severe and Profound Mental Retardation" covering the years 1955 to 1974, several hundred references were given. Table 2-1 below reflects the major interest topics based on the number of studies cited.

From an examination of Table 2-1, if we consider that aggression can be intrapunitive (directed against self) or extrapunitive (directed toward others or objects),

Table 2-1

Index of Behavioral Researchers' Interests

Research Topics	Number of Studies
Elimination of Stereotyped Behaviors	25
Modeling-Imitation Learning	16
Problems Associated with Eating-Drinking	14
Elimination of Self-Stimulation	14
Elimination of Self-Injurious Behaviors	13
Measurement of Adaptive Behavior	10
Ethological-Based Studies	10
Effects of Music	9
Inducing Self-Help Skills	9
Communication Skills	8
Rumination, Vomiting	7
Programming	6
Eye-Fixation-Conditioning	6
Building Design	5
Control of Aggression	4
Improving Ambulation	4
Developing Motor Skills	4
Sleep and Bio-Rhythms	3
Mortality-Longevity	3
Use of Tools in Problem Solving	3
Theoretical	3
Games-Toys	3
Pica Elimination	2
Psychosis in PMR	2
Gustatory Processes	1
Dental Problems	1
Depth Perception in PMR	1
Pain Reactions	1
Extinction of Exhibitionism	1
Speech Training	1
Sensory Deprivation in PMR	1

"self-injurious" studies plus "control of aggression" account for 17, or the second highest total. Let's examine aggression in greater depth. It deserves our continued research and professional interest.

Rago (1976), Cleland (1978), and other investigators have characterized the social interactions of the profoundly retarded as highly aggressive in nature. Direct evidence of the effects of aggression in the institutionalized PMR is readily observed via physical inspection for scars, bites (Butterworth & Bower, 1959), bruises (MacAndrew & Edgerton, 1964b), and so forth, and indirectly by noting the frequency of injury reports filed in the master records. Some injuries incurred, of course, are due to the high incidence of epilepsy among profoundly retarded persons. Nonetheless, the two basic forms of aggression, extrapunitive (outward aggression) and intrapunitive (aggression turned on oneself) are quite a concern for individuals who work with this population. What are some events or situations that induce aggression and how can it be minimized?

One possible reason aggression is high relates to the oft-noted impairment in one or several of the special senses (Cleland & Clark, 1966; O'Grady & Talkington, 1976). In addition to impairment of sight, smell, touch, taste and hearing in a large number of the profoundly retarded (relative to normals), there is the thought among many workers that the PMR, relative to normals, have a higher threshold for pain. Although most literature on the subject of pain perception is clinical-anecdotal rather than empirical, it is likely that quite a number of PMRs do have differentially elevated pain thresholds. If so, would the higher pain threshold argue for a lower threshold for aggressive behavior? Possibly, since the person who perceives pain easily (low pain threshold) might be expected to be more cautious about attacking another person, that is, he or she has learned that attack yields counterattack and subsequently, pain. Alternatively, failure to respond quickly to a painful stimulus, especially when the person is profoundly retarded, could be due to an extremely delayed response--a not uncommon occurrence among the retarded (Baumeister & Kellas, 1968). Thus, if a PMR touched a hot surface, did not remove his hand until a caretaker paid notice and removed it, it is possible (though speculative) that the perception of pain could register a minute or even five minutes subsequent to the stimulation. If this does occasionally occur, it would be easy for direct-care or professionals alike to be duped into the belief that PMRs "don't feel pain."

I would favor the hypothesis that some PMRs have very high pain thresholds. It would seem reasonable to include the hypothesis "a high pain threshold would argue for a low threshold for aggression" as one index as to why aggression is commonly seen in the profoundly retarded. It should be clearly understood, however, that individual differences in pain thresholds, as among normals, do exist in PMRs.

Another possible cause of high aggression in the PMR ranks could be related to various aspects of feeding or eating. Both frequency of feeding and the spacing of individuals (distance from others) during meals could augment aggressive behavior. In the literature on animal behavior (Hinde, 1970) food deprivation frequently leads to heightened aggression. In Key's, et al. (1950) classic study of the effects of semi-starvation on conscientious objectors in W. W. II, similar effects were noted. Irritability, crankiness, and the disappearance of humor were all observed in these men who were maintained on a diet of only about 1,500 calories daily. When Watson (1973) provided profoundly retarded males (SQ range 9-16; CA range 16-20) six minimeals instead of the customary "3-square," she found that although caloric intake was unchanged, her subjects gained weight and their behaviors unexpectedly improved. Her study more closely approximates the demand feeding of normal infants and shows, in some ways, the PMR late adolescent and young adults (with infantile mental ages) appear to manifest similar feeding needs.

Hunger among the profoundly retarded could, if not directly, indirectly augment aggression. Since they are dependent on others for food and unable to tell us "I'm hungry," we may inadvertently miscue. If so, and hunger exists in some, activity levels would increase. For, as Wald (1965) concluded from a review of the literature from protozoa to man, "the universal sign of hunger...is increased activity" (p. 38). Thus, in mass living settings such as institutions or in the public school class, heightened activity would also increase the likelihood of body contact and possible injury to others. While only an indirect, rather than a direct cause of aggression, hunger's occurrence among the PMR should be avoided. That activity levels among the profoundly retarded are cyclic in nature has been noted by Kaufman and Levitt (1965) and Cleland, McGavern and Case (1976). In the Kaufman and Levitt study, activity levels increased just prior to lunch and Cleland, et al. noted that night disturbances occurred during a period of relative food deprivation, that is, the last feeding was at 5 p.m. and the next at 7 a.m.--this was the longest daily stretch between feedings. Activity levels in normal human infants are also greatest prior to nursing and lowest subsequent to feeding (Keesler, 1966).

Another variable that can increase aggression among the profoundly retarded is boredom. Consider the many activities or boredom antidotes normals or very bright people come up with. There is raiding the icebox, doodling in faculty meetings, and so on. However, the PMR is very limited in creating boredom antidotes. For the PMR, Murphy (1964, p. 30) states the case: "The child's first expressions are of emotions and the language of emotions is primarily a body language. Some severely subnormal never progress beyond this level of communication." Fenichel also provides a hint for us to consider in our work with the profoundly retarded, albeit he was speaking of infants. Fenichel (1945) points out that "primitive perception is precisely characterized by its closeness to motor action." Thus, it does not stretch the imagination too far to consider the bored PMR will aggress, masturbate, or conceivably resort to coprophagy (Cleland, Rago & Jones, 1978). In their limited repertoire of behaviors that may be expressing boredom, other signals may be seen such as increased urination or defecation, and both of these eliminative behaviors will usually get increased attention from their caretakers. In those among the PMR ranks who likely suffer the greatest amount of boredom, the bedfast employ urination or defecation as the equivalent of the general hospital's "call button."

One could reasonably inquire "Do the profoundly retarded experience boredom?" They cannot, of course, verbally report that they do but motorically they can. For example, Klaber and Butterfield (1968) conducted a study of stereotyped rocking behavior in profoundly and severely retarded children. They hypothesized that the percent of residents engaged in rocking would reflect on the adequacy of ward care provided. Rocking, as well as other stereotypies, is viewed by certain researchers as an attempt to gain added sensory input or self-stimulation (Cleland & Clark, 1966). Enforced quiescence or verbal rebuke were found by Klaber and Butterfield to increase rocking behavior, and these authors suggest that rocking is mediated by enforced quiescence and/or verbal rebuke and that it occasions an internal "feeling of discomfort or anxiety on their part" (p. 19). Earlier, investigators had noted that stereotypy is reduced if toys are made available, especially highly preferred ones (Davenport & Berkson, 1963). It would appear, from Klaber and Butterfield's work as well as Berkson and Mason's (1963) study that boredom is an emotional state that the PMRs share with normals and that it can augment stereotypy, aggression, and other undesirable behaviors. We will discuss pica and coprophagy as possible outcomes of boredom in Chapter 3 in more detail.

Another intrusive problem in institutional settings (and community residential areas too) is that of noise. In institutions where wall surfaces are usually sound reflective rather than absorbent, the noise levels can be quite high and generally, the lower the level of occupants, the higher the noise level. If you will reflect for a moment on "cramming for an exam" and the apartment dwellers next to yours having a rowdy party, you will readily sense the role of noise in augmenting aggression. Noise levels that are excessive can also mask speech and frustrate communicative efforts. Glenn, Nerbonne and Tolhurst (1978) studied word intelligibility by a perception identification test under quiet and noisy conditions in a Massachusetts state school for the retarded and found 73.9% correct perceptions occurred under quiet, but only 44% in the noisy condition. They concluded, "residents who already had a primary language-learning handicap, were being subjected to a possible secondary impediment resulting from the living environment" (p. 594). Double-jeopardy in the ranks of the profoundly retarded is insured by a variety of dynamically interacting forces.

Although many other reasons could be cited as productive of high levels of aggression in the profoundly retarded, we will give only one other before turning to some approaches to minimize aggression. We turn now to Dollard, Doob, Mowrer & Sears' (1939) frustration-aggression hypothesis. Think now of a prime characteristic of the PMR--their extremely limited capacity to communicate. Imagine yourself suddenly unable to be understood by those around you. You may desperately need a drink of water, but your teacher or caretaker misunderstands and takes you to the bathroom! Over and over this kind of communication hiatus occurs and in my opinion spawns enormous frustration in the ranks of the PMR. Talkington, Hall and Cleland (1971) compared 60 retardates having poor or no communication skills with 60 communicatively adequate peers. The groups were matched for IQ, age, and length of institutionalization. Ten behavioral categories were studied and the noncommunicators rated significantly higher on the behaviors of aggression and preference for solitude. The adequate communicators rated high on interaction, participation, feeding skills, and dressing skills. While these subjects were moderate and severely retarded, not profounds, it illustrates the possible consequences of frustration over being misunderstood. Talkington, et al. invoked the Dollard, et al. frustration-aggression hypothesis to partially explain the results. This hypothesis initially indicated that frustration always leads to aggression (Dollard, et al., 1939), but was later modified to acknowledge that other reactions to frustration, aggression included, were possible (Cofer & Appley, 1964).

AGGRESSION ANTIDOTES

The reduction of aggression among the PMR must be accorded high priority if the foregoing discussion has validity. Let's first look at the hypothesis regarding pain thresholds. Recall that I suggested that "persons having a high pain threshold should have a low threshold for aggression." However, to my knowledge, there is no empirical evidence to support this statement--it just seemed to be reasonable on the surface. So, as an initial task, we would need to put the hypothesis to a test. It could be tested in several ways. One approach would be to isolate via interviews with dentists, physicians, and experienced houseparents those profoundly retarded thought to have very high pain thresholds and those whose threshold for pain appears "normal." We could then isolate the highly aggressive by reference to ward daybooks, master records, and behavior ratings such as the AAMD Adaptive Behavior Scale-Part II. The ABS-Part II consists of 13 behavioral domains: <u>violent and destructive</u> behavior, antisocial behavior, rebellious behavior, untrustworthy behavior, withdrawal, stereotyped behavior and odd mannerisms, inappropriate interpersonal manners, unacceptable vocal habits, eccentric habits, <u>self-abusive behavior</u>, hyperactive tendencies, inappropriate sexual behavior, and psychological disturbances. The two underscored behaviors would, of course, be those most directly relevant to testing the hypothesis on pain thresholds. Another method of approach would involve direct observation. Still other methodological approaches could be developed by readers interested in testing this hypothesis.

What this section is all about, however, is ways to prevent or reduce aggression. Suppose it becomes clear that high pain thresholds do correlate highly with aggression--there is little we can do, or is there? Since pain is activated by special sense organs in the form of free nerve endings in skin, internal organs, and blood vessels, and its sensation is conducted via the hypothalamus and reticular system (Goldenson, 1970), it would appear there would be little intervention possibility. However, by isolating those with the high pain thresholds, we could at least have made a contribution to diagnosis, that is, it could point to damage to the hypothalamus, reticular activating system, or both. It could even point to early childhood, child-rearing practices. Recall, from Chapter 1, Pratt and Sackett's abnormally reared monkeys and their later preference for only those similarly reared? Others have also learned that when isolation-reared monkeys first encounter peers, they tend to behave very aggressively toward them. Melzack and Scott (1957) demonstrated that dogs, lower in the phyletic order, who were isolation-reared and understimulated failed to respond to shock, pinpricks, or other painful stimuli in a normal emotional manner. If it were determined that isolation-reared (and the PMR) would, somewhat naturally, be shielded more than normals from contact, then it would be important to advise parents very early on the value of stimulation <u>and</u> some exposure to age peers. For, if individuals are relatively isolated and later placed in an institution, aggressive behavior toward others could lead to "snowing" by drugs or other efforts to control the behavior. All of this, of course, is highly conjectural and the leap from animal studies to man was introduced merely to augment the reader's curiosity and/or hostility to the point of demonstrating the author is "all wet."

At a less speculative level, let's look at feeding and eating behaviors, as these may serve to generate aggression. One behavior that can instigate aggression at the dinner table is that "bane of the institutional mess-hall," the pirate. Pirating of others' food can cause the pirated one to attack, or more often simply to lose weight. Pirating is augmented by spacial proximity, but since space is finite in one's own dining room as well as in the institution's, how can we avoid pirating and reduce aggression? Since the 4-seater table of about 3 x 3 feet is perhaps modal and permits face-to-face seating, we redesign the table. The new design would be circular and would look like a doughnut. A hinged portion would allow four to enter, but they would be seated back-to-back and facing out from the doughnut. The presumed advantage would be, first off, that one individual's food would be behind another's and "out of sight is out of mind." Another possible advantage would be to food servers--they would approach from the front and not come from behind a PMR, and the skittish PMR would be less likely to throw his food tray at the server. In any event, it could be worth a try.

We have already referred to Watson's (1973) mini-meal study and the finding subsequent to initiation of six instead of the traditional three-square meals daily that her profoundly retarded surprisingly showed improvements in behavior and weight gains as well. Thus, frequency of feeding can serve to diminish aggression.

Recently, Keyes (1978) introduced a pilot aggression reduction program in an Illinois institution. Major features included greater living space, improved employee-resident ratios, and better recreational programming. Within 60 days of the program's inception, injuries declined 28%, destruction of property fell 87%, and aggression declined greatly. Food and soft drinks in a unique atmosphere were also cited as beneficial.

Comparative and social psychological literature can help us understand why eating and feeding conditions sometimes spawn aggression. Scott (1958), Southwick (1967) and Platt, Sutker and James (1968) all indicate that when feeding areas become heavily populated, individuals eat more and faster and often become hostile toward peers. Crowding during meals has often occurred in mass care settings. Thus, another key in reducing aggression is the manner in which meals are served and the numbers served at one time. Case, Harris, Sarma, and Lance (1975) studied speed of eating in relation to aggression and length of institutionalization (LOI) in 66 subjects having IQs below 19 and whose ages ranged from 18 to 31 years. They hypothesized a relationship between rapid eating and aggression and LOI. However, neither aggression nor LOI was significantly correlated with speed of eating, although the correlations were in the predicted direction. The speed of eating time ranged from 2.2 minutes to 26 with a mean of 7.5 minutes! I had earlier asked these students the question, "Are there gourmets among the PMRs who do not wolf their food but slowly savor it?" They found few gourmets but the answer to my question was "yes." Referring back to Table 1, Chapter 1, the reader will note that food aspiration accounted for over 3% of PMR deaths--a 2-minute meal must be guarded against! The eating behaviors of today, we suspect, are not greatly different from those MacAndrew and Edgerton (1964b) described over a decade ago:

> Whole hard-boiled eggs are eaten at a gulp, oatmeal with milk is eaten with the fingers, prunes drop to the floor,

trays are overturned, neighbors have cups of milk poured or sloshed on them, and so on. (p. 314)

Goethe once said, "Man is what he eats," and Conolly (1847) noted the importance of food in the satisfaction of mental patients and observed that food and eating can communicate. If appetites change dramatically, this can even herald illness (Cleland & Swartz, 1969; Cleland, 1978). By this point in the discussion, the reader has either developed an appetite, boredom, or both. Let's examine now some boredom antidotes to see if aggression attributable, in part at least, to boredom can be alleviated.

Taking a molar approach first and thinking of the campuses of many state institutions, can we develop a stimulating, interesting, and enriched environment that is antithetical to boredom? The following fictional account may help us think more in terms of Maslow's higher order needs.

Fiction: An Approach to Institutional Design and Programming

For the profoundly retarded, the rarest and most severely impaired of all retarded, institutions are home to over half their number. This is so because at 20, 30 or 40 years of age, they will still have the mental age of infants and few will ever speak an intelligible word in any language regardless of what language they hear. Institutions are also home to a considerable number of the severely retarded--those who at adulthood will not exceed a mental age beyond that of a child of 3 or 4½ years.

Perhaps we can see why everyone who is retarded cannot live in the community if we think about geniuses. I once asked the following as an exam question: Suppose you had several million dollars to spend as you saw fit. I want you to tell me how you'd spend all or part of it in a way that would or could let you know how it would feel to be mentally retarded. You may think you know, but how could you be even more certain? The A+ went to the girl who wrote: "I'd charter a large yacht and invite as paid guests only people like Einstein, Buddha, von Morgenstern, Santayana, George W. Carver, Aristotle, Plato, etc. Only, they would all be geniuses who were living, naturally. I would be the only person on the ship who was of just average intelligence and if, at the end of a three-month cruise, I hadn't lost my mind because I had no one to talk to that I could understand, then I could tell you how a retarded person must feel in a world of normals!" So, not all retarded people can stay out of institutions as the deinstitutional enthusiasts insist. Some, like most of us, enjoy being around people who are not too much smarter, nor duller intellectually than they are. The philosophy of normalization and/or mainstreaming gets tested regularly in my classes when I ask for a show of hands to two questions: "How many of you when you had your last party invited mostly people your age?" Almost all raised their hands. The next question, "How many of you invited someone you knew was mentally retarded?" No hands went up. Integration on lines other than intelligence is reasonably established, but when we talk of integration on the basis of intelligence of various levels, there is still a grain of truth in the old cliche, "Like seeks like." That's the real reason why institutions exist--they meet some needs the community cannot, and some retarded people like them, and for some, they are home! Home, in turn, has been described or defined as the abiding place of the emotions. If any of what I have said thus far is true--the state school is, for some, a home and that some like it--let's see how we can make them like it even better. To do this, I will pretend I am profoundly retarded and that the rest of my days will be lived in an institution. In a sense, since few ever speak, the author will speak for them. Following are the comments of a profoundly retarded person about to be enrolled in Itard State School. "My parents are sizing the place up and have driven up and down Seguin Boulevard several times--they talk but I look. What I see is that it's very flat land and I think, "The excavation of dirt from that new building could have been used to put up a hill--I don't see why an institution couldn't have a hill to climb and to roll down--it could be fun! People passing by might be startled to see a manmade hill where none existed but it wouldn't hurt anything. Another thing, my folks've visited at a lot of these schools and we see different things. Something I've not seen, though, is an institution with a bridge--even a little decorative bridge would be different and fun for kids to walk over. It would sure startle visitors to see that we were the only institution to sport our very own bridge--none of 'em to my knowledge has got one but Itard State School could have one and if there's a low spot on campus that fills with water when it rains hard, that's where I'd put it! Some towns have some neat statues in their parks. If I go to Itard State School, I'd sure like to see some outdoor statuary to make the place different and prettier than people seem to think all state schools are supposed to be. A little decorative statuary wouldn't hurt anything but it might change people's minds about institutions though--that's dangerous! The folks are gonna drive past Itard State School again; OK, well, I can look some more. Wow! Imagine how the folks in Wallintown who don't work at State School would be surprised if they drove by some night, and we had a couple of big water fountains shooting water into the air and all lit up with a color-wheel making the water fountain turn all colors. Gee, that'd be real pretty for everybody inside and out to see. Well, while I'm dreaming, I'd just as well go first class. I've never seen an institution with its own high-rise building--mainly just flat one-story jobs so's they can get us out safely if there's a fire. Wouldn't hurt to put up a high-rise administration building though--kinda like all the big bank buildings in big towns where they have a restaurant at the top. If Itard State School had one, maybe they could let us eat at the top too and get to look down on somebody--see pretty views once in a while--bet people have spent money on stuff a lot sillier than that. Wow--a sunset from the top of the Itard State School High Rise--that would be awe-inspiring--might even see the ocean too! Well, if they can't do that the next best would be roof gardens where we could sunbathe and watch the clouds go by--heard my folks talk about roof gardens where they used to dance--I won't be dancing but I can see birds on the wing, clouds, and maybe even once in a while the moon come up--don't see it would hurt anything. Some of us, like other people, are night people--I like to stay up late. Maybe they could just watch and see which of us go to sleep early and which of us are not asleep till late and just have staggered bedtimes.

Another thing I like is music--real, live music, not listening all the time to records. I wish they'd put up a bandstand and throw an outdoor concert every once in a while--we could have all kinds of music like mariachias, German bands, country western, marching bands--the whole bit! I like to see bands and the colorful uniforms musicians wear--it's real exciting to see and hear real, live musicians.

I remember once the folks took me to San Antonio and got a paddle boat and took me riding on the river--it was fun!

Wonder if some institution could put in an artificial creek, plastic lined and not very deep so's the residents could ride in paddle boats? It might be a little risky but I'll bet a lot of kids that haven't got very strong legs would really try to paddle so they could get the boat going. I see Itard State School already has a swimming pool so they probably wouldn't want to build an artificial creek but if you're gonna have little bridges, a creek would be neat to have.

Heard my folks say somebody sells feather-lite rocks that look like the real McCoy. People use 'em to put in their backyards and make little pools and waterfalls. Folks say it makes you feel like you're out in the forest somewhere instead of in a crowded town. Yes, sir--I'd really think Itard State School ought to have some waterfalls and pools. They could even put those big Japanese perch in the pools--they tell me they come in all colors. Course, people would think we'd all drown but they could put clear plastic shields around so's we wouldn't fall in--we could still see, and it would sure surprise a lot of people that don't like institutions to see Itard State School after it's all gussied up. Another thing that would break the monotony would be some groves of trees here and there with picnic benches so our folks could take us picnicking right on the Itard State School campus.

Somebody told me about two guys at The University of Texas named __________ and __________ who bought 600 pounds of pecans, scattered these over a wooded area of the ________ State School very early one morning and held a pecan hunt for the retarded residents in March! This was a great surprise cause all those residents were older and not nearly as retarded as me and they _knew_ pecans can't be harvested in March. Fact is, they were _so surprised_ that they whooped and hollered and really had a big time. Surprises are nice if they're not bad news. Why not get the Itard State School volunteers to dream up surprises--don't see it would hurt anything to have an off-season Easter egg hunt say along about late October. I couldn't find any but a lot of the residents would really go bananas over such surprises. Kinda like the tooth fairy.

The folks are finally gonna drive in--thought they never would. Well, looks like they're gonna put me here at Itard State School. I'll be on the bedfast ward cause I can't do anything but sit in a wheelchair and have to be strapped to sit in that even. Wish they had glass roofs so we could see the birds fly over--watching seagulls is fun. They could have a rollaway roof-cover in case of storms or if the sun's too hot but wouldn't it be neat to see the birds and clouds, airplanes, and moon and all kinda things. The folks read a lot about institutions and I heard them talking about two guys named __________ and __________ who proposed a really different kind of building for bedfast people--maybe some day the state will cough-up enough to erect one of these experimental bedfast buildings. Who knows? There are lots of things a person could do to make the people who live here happier.

Everybody gets mad and angry at times and retarded people are no exception--I know cause I'm retarded. Why not, for the retarded who are so destructive they are always tearing things up, a weekly or monthly car-smash? Get an old car out of a junk yard and put some shielding type glasses on the residents and let 'em have so many hits with a sledge hammer. Carnival midways always have a ducking stool where you pay to get to throw balls at a target and if you hit the target, the guy or gal flops into the water tank. If people didn't have some hostility in 'em, then why would they pay good money just to give another person a bath, I ask you? At any rate, the employees would have to figure out how often such a gimmick should be used--else, the residents might get even more hostile. Some way to get the old anger out oughta be a part of places like this though!

Folks, I've gotta quit this fantastic stuff--or is it fantastic? Everybody knows that retarded people are not good at thinking. However, we do feel and have emotions like everybody else. We laugh, cry, and express surprise. What I've been talking about is how to make laughter, surprise, awe or wonderment, joy and even anger be more easily experienced and expressed. Very few people have days when all the emotions they experience are truly great. It's the little things you normal people take for granted that make life livable. The sunsets, the moonrise, an exciting thunderstorm, a good healthy laugh over a little funny or a pleasant surprise--these are the antidotes for the worst disease of all--boredom! The hill where none existed, the incongruous high-rise where society thinks none should exist, a waterfall or lighted fountain offer new vistas for residents and employees alike and, to the passerby who will never even come into the Itard State School, a little beauty here and there wouldn't hurt their eyes either. And now, I return you to the author.

Noticing emotions and their expression in man or woman is hardly something that would qualify as unique, since Darwin (1872) beat me by over a century. What is proposed is a program to elicit pleasant emotional expressions or an antidote for boredom. It could, in some respects, also be termed a disguise for institutions, so they can escape being detected as institutions. Some retarded people like the life in institutions, and I have offered some ideas on how to make them, and perhaps employees too, like it even better. I hope the reader will expand on these ideas. If we can systematically institute an environmental and behavioral program for emotional elicitation from the institutional residents, then we will have gone a step beyond feeding and toilet training.

The foregoing approach to institutional design addressed, in large measure, the aesthetics of institutions--the dwelling place of at least half of all PMRs in the U.S. It attempted to instill beauty into the everyday life of many PMRs, for an aesthetically pleasing and novel environment can assauage boredom.

Aggression inspired by boredom can also be alleviated by getting PMRs psychologically off-balance and by contagion. Mention was made earlier of the fact that laughter and aggression are incompatible responses, and if the classroom or ward mood is ominous or threatening, what can be done?

One of the most heterogeneous yet congenial crowds I ever encountered was in a large department store some 15 Christmases ago. In the large toy department a huge crowd was gathered very close to a large shelf--I grew curious as to what was causing the gales of laughter. I soon learned and became one of the side-splitting laughers. The cause was the "sack-full of laughs," which was activated when turned upside down. All types, ages, etc., were trying them out and the "ho-ho, ha-ha's" that came from the sack were very, very contagious--the entire crowd was infected. A German inventor had recorded laughter, male and female of all ages, and sacked it up! If the spontaneity of laughter and the size of the crowd was an index to sales, the department store did very well on this unique toy.

Such a toy, used sparingly but at critical times, could possibly augment the teacher or attendant's store of "weapons" to be used to restore a joyous mood and minimize occasions when boredom is awesome.

Numerous other variations can be conceived that dispel boredom. Perhaps even the ward or classroom odor itself can contribute to monotony, ennui? If this sounds plausible, a simple expedient would be to try out a new odorant or aerosol bomb. While the residents or students are on a bus ride and just before their return, spray a new odor into the environment and observe the returnees to see if any notice is given, and, if so, were the reactions generally pleasant? This may sound implausible but women on occasion vary their perfumes and at least partly because the same scent, day-in, day-out, may lead to disinterest on the part of the mate or lover. Also, the ward odor is reasonably homogeneous--lysol or other disinfectant mixed with the odor of urine or feces. It could even influence a change in employees' attitudes.

Noise also contributes to aggression, as mentioned earlier. The school or institution might benefit from the help of a consultant sound engineer or an acoustical physicist. Where in dormitories or classrooms are sound levels highest and what time of day is noise at peak? Acoustical shielding could help in certain areas. In dining rooms, replacement of metallic dishes with autoclavable plastic could also reduce noise or unwanted sound. Also, since the dining rooms are usually noise factories but are unoccupied much of the time, this could be a target area where acoustical treatment might best be employed. As a further consideration, I would advocate high ceilings rather than the low ceilings often found in single-story dormitories. Why? Because the acoustical tiles in low ceilings are, if PMRs are given toys or balls, often knocked out of place. A high ceiling would avoid this continual maintenance problem, give more space and an airiness to the dorm, and let sound abate more readily. Finally, though these suggestions are not exhaustive, an anechoic (soundproof) room on PMR dorms might be advised. Here, those whose forte is noise-making could be periodically assembled in small groups for the discharge of this apparent need. There are quiet and contemplative PMRs and noisy ones--each deserves individually tailored programs. If the anechoic room allowed noisemakers periodic discharge, it is conceivable this need to produce noise would abate somewhat.

Frustration is often the lot of the PMR. Some method is needed to permit them to vent pent-up hostility before aggression occurs. <u>We</u> can write a hostile letter or assault our enemies verbally--they can't. PMRs need a safe outlet. Perhaps allowing PMRs to physically assault surrogates of the human figure would help. Symonds, cited in Cofer and Appley (1964), provides a series of events in the normal life cycle that are frustrating. "These include the restriction of infant activity, thwarting of autoerotic expression, loss of attention and care, unsatisfactory nursing experiences, weaning, toilet training, loss of love or security and support, forced independence in adolescence, and adult economic hardships and other losses, including those due to death of loved ones or anticipation of one's own death" (Cofer & Appley, 1964, p. 417). Of the foregoing, autoerotic expression and toilet training are perhaps the major concerns with PMRs. When a profoundly retarded male or female masturbates, it is often not done in private. Not infrequently, vigorous attempts by teachers, houseparents, or others are made to abolish this practice. Frustration or thwarting of the sex drive can lead to aggression, and when one considers the PMR of age 18 or above (legal voting age), the question arises as to whether we should so vigorously try to stop masturbation. Sexual mores relaxation during the past decade notwithstanding, the PMR of legal adult age is still regarded, when sex is the issue, as an infant, and their efforts at sexual release via masturbation are still largely frustrated or thwarted. That conservative sex attitudes are still prevalent in institutions is supported by a recent study of staff members' attitudes in three California residential facilities. These researchers indicate, "one crucial finding was that a large percentage of staff members feel that no sexual behavior on the part of residents is acceptable" (Mitchell, Doctor & Butler, 1978, p. 295). The issue of sex motivation in PMRs will be discussed further in the section on subgroup differentiation.

> Aggression and laughter are incompatible responses. In the management of an obstreperous and very negativistic retardate, I learned from a sophisticated attendant many years ago the value of humor and laughter in eliminating such unvalued behaviors. While engaged in my first job with the mentally retarded, I was instructed to get "all the men (CA's 18-49) to school after their lunch break." One, reclining in his room, refused and instructed me quite forcefully and with all the authority bestowed by his great size to "go to...." In my ignorance and zeal to "do good," I forcefully countered with, "You're going to school now," and in only a few minutes the situation had deteriorated badly...I was losing. The experienced attendant stepped into the room, sized up the

situation, reached and tickled the big fellow's ribs. Instantly, the antagonist burst into laughter and said, "You know if you get me laughing, I'll do anything you want," and went happily off to school. The seriousness of the situation literally dissolved due to the experience and knowledge of the attendant and the strategies that would "sell" unpalatable services (school for this particular subject) to his customers.

While this case involved a mildly retarded male, it does hint at another possible aggression antidote--tickle.

Many variables in institutional settings are complex in their effects on behavior and are only recently being given serious study. Talkington and Riley (1971) isolated one variable that significantly augmented resident aggression--reduction diets. In this study, which employed young adults of moderate and mild levels of retardation, frequency counts of aggressive incidents subsequent to placing 32 persons on medically ordered reduction diets were tallied. A matched control group on regular diets was employed. For six months aggressive incidents were recorded and the diet group's frequency of aggression increased significantly while the non-diet group's aggression remained relatively unchanged. The researchers suggested that blocking of the primary drive (food deprivation) instigated frustration, and the resultant increased aggression conforms closely to the frustration-aggression model of Dollard, et al. (1939). Since certain medical problems, such as diabetes, cardiac problems, necessitate reduction diets, the investigators suggest several aggression preventatives. Counseling, separate dining areas for dieters, and reinforcement for weight loss could all prove beneficial.

Although the subjects in the above mentioned study were of mild and moderate level, the profoundly retarded would certainly not be immune to the effects of a reduction diet. In summarizing to this point, we have seen something of the antecedents of aggression and have suggested a few possible ways to minimize the problem. Let's next examine some goals and objectives in helping the profoundly retarded.

GOALS AND OBJECTIVES IN HELPING PROFOUNDLY RETARDED

In conversation with Coates Stuckey, a long-time Superintendent of the Pinecrest State School in Louisiana, he inquired, "The behavior modification programs have accomplished quite a lot in training PMRs basic toileting and feeding skills, but where do we go from here?" Before answering, I mused "A damned good question and an echo of what Mr. Leath and I talked about--namely, where do we go from here? Concerned professionals the country over, more specifically those experienced in working with the PMRs, are pondering and scratching their heads over the same issue. Why? Because at gut level we know that even if we teach the ambulatory PMR to deposit their body wastes in the proper "bank," such a self-help skill addresses only a lower order need, and one that they themselves, could they articulate their desires, might reckon a rather silly waste of time. While few would deny the importance of sanitation practices, this writer would venture that we teach toileting with great zeal principally to serve our own ingrained social overlearnings. "It's nasty, revolting, nauseating to see people over the age when toilet skills should be established discharging body wastes wherever, whenever the urge strikes." We tolerate these "excesses" in normal infants but fail to realize that PMRs, of whatever life age, remain infants mentally. So, to repeat, are there not more humanizing feats for us to set our sights on than toileting and feeding?

In an introductory text on mental retardation (Cleland, 1978), an effort was made to address the quality of life of those humans about whom we know least. Throughout this earlier work, normalization and humanization of the retarded individual was addressed, guided heavily by Maslow's (1954) self-actualization theory of human motivation. To date, I have found no better theoretical underpinning to guide us in providing a quality life for the profoundly retarded person. Let us examine briefly some key features of Maslow's theory.

Man, of every kind and everywhere, is motivated by an interrelated series of needs which are ordered into a prepotent hierarchy. The five postulated needs in the hierarchy encompassing most human needs or motives are:

physiological needs
safety, security
love and belongingness
esteem needs
self-actualization

A significant point of emphasis in Maslow's development of theory is a focus on fully functioning and healthy human beings as opposed to other theories that have arisen from primary concern with mentally ill or neurotic subjects. This departure would appear most significant for those concerned with humanizing and normalizing the environment for the profoundly retarded. For, as we all know, an enormous amount of attention given the PMR is focused on pathology. Let's try Maslow's approach.

What then, in Maslow's views, prevents individuals from becoming self-actualized? Very simply, the dominance of needs lower in the hierarchy. One cannot reach a higher-order need such as love-belongingness if there is little or no gratification of the safety needs. Thus, although it is evident that physiological needs (thirst, hunger, elimination of body wastes, etc.) can never be gratified entirely away, satisfaction of love and esteem needs can free the individual to ascend further up the need hierarchy. If the need for love, both to be loved and to love, is reasonably satisfied, this more or less eliminates this need from further organismic concern. One's life then from a self-actualization viewpoint is not equilibrium or homeostatis oriented, but rather is guided by growth principles.

To illustrate at a more concrete level how such a conceptualization might apply to mentally retarded, a few examples are offered. In our society, unlike some countries where hunger haunts a large segment of the population, most people are not in such abject poverty as to constantly think food and drink. Programs in public schools or institutions provide adequate nutrition, and this reflects one way this particular physiological need is gratified. Theoretically at least, few retardates, institutionalized or not, should be hungry and thus unable to move from physiological needs to the next order need--safety. Maslow (1954) indicates a child's need for safety is reflected in his preference for some degree of order and routine. Examples of how the safety needs are met in a school setting would include "instruction in perception and by neutralizing apparent dangers through knowledge about them" (Romig & Cleland, 1972). Again, since one's world is being modified daily and there is some need for order and routine, departures from routine should, when possible, be announced in advance (see illustrative case, "PMRs Reschedule Us," later in this chapter). Next in hierarchical order come the love and belongingness needs which theoretically come into play when physiological and safety needs are relatively quiescent.

Often, this need is frustrated. The last basic need the child should fulfill before reaching self-actualization would be the esteem needs. Such needs, in Maslow's thinking, reflect "a need or desire for a stable, firmly based, usually high evaluation of themselves, for self-respect, or self-esteem, and for the esteem of others" (Maslow, 1954, p. 90). For the profoundly retarded, this will be difficult, but perhaps not impossible.

As the reader has observed, once the physiological needs have been successfully addressed, the gratification of needs becomes ever more difficult and complex for attendants or teachers to meet. However, it should be noted that the hierarchy is not necessarily fixed nor is it essential that a lower order need "be permanently and finally gratified" (Cofer & Appley, 1964, p. 677). As Ardrey succinctly phrased it," the pursuit of security bears reward only when you do not have it. And even possession of a slimmest portion may free us to seek impenetrable skies, imponderable answers, and a human dignity beyond definition. It is what youth in its ignorance knows, I believe, and we in our habituation do not" (Ardrey, 1970, p. 187).

Normality, for Maslow, is equivalent to self-fulfillment, and it is clear from his writings that self-actualization is potential in anyone. At length, a person whose maintenance needs (physiological and safety) and higher order needs (love and belongingness; esteem needs) have been reasonably gratified reaches the highest-order need, self-actualization. The characteristics of a fully self-actualized person as Maslow (1954) presented them include:

1. More efficient perception of reality and more comfortable relations with it
2. Acceptance of self and others
3. Spontaneity
4. Problem centering
5. Detachment; the need for privacy
6. Autonomy; independence of culture and environment
7. Continued freshness of appreciation
8. Mystic experience or the oceanic feeling
9. Social interest
10. Interpersonal relations
11. Democratic character structure
12. Discrimination between means and ends
13. Sense of humor
14. Creativeness

15. Resistance to enculturation

Preposterous, humbug, impossible to implement with the profoundly retarded! Difficult indeed--but isolated fragments of the 15 characteristics cited above do appear in the profoundly retarded albeit they appear dim or veiled relative to their expression in normal persons. There is evidence, though of limited quantity, that reflects certain of the self-actualized characteristics among the profoundly retarded. Undoubtedly, more evidence would be observed were we not overwhelmingly focused on pathology. Here then are a few shreds of evidence of valued human attributes in the PMR.

Rago and Cleland (1978) describe an instance of altruistic or empathic behavior in two institutionalized males. Reuben was 38 years old and had a Vineland Social Quotient of 17; John was 41 at the time of the observed event and had a Vineland of 10. The altruistic behavior pattern was observed on a weekday morning during a period of time in which the entire group was being observed for a research project concerned with territorial behavior and spatial dispersion. The residents were in their recreation room which was 5.49 m by 8.23 m. The periphery was lined by 1.83 m plastic benches; otherwise, the room was empty. John was sitting on a bench against the wall, his usual position within the room. Reuben was sitting on a bench which was against a wall perpendicular to the wall against which John sat. Reuben was approximately 4.57 m away from John. During this time, with our subjects seated, the group attendant randomly distributed 4 magazines to the 14 residents (a relatively untypical behavior). John received a magazine and Reuben did not. However, another group member, apparently disgruntled with not receiving a magazine, walked across the room directly toward John, snatched the magazine from John's hands and returned to his seat on the opposite side of the room from where Reuben was seated. Reuben, after apparently observing this series of events, got up from his bench, and, with apparent calm, simply walked across the room, retrieved the magazine, walked to John's bench, and handed the magazine to him. Reuben then proceeded to where he had been sitting, terminating the altruistic behavior pattern. The most striking aspect of this behavior was the apparent simplicity and spontaneity with which it occurred.

Earlier, MacAndrew and Edgerton (1966) described the existence of friendship and altruism in two severely retarded adults, but to our knowledge, the Rago-Cleland account is the first documented case of altruism in PMRs. This demonstrates, at least rudimentarily, acceptance of self and others and social interest--two of Maslow's big "15."

Another illustration of social interest is seen in Altman, Cleland and Swartz's (1972) study of what ethologists classify as an appeasement gesture; reference here is to the handshake. The subjects, of late adolescence and early adulthood, had an average Social Quotient of 9.9. Twenty of 26 subjects shook hands and the handshake was elicited from one subject having a Social Quotient of 1! Several facts of interest mark this study. First, it was almost 90% certain that few, if any, had ever received specific instruction in handshaking, albeit they may have witnessed its occurrence. Thus, some support is given to the ethologists' contention that the handshake is an instinctive inhibition against aggression. Secondly, only extreme patience elicits the handshake from some PMRs--most had an extremely delayed response (perhaps this is why few politicians solicit votes from PMRs?). However, like normals, once they "pressed the flesh," almost all who shook hands also smiled broadly. Finally, although Doll had earlier noted the prevalence of left-handedness in higher-level retardates, Altman, et al. found over 25% of their profoundly retarded to be southpaws. Individuals working with the profoundly retarded should offer reinforcers to the PMR's preferred hand.

Quite recently two doctoral students at The University of Texas at Austin have catalogued yet another self-actualization characteristic among the profoundly retarded--sense of humor. These investigators observed 55 PMR males over a three-week period and found novel situations elicited much laughter and smiling as did situations wherein subjects had a triumph or accomplishment, that is, successful use of their own powers, such as kicking a ball and then smiling. They also found "more humor responses occurred during interactions with attendants" than in peer interactions (Jones & Shirley, 1978). Thus, since humor (laughter, smiling) is largely incompatible with the expression of aggression, novel situations that occur naturally or are staged, should be employed with considerable frequency with the PMR. It should be carefully noted, however, just what response various novel situations evoke since some PMRs may be made fearful while others may laugh. Individual differences in reactions to novelty should be carefully catalogued in order to ascertain which class of stimuli are universally productive of mirth or humor and which seem to elicit fear. Readers interested in laughter, humor, mirth and play should consult Berlyne (1969),

Chapman and Foot (1976), or Levine (1969) for a more comprehensive and detailed discussion.

Elsewhere in this text mention was made of tool usage in certain profoundly retarded persons. The Vineland researchers Aldrich and Doll studied problem-solving and tool use experimentally and Cleland, Rago and Mukherjee (1978) collected instances of problem-solving and tool use in the profoundly retarded person's naturalistic setting. Both problem centering and creativeness are involved in tool use and, relative to their degree of intelligence, this writer would argue that such an accomplishment is dramatic indeed.

The foregoing reflect on the question posed by Coates Stuckey at the beginning of this section, "Where do we go from here?" It seems clear that Maslow provides us a theoretical guide and we have seen a few examples of characteristics of self-actualized, or metamotivated, profoundly retarded persons. Hopefully, the author's message has been clear enough--we must not be staggered by the enormous physical and behavioral pathology the PMRs exhibit. Our senses must be open to receive, and systematically catalogue every instance of normal, or for the PMR, supernormal behavior.

Surprise sometimes can violate the safety and security needs of profoundly retarded persons--are we clever enough to provide the PMR with schedules-announcements so they too can "know what's up" and have some routine and order in their daily life? Consider the following as the author's attempt at a model for upholding PMR's security and safety needs.

The PMRs Reschedule Us

To never know "what they'd like for Christmas, or whether they'd like bacon better than sausage, guacamole better than onion dip, or whether they like polka better than big-band music" are questions that must be faced or we can never give the profoundly retarded an individuality or a life to their liking.

Some parents, researchers and some houseparents or teachers come, over time, to understand what some of the PMR's unintelligible grunts, gestures, squeals or cries may mean. Like the mother who comes to know her own four- or six-month normal baby's behaviors and their meanings.

However, many who come to work with PMRs don't stay long enough to ever learn what each PMR is trying to express--is it sickness, anger, curiosity, humor or what? The mother with a normal baby has another advantage over those who work with PMRs of 6, 12, 18 or 30 years of age. Because the baby is tiny, there's little chance it will harm itself or others. When the profoundly retarded grow large but still have no recognizable speech, a knowledge of their intentions, meanings, likes and dislikes becomes urgent--they can now, and often quickly, harm themselves or others. The knowledge a mother has of her baby's non-verbal behavior (knowing how he/she behaves when sick, etc.) is likewise, very restricted. That is, another person, say a teenage babysitter or even another mother, can't be instantly told what to look or look out for. So, what is needed is some kind of <u>new</u> but very simple communication form by which the mood states, likes and dislikes of the PMR can be relayed or translated in a systematic way to others, and quickly.

There are many approaches one could take. People in different times or cultures often employed substitutes when distances were too great for the human voice to carry. Some islanders in the Mediterranean employ a whistle signal system. American Indians employed smoke signals, while some African tribes used drums as a means of informing others at a distance. Before modern radiotelephone was developed, elaborate foghorns were developed by acoustical physicists to warn sailors of heavy fog and shallow water when the lighthouse was drowned out by the fog's density. Animals often signal (or communicate) to others "keep out, this is my territory" by means of scent or <u>odor</u> marking. Humans, man and woman alike, also signal by smell and often use other odors to "mask or disguise" their own. Thus, mouthwash and the use of after-shave or perfumes may signal others of the opposite sex, "I'm approachable, I smell good and don't stink." <u>Heat</u>, or the thermal sense, also can be employed to communicate as when a radiantly heated path leading to a dormitory restroom signals to a blind person, "This is the right way to the restroom." <u>Touch</u>, as in teaching the blind to read by the Braille method, can also be employed usefully in other ways, such as hand-holding to convey the delicate emotion of love. All the senses that are <u>intact</u> in man then are available in our effort to convey meaning or messages to the profoundly retarded. Further, technology has greatly amplified our ability to use our senses and the infrared movie camera allows taking pictures of living creatures at night by means of the heat they radiate, hearing aids greatly amplify sound for the benefit of the deaf, and voice spectrography has been used to diagnose and differentiate between the Down's Syndrome and Cri-du-Chat Syndrome in mental retardation. With all this technology plus the inventiveness of humans, why is the profoundly retarded still a private person? Can't we somehow "get through" with our questions, information and above all meaning so that their lives can be richer and fuller? Perhaps we can try to find the Rosetta Stone that will help us all to understand their needs, wants, desires--the things many may take for granted. How do we proceed?

First, think of yourself and how you know your own world--the work world, the home world; in short, the way organization of your daily life occurs to help you get through as best you can. One way you manage is to attempt to reduce your uncertainties, anxieties or fears. Thus, you set up a schedule of what's coming up on an hourly, weekly, monthly or yearly basis. We cannot foresee everything that will happen and, occasionally, we're surprised or caught unawares. Depending on one's personality, intelligence and whether the surprise is pleasant or unpleasant, we respond adaptively or maladaptively. Even insignificant happenings can loom to us as major events. For example, you *expect* on return from work that your chair will be in its proper place, ditto the TV, and so on--they aren't! For some of us, it's a major upheaval--for others, it gets slight notice.

All people of normal intelligence when knowledgeable and informed about some forthcoming activity or event will change pace or stride (mentally or physically) in preparation for it. We will, if we know what's up next, get set or ready to face it. Now, what about the nonverbal, profoundly mentally retarded? Let's ask a question for these nonverbal people. "Why can't we have some signal that tells us what activity or event is coming up next so *we* can get ready and *set* for whatever it is you've scheduled for us?" Readers may think the idea is absurd--why, suppose you walked into a room full of PMRs and said "You all get ready now, we're going on a bus ride and then go picnic," what might happen? Nothing! In all likelihood they would continue doing as they were. However, let's suppose that *invariably* when *you* (no other teacher or houseparent) enter the room *you* turn a rheostatically controlled light to very bright, simultaneously say loudly "bus ride-picnic" and spray a constant odor into the air--then what? It could be that if every time you did what was just described and did shortly thereafter load them into a bus and go to a park and picnic, they'd learn that you plus bright light plus the words "bus ride and picnic" and the odorant would mean ride and picnic. Through repeated occurrences of this unchanging sequence they would learn through association the upcoming event you had scheduled. It could even be that "bus ride and picnic" could come to stand alone as the announcement. Take another scheduled event--lunch. Here we probably don't need to announce this scheduled event since stomach contractions and many repeated feedings at the same time have caused them to know it's coming soon (Cleland & Swartz, 1969).

Let's look at self-help skills such as learning to get dressed. This is a major chore for PMRs that can best be taught by behavior shaping or modeling strategies. However, if we announced that the learning to dress class is coming next on the schedule, the profounds might in their rudimentary way know what to expect and thus establish a "set to learn." The class itself would now come as no surprise and if some get upset by not knowing what's up next, it could lengthen the time the behavior modification expert expends--emotional upset is a great deterrent to learning! What is suggested is that in institutions or public school classrooms where the PMR may be found, we develop schedules and make them understandable to our PMRs.

The approach and example cited addressed the safety needs of the profoundly retarded. It's designed to reduce their fears and uncertainties. If we can train them to know that they are going to the barber shop, to the play park, to a picnic or whatever, we've made a quantum leap in caring for their needs. Suppose we do train them to know that a certain person, a word, a special odor, etc., means a bus ride; while a different person, a different word, odor and so on, means the swimming pool. So what? It will mean that by their behaviors (smile, frown, becoming upset, having a seizure or even vomiting) we, through detailed observation, will learn their preferred or detested activities and perhaps even their favorite foods, etc. In other words, they will then schedule us rather than us scheduling them. Both the grossly misunderstood profoundly retarded and all who work with them should feel better. They, in turn, could stop being taken to the toilet when their grunt, cry or behavior actually meant they wanted a snowcone!

This admittedly sketchy model is untried but when our knowledge and treatment strategies are meagre, then Maslow's advice deserves attention. "The proper place for a scientist is in the midst of the unknown, the chaotic, the dimly seen, the unmanageable, the mysterious, the not-yet-well-phrased" (Maslow, 1954). This is largely where we stand in relation to the profoundly retarded--they, to most people, are still "the unknown." What this writer has proposed is just the skeleton of a plan to decipher their unknown words or actions. If any measure of success in meeting their safety needs occurs, we'd then aim to meet their higher needs also.

If, through associations that pair odor, light, sound (human voice), touch, etc., we can establish reliably that they have come to understand what is next up, then the next effort would entail fading out of all stimuli save the human voice. Should they still reliably and correctly behave in response to very abbreviated announcements "bus ride-picnic," then rudimentary receptive language has come into being. One could even conceive of a very elementary preference test after a number of activities have been experienced and learned. By presenting the "bus ride-picnic" announcer simultaneously with the "go swim" announcer, facial expressions or assembling at one versus another announcer's side could tell us which activity is preferred.

If we give serious consideration to the Maslowian approach and attempt to go beyond the toilet and table, perhaps we could accelerate our progress by an oblique approach. In the above example, an effort was made to let the PMR reschedule us and thus help to meet their safety and security needs. In the following "confrontation of opposites," the outcome, in terms of meeting some higher-order needs of PMRs, could be outstanding.

Confrontation of Opposites

Imagine what we might learn, and all the more quickly, were we to import, draft, or pay several outstanding geniuses to study the profoundly retarded. A genius, a person of transcendent mental power and extraordinary creativity, possesses also a uniquely potent curiosity drive. Such individuals manifest an itch or urge to investigate, especially when the phenomenon encountered is novel or unusual (Goldenson, 1970). John Rader Platt in an interesting article entitled The Coming Generation of Genius underscores the awesome ability of an individual of 180 IQ. He maintains that "to prove the germ theory of disease or to make the first atomic pile" at least an IQ of 180 would be needed. He also says that it would be futile to assemble dozens of 170's or even hundreds of 160 IQs to tackle such problems. Phrased another way, Platt indicates "Seventeen Jonsons and Popes will not make a Shakespeare."

In many respects, a genius represents the polar opposite of the profoundly retarded person. Leta Hollingworth, a famous psychologist, has defined genius as stringently as anyone and says a genius is a person with an IQ of 180 or above plus an outstanding achievement. Historical figures that would meet Hollingworth's criteria as revealed in Catherine Cox Miles' study include J. S. Mill, Galton, Voltaire, Goethe, Pascal, Leibnitz and Hugo Grotius. The most notable genius of recent times would undoubtedly be Einstein. The reader, by this point, will likely have raised the question, "Why, in a book devoted to the profoundly retarded, are we addressing genius level people?" Because the author believes they can be of benefit to our understanding of the profoundly retarded and in the clarification and elaboration of their needs.

For a number of years the author has asked his college students to raise their hands if they had heard of, or knew about, the following people: Plato, Galton, Seguin, Einstein, Goethe, Montessori, Aristotle, Itard, Darwin, Mozart, and Von Braun. The underscored names are famous names associated with mental retardation research and writing. Compared to the non-underscored names, our most illustrious mental retardation researchers were known hardly at all to the students in my Introduction to Mental Retardation classes. Nearly every secondary schoolboy or girl, however, is familiar with the titans of physics, philosophy, literature, music, botany or zoology, mathematics and chemistry. Thus, our most illustrative scholars in the field of mental retardation, outside the field itself, are unknowns--their fame is circumscribed! By contrast, the true genius transcends space and time. Is it possible that the greats (the famous) in mental retardation are less intelligent than the people of genius in other fields? The answer, without denying the great capabilities and achievements of our mental retardation greats, would undoubtedly be yes. First, genius of the level of 180 ordinarily flowers early in life. Goethe, for example, by age 8 had produced literary works of adult quality while Voltaire produced verses from his cradle at age 2! In the biographical material available on Itard and Seguin, no such spectacular achievements were noted in early childhood or adolescence. While Itard and Seguin's contributions made in their adult years are original and pioneering, these contributions fall far below Darwin's theory of evolution or Freud's discovery of the unconscious. For, as Koestler describes Darwin and Freud's impact, these are the makers of the Modern World! Finally, a panel of three clinical psychologists were asked to estimate the IQs of our mental retardation greats--their estimates ranged from a low of 140 to a high of 160--well below that of the geniuses of the IQs estimated 180 or above.

Although it has been a circuitous route to the point of this section, our plan can now be laid out. If we assume the foregoing discussion is valid and that few, if any, true genius level people have studied the unfathomable PMR, what can we do? If one IQ 180 exceeds every IQ 140 that ever lived in mental prowess, let us persuade or purchase some time from several contemporary geniuses. We are trying an untried experiment in the field of mental retardation--literally, we will attempt to purchase some brain time from geniuses. If success is met and we gain their participation, what do we hope to accomplish and how do we proceed?

As an initial step, our "hired brains" will be provided selected research literature on the profoundly retarded. The four volumes of Proceedings of the Western Research Conference would serve nicely to sensitize them to the massive problems of everyday care and familiarize them with the parameters of knowledge about the PMR. While prevention of mental retardation might be their primary interest (and, of course, prevention is the overall major goal), our interest and the task presented our geniuses is "how to improve the lives of the PMR who are now living?" To do this means we must understand their primitive communicative efforts and with this problem, we should expect considerable help from our superbrains. To help orient our brain trust, sound movies of the PMRs in everyday life (awakening, toileting, eating, etc.) will be shown subsequent to their reading assignments. Without odors or screams to traumatize our consultants, their objectivity and perception should be relatively undistorted. The last phase will be the actual confrontation with their intellectual opposites (a novel event). At least one week of observation, perhaps every other day of 14 days, would seem indicated. After their blitz training, the brain trust would then commit their observations and impressions to writing--a sort of diary of life with their intellectual opposites. Finally, our consultants would spend two weeks or more in interaction with the research and professional elite of the mental retardation establishment to exchange ideas and chart the outlines of a strategy to enhance the lives of the PMRs who are living now. Methods by which the PMR's nonverbal communicative efforts could be deciphered would, of course, be the keystone of how we could improve their lives and meet their needs. The foregoing is incomplete and only presents the bare outline of a different sort of engagement--the confrontation of opposites. What if it could be staged? Exciting things could happen. Great progress could occur! And what a great thing it would be for these people of genius to share their enormous endowment with those who fared so poorly.

A human having a herculean intellect and a matching curiosity drive had a confrontation with honeybees. This encounter led Karl von Frisch to the discovery of the bee's mode of communication, and the Nobel Prize! Where is the Karl von Frisch of the "back-wards"? This brief and speculative section suggests a method by which the discoverer-translator of the PMR's communicative mode(s) may be identified.

3

Difficult Problems and Remedial Efforts

PICA AND COPROPHAGY: IMPACT ON HEALTH AND EMOTIONS

Two habits, not infrequently observed in the profoundly retarded and in certain regressed schizophrenics, serve to alienate houseparents and professionals alike and also constitute major health hazards. Reference here is to pica (eating of objects such as dirt, paint or other objects having little nutritional value) and coprophagy (the ingestion of feces). Abhorrence of coprophagy in humans has served as an effective barrier to research and little is known about its genesis. However, in primates below man, considerable attention has been accorded coprophagy because it is one of the most difficult problems facing zoo-keepers (Mitchell, 1970). Gorillas and rhesus monkeys alike frequently turn to coprophagy in captivity and Shaller's (1963) extensive studies of gorillas in the wild revealed not one instance of coprophagy. Primatologists have concluded that coprophagy "is a condition occurring in captivity" (Mitchell, 1970), and boredom has been causally linked to its expression.

Because our programs for the profoundly retarded, nonverbal, institutionalized persons are far less adequate than those for verbal retardates, and since early institutionalization (captivity) is so often the case, it seemed reasonable to Cleland, Rago and Jones (1978) that conditions leading gorillas, monkeys or PMRs to coprophagy were basically similar. In monkeys, "the longer, the earlier, and the more severe the captive situation...the more frequently coprophagy occurred" (Mitchell, 1970). Cleland, Rago and Jones (1978) studied two groups of PMRs--the coprophagics' mean Social Quotient was 11.3, the non-coprophagic SQ mean was 10.8, and the coprophagics' length of institutionalization was 18.2 years, the non-coprophagics' LOI was 16.45 years. The hypotheses guiding the study were that the coprophagics would be brighter (as measured by Intelligence Quotients or Social Quotients) and that coprophagics would be those having longer institutionalization. Although the coprophagics scored slightly higher on The Vineland Social Maturity Scale (Doll, 1953b) and did reside in the institution 1 year and 8 months longer than the non-coprophagics, the differences failed to attain statistical significance. However, when these investigators checked furlough records back to the date of admission for both groups, it was discovered that no coprophagic received a single furlough in contrast to the non-coprophagic subjects' total of 2.6 years out of the institution! Although the boredom-intelligence and length of institutionalization was not statistically significant, the trends were in the predicted direction. These investigators could only locate 8 coprophagics but their non-coprophagic sample size was 30. Had they had comparable size groups, it is likely their hypotheses would have received support. The authors speculated that if odor of feces was an attractant, then cheese snacks of tilset, Port-Salut or Limberger might prove to have substitutive value (Gorman, 1964). The only cheese foods on the menu were mild cheddar and cottage cheese.

In the event boredom and coprophagy are found in future research to be causally linked, it could lead to improved programming for the PMR. How? If one facility has a very low incidence of coprophagy among its PMRs, while another has a very high incidence then, by carefully noting differences in programs, appropriate changes could be made. Suggested here is that frequency of coprophagy could be one index of the quality of care given by various facilities.

If coprophagy could be reduced, then hospitalization due to diarrhea, cholera, shigella, dysentery, or other bacteria-related problems could be more readily controlled. Additionally, it would undoubtedly help to reduce attendant turnover--a major economic problem and an even greater problem in providing the PMR consistent mothering or fathering.

A recent and interesting study by Tillman, Grot and Steinke (1978) further testifies to the problems presented by the profoundly retarded who have pica appetite. These investigators noted that, although studies of blood lead levels had been conducted on noninstitutionalized children, none had been conducted with institutionalized retarded children. Using a sample of 1632 retarded residents, the authors found a much lower incidence of undue lead absorption than occurred in surveys of "normal" communities. Of interest, however, was that 95% of the institutional sample having unduly high blood lead levels were those functioning at the profoundly retarded level. And, of the four residents whose blood lead levels were in the toxic range, three were blind, profoundly retarded, and possessed of pica appetite. The authors point out that the PMR, ambulatory blind are at high risk since they explore their environment orally and they should be placed in buildings-areas having the lowest lead content. As they further indicate, older institutions still have areas where lead-based paint exists and, the oldest buildings are often those housing the lowest functioning resident. In an extensive survey of institutions conducted in 1974, it was very apparent that the PMR was still the victim of the out-of-sight, out-of-mind approach (McGavern, Cleland & Swartz, 1974). Such practices as back-ward placements for PMRs, as noted elsewhere (Cleland, 1978), are unlikely to foster our knowledge of this retarded subgroup.

RUMINATION AND VOMITING

To ruminate means to chew the cud; to chew again what has been chewed slightly and swallowed (Webster, 1949). A second definition Webster provides is "to bring to mind and consider again and again; to muse, ponder." Hinsie and Shatzky (1953) define rumination or Merycism as "the act of voluntary regurgitation, remastication and swallowing again." This latter definition is a psychiatric definition and, as in Webster, these writers give as a second meaning, "meditation." Kanner (1950) indicates the syndrome was initially described by Fabricus in 1687, and the intellectual range of ruminators spans from profoundly retarded to near genius. The syndrome occurs in infancy and in adults as well, and

Kanner (1950) reported that of 52 ruminating infants seen at the Harriet Lane Home, 11 died "from the results of rumination." The syndrome appears to manifest itself oftener in psychiatric or mentally retarded groups although, as Kanner (1950) points out, many ruminators are intellectual people such as physicians. Aside from the life threatening aspects of rumination (Overbeck, 1977; Libby & Phillips, 1978), the syndrome is most revolting to those who must witness it as the following case illustrates:

> __________, an ambulatory, profoundly retarded male whose Social Quotient was 9, was a chronic ruminator. He also displayed pica appetite and was once caught eating an ink bottle he had broken--glass and ink appeared equally appetizing. His rumination usually followed meals by about 15 minutes and, when out of doors in summertime, flies covered his mouth. To compound the problem, __________ would occasionally vomit and another profoundly retarded male would join __________ in eating the vomitus!
>
> Nearly all treatment strategies had been employed to break __________'s intractable habit, all to no avail. Since the above case occurred in 1951, treatment or therapeutic interventions included isolation, physical restraint, drugs, and even electroshock. __________'s physical status was deteriorating badly and weight loss was marked. The school authorities asked me if I had any suggestions that had not already been tried. My suggestion was to add, to the ruminator's food, a non-toxic color additive such as red or purple to see if this might extinguish the habit (Cleland & Swartz, 1969). Whether it was tried, or successful, cannot be answered since I left the area soon after suggesting this "remedy."

What is rumination's etiology, and what theories have been proposed to explain its occurrence? Kanner, citing Holt and McIntosh (1933) indicate it to be a functional neurosis and this psychological, rather than organic basis, would likely be the current consensus on its etiology, although undoubtedly some cases have organic roots. Theoretical explanations range widely as Kanner (1950) indicates and a few of these are: "atavistic analogy to the rumination of herbivorous animals; heredity; dilatation of the lower end of the esophagus; dilatation of the stomach; aerophagy; and boredom analogous to 'cage sickness' of animals" (p. 469).

Insofar as treatment success goes, two recent studies, both successfully diminishing the habit and both employing a food satiation strategy, point also toward a functional etiology. Overbeck (1977) adopted Jackson, et al.'s (1975) strategy of giving excessive amounts of food and ultimately fading out the nutriment excess. Overbeck indicated an almost instant accompaniment of the decreased rumination was an increase in sociability. Overbeck's (1977) study involving the staff in the research as an integral part of the ruminator's ecosystem shows both sensitivity and sophistication in seeing that employees too have needs. This highly successful account of the elimination of rumination in a profoundly retarded female should be read by every serious student for its procedural aspects. Another, more recent success, also involving one subject, is credited to Libby and Phillips (1978). These investigators, via satiation procedures, eliminated rumination and, like Overbeck, reported increased sociability, curiosity, and amenability to programming as side effects.

Returning briefly to theoretical aspects of rumination, let's consider first the "atavistic analogy to the rumination of herbivorous animals." On the surface, it sounds rather ludicrous. Man, unlike ruminants, is constructed differently--we do not have complex, four-part stomachs. However, the theory has been around for a very long time, so let's look at some recent evidence coming from research on altered states of consciousness, namely sleep research. Jouvet (1967), studying a variety of animals, as well as humans, says, "We find a fairly strong indication that the hunting species (man, felines, and canines) enjoy more deep sleep than the hunted (rabbits and ruminants)." Suggested, on the basis of Jouvet's work as this may relate to human ruminators is underlying fear or anxiety? For mass-living, profoundly retarded ruminators, are these the nondominants--fearful of predation by others diurnally or nocturnally? Would PMR ruminators' sleep stages reveal a lesser amount of deep sleep? Eating (or ruminating) can, according to frequency, mean several things. Frequent eating could mean an assuagement of anxiety, a substitute for love, it could mean the person is bored. In rumination, older children and adults "show a remarkable selectivity, bringing up only their favorite food while disliked substances are not regurgitated" (Kanner, 1950). Among a high school honors group, members used to call each other and invite them "to come over and chew the cud." What they meant was to come over and discuss various intellectual topics or controversial issues. While analogies do not support the issue of atavism, the bridging or linking to the second meaning of rumination is clear. Finally, in thinking of reflective or contemplative types of people as opposed to impulsive types, it is interesting to observe the two types at meals. To the writer, it seems that the more reflective/contemplative person chews slowly, deliberating as it were, while the impulsives tend more to be wolfish in devouring their meals. This latter thought is, of course, mere speculation. The evidence for an atavistic theory appears best supported by Jouvet's sleep research and, of course, this evidence is indirect. To conjecture about the bringing up of only preferred foods by ruminators--perhaps, for nonverbal PMRs who ruminate this could be an oblique way of isolating their food preferences?

The boredom theory has been advanced to explain several eating disorders, and coprophagy and rumination are representative. In their test of boredom and coprophagy, Cleland, Rago and Mukherjee (1978) failed to support the boredom position although the trends were in the predicted directions. The two ruminators studied by Overbeck (1977) and Libby and Phillips (1978) were institutionalized at ages 9 and 5 respectively, and their ages at the time of the two studies were 32 and 17. In Jackson, Johnson, and Ackron's (1975) study involving two profoundly retarded ruminators, both appeared to have been institutionalized very early in their lives. It is known that in higher primates, the longer and more severe their captivity, the more likely they are to become coprophagic. Based on the knowledge that institutions were much less stimulating and also poorly staffed 15 to 20 years ago, the boredom hypothesis of rumination appears to the author to have the leading edge over the atavistic thesis. We hope that young PMRs being institutionalized today may not develop the rumination syndrome.

Vomiting can have organic bases or psychological origins. Speaking of infant's feeding disorders, vomiting included, Kanner (1950) maintains that "the most potent psychologic factor...is an agitated, uncertain parent or nurse" (p. 455). And, as noted elsewhere in this text, turnover, absenteeism, and days off almost insure the institutionalized PMR of some pretty uncertain parent surrogates. When it occurs in a PMR whose medical history reflects little of this, vomiting can signal illness or a brain tumor and should receive immediate medical attention. Projectile vomiting not infrequently is associated with a brain neoplasm and may, in part, be the genesis of the old institutional cliche, "When the hydrocephalics start to vomit, you'd better start measuring their heads" (Dingman, Cleland & Swartz, 1970). Vomiting can also be caused by motion or car sickness, overexcitement or overeating. If direct care workers carefully note the time of day, frequency, and situation in which vomiting occurs, stimuli that serve as triggers can be avoided. On occasion, vomiting occurs as an attention getting vehicle. Vomiting, like rumination, can be life threatening. For this reason, it is important to seek the cause and take therapeutic action.

ENURESIS AND ENCOPRESIS

The frequency of enuresis and encopresis among profoundly retarded persons is extremely high compared to normal individuals and constitutes a major problem in care. In concert, these disorders also extract an economic toll since soiled clothing and bedding keeps the laundry in constant activity. Enuresis usually is defined as the involuntary passage of urine after the age of three (Thorpe, 1955; Kanner, 1956; Goldenson, 1970) and occurs most often in males. Encopresis refers to involuntary defecation after the age of two, and again males significantly outnumber females. Both conditions from an etiological standpoint entail a significant functional or psychogenic component, although some enuretics and encopretics do have an organic basis. And, as Kanner (1950) and Goldenson (1970) indicate, individuals having organic brain damage, as many PMRs do, would be expected to exhibit a higher frequency of enuresis and encopresis than normals. This notwithstanding, most cases of either condition are thought to entail a strong psychogenic component. How many profoundly retarded are enuretic? Based upon several sources, a reasonable estimate would yield over 85%. The number of encopretics among PMRs would probably amount to 75% although this estimate is less reliable than for enuresis.

Historically, these conditions have occasioned a variety of remedial measures, but it was not until 1963 that a really systematic approach was presented by Ellis. Ellis's approach entailed a stimulus-response reinforcement analysis, and it has since enjoyed widespread application in numerous residential facilities. Since this approach is well known to most readers, it will not be further considered here but readers unfamiliar with this method are referred to Ellis (1963).

The author's interest in the problem of enuresis and encopresis arises out of familiarity with the work of ethologists and their emphasis on direct observation in natural settings of both animals and humans. When we consider a typical ward or dormitory housing the profoundly retarded, certain facts stand out. First a PMR dormitory is characterized by a very static population. There is little by way of discharge or furlough to disturb the equilibrium, and the major cause of resident turnover, at least in adult PMR dormitories, is likely death. Discharges or transfers would probably be the second highest cause of turnover. Another fact about PMR dormitories concerns new admissions. Usually, institutions have a waiting list. When a vacancy occurs due to death, discharge or transfer, a PMR from the list is admitted.

Keeping in mind the above facts and combining them with the knowledge that male enuretics and encopretics outnumber females appreciably led the author to muse about certain ethological studies on territoriality, scent-marking, and aggression in animals. In animals below man, territorial defense is primarily a male function, and it is invigorated if a strange male of the same species invades an established territory (Ralls, 1971). In another study Müller-Schwarze (1971) maintained that "the terrestrial mammal has still to be found in which urine does not play a role in a social context or in marking the environment." He also mentioned children's bed-wetting under emotional stress "even though olfaction may not be involved." Since the PMR cannot easily vent anger toward attendants, and they have no verbal means to tell us their space has been violated or how much they need, we asked "Can nocturnal urination and defecation among PMR males be interpreted as territorial defense (and aggression) by means of scent-marking?" If so, spatial enlargement, cessation of new admissions (strange male invaders), and visual boundaries between their beds should reduce both urination and defecation.

Nine chronic noctural and diurnal enuretic and encopretic males (mean CA = 25.11; mean SQ = 12.0) were, subsequent to baseline measurements, provided a 64% spatial enlargement by removing 16 residents from their 13.7 m x 9.4 m sleeping area. During the test phase, no new admissions were allowed by administrative order. As predicted, a marked increase in the number of dry and clean beds occurred. These findings strongly suggest that territorial defense may be a motivating force in human as well as animal behavior (Hereford, Cleland & Fellner, 1973). Paluck and Esser (1971) had earlier studied territorial behaviors in severely retarded, Tucker (1972) studied college students and spatial behaviors, and Rago (1976) has extended our knowledge of the territorial behaviors of profoundly retarded persons. What these studies demonstrate is the utility of the ethological model in extending our knowledge of the spatial needs of nonverbal humans and an alternate approach to reducing soiling and wetting. In combination with an approach such as Ellis's which entails daytime training, the approach taken by Hereford et al. would perhaps significantly reduce the problem posed by incontinence.

ANXIETY IN THE PROFOUNDLY RETARDED

There is a general consensus among mental retardation authorities that the feeling of anxiety is universal among humans (Hutt & Gibby, 1965; Robinson & Robinson, 1976). There is also a fairly good agreement that retarded persons are characterized by higher levels of anxiety. When it comes to an operational definition of anxiety, disagreement is widespread and opinions differ on the varieties or types of anxiety. However, as English and English (1958) warn, "Anxiety must be read with great vigilance for an author's meaning or, more often than not, his several meanings." Goldenson's (1970) definition, "A diffuse feeling of dread, apprehension, and impending catastrophe," seems appropriate for present purposes. As Goldenson points out, anxiety differs from fear in that its source is largely internal and only vaguely perceived whereas fear usually involves a known source of external danger. Hutt and Gibby (1965) discuss from a psychoanalytic viewpoint some of the thoughts on the origins of anxiety. Great emphasis is placed on the birth process and Freud viewed birth as the first danger perceived by everyone--a radically different environment is encountered from that characterizing uterine life. As such, Freud postulated that the birth process was the physiological model for later anxiety. Rank (1929) in The Trauma of Birth indicated that birth is both psychologically and physiologically shocking and thus becomes the source of anxiety. Another prominent psychoanalytic writer, Phyllis Greenacre, holds that "constitutional factors, prenatal experiences, the birth process, and the situation immediately after birth" all are involved to predispose a child to anxiety (Hutt & Gibby, 1965). As the Robinsons (1976) maintain, "...anxiety is an extremely difficult, if not impossible, concept to define or to differentiate operationally from any other high state of arousal" (pp. 185-86).

From this brief discussion of anxiety, we see that the birth process occupies a place of prominence relative to the genesis of anxiety and that most studies of the retarded indicate the retarded are characterized by a higher level of anxiety. Since almost all studies of anxiety in the retarded have employed mildly retarded, we can only speculate about anxiety levels in profoundly retarded subjects. However, if we consider Greenacre's position that invokes constitutional factors, prenatal experiences, the birth process, and the situation immediately after birth as <u>all</u> involved in predisposing one to anxiety, perhaps we can tailor a longitudinal study to ascertain whether PMRs are more anxious than mildly retarded persons.

On the surface of our question about the anxiety levels of PMRs, it would appear easy to argue that they would be the most anxious of humans. Why? If birth is traumatic to all humans and the trauma (stimulus flooding) is overwhelming and generative of anxiety, think of the plight of the PMR. An overwhelming number of PMRs have organic brain damage as an etiological component whereas the mildly retarded generally do not reflect any demonstrable physiological defect. Thus, among PMRs it would appear that many of their births were excessively traumatic compared to mildly retarded or normals. Recall here Pasamanick and Lilienfeld's "continuum of reproductive failure," and it is apparent that the insult to the PMR during prenatal life or during birth must have been substantial to yield this degree of intellectual and, often, physical defect. As one effort to determine anxiety levels in PMRs, we could draw a sample of PMRs where an extremely difficult birth is known to have occurred, another group of normal children whose birth was adjudged "easy, effortless, etc." (as in cases where mothers elected the Leboyer or Lamaze natural childbirth methods designed, among other things, to minimize mother's anxiety about birth), and perhaps a group of mildly retarded children having no history of difficult birth and no demonstrable brain damage. Since the PMRs are nonverbal, physiological and clinical measures or indices of anxiety would be necessary such as heart-rate monitoring, palmar sweating, rapid breathing, muscular tension, frequency of urination and defecation, and so forth. As mentioned, such a study would be both comparative and longitudinal in nature. We might include twins or triplets among the subjects, since this is a rare occurrence in humans, and it is known that individuals of multiple births are more at-risk for a variety of pathologies, mental retardation included (Cleland, Case & Ford, 1977).

The above proposed study is purposefully sketchy and incomplete. The students and instructor are challenged to criticize it as to the potential or lack of same and to suggest possible ways of improving on the basic idea provided. I believe it important to learn more about the nature and extent of anxiety in the profoundly retarded. For, if they are suffering intense anxiety and we can discover valid ways of measuring it, then program changes that reduce anxiety can be detected and program changes that increase anxiety can be discarded. If the foregoing approach to studying anxiety as it relates to various styles of being born seems to have merit, it may be possible to shed some light on theories relating to the origins of anxiety.

GYNECOLOGICAL PROBLEMS

Toilet training the profoundly retarded is a major undertaking, but training is even more difficult in the matter of a cyclic (monthly) occurrence such as menstruation (Pattullo & Bernard, 1968). While a considerable literature on the gynecology of normal females exists, hardly any interest was shown in the profoundly retarded until the Cooke and Weaver (1948) report. Numerous abnormal gynecologic conditions were reported among the 1,014 females in their study. Of those beyond 18 years of age, the survey revealed that 244 had intact hymens. While all four levels of retardation were included in the Cooke and Weaver study, they estimated about one-third were profoundly retarded. Among the abnormalities noted, congenital absence of the left adnexa, midline vaginal septum with a biforis, transverse vaginal septum, congenital stenoses of the vagina represent only a few of the 1,262 abnormalities noted in their sample of 1,014 women. It is an interesting and recurrent finding that although the PMR females have the shortest lifespan of all women, no cervical cancer has been reported on institutionalized (hence virginal) PMRs (Gagnon, 1950; Cooke & Weaver, 1948; Cleland, Powell & Talkington, 1971).

In a lecture to my seminar on profound retardation about a decade ago, I remarked, "We probably know more about menstruation, cycles, and sexual behavior in primates than we do about such issues in the profoundly retarded."

Jane Lee, a student in the seminar, promptly embarked on a dissertation study and in 1971, her results were in. Lee's (1971) study involved 322 profoundly retarded women whose mean age was 22.01 years and whose mean IQ or SQ was 9.82. Of interest was the finding that not one of her women attained menarche under age 10 and only 3 did before age 14. She found that premenopausal menstruation cycles occurred at about 34 years as constrasted to normal menopause at around 47 to 50 years. Interesting too was the fact that no subject beyond age 29 menstruated regularly. In support of using intelligence quotients at this lowest functioning level, Lee found her regularly menstruating subjects had higher IQs (more scoring above 10) than irregular or amenorrheic subjects. This could also represent another method of subgroup identification within the IQ range of 0-19 (a topic more fully addressed in the next chapter). Finally, Lee points out that the profoundly retarded experience behavioral changes associated with the menstrual period, such as increased seizures, crossness, more biting and spitting, more wildness, more hyperactivity, more vomiting, and increased aggression. Readers interested in Lee's extensive study of the gynecology of the profoundly retarded should consult the original work.

In 1976, Rago, Case and I attempted a study of whether or not menstrual synchrony occurs in the profoundly retarded as has been noted in communally living normal women (McClintock, 1971). The study failed to materialize since the institution embarked on a massive moving of residents into new dormitories which, of course, would have invalidated the study. A synopsis of this proposal appears in Appendix C. Readers interested in an excellent historical account of menstruation should consult Delaney, Lupton, and Toth (1976).

OBLIQUE APPROACHES TO TOILET TRAINING

Many indirect approaches to toilet training emerge if we carefully scrutinize the heterogeneous behaviors of PMRs. To most observers, staring fixedly at a bright light, twirling a string incessantly, or urinating on another person or into an electrical outlet are grossly deviant actions. To experienced workers, such acts are examined for their possible meaning to the initiator, that is, what response does the act evoke? When PMRs stare into sunlight or an indoor light it is often noted that they wave their arm and hand before their eyes to obtain an alternating pattern of bright and less light. If interrupted or restrained in this activity, their countenance mirrors irritability, or a smile is replaced by a grimace or frown. Most plausibly, the activity of staring-waving at the light source means pleasure or reinforcement to them. The power of M&M's notwithstanding, a number of reinforcers exist beyond food or drink. Halting PMRs from string-twirling also evokes signs of displeasure.

When consideration is turned to the PMRs who urinate on an electrical wall outlet or another person, what do they gain? In some PMRs, as we have noted, pain thresholds may be quite high, and the shock received from urinating into an electrical outlet may, instead of inducing pain, enhance pleasure. Despite the danger inherent in such a practice, the sensation received could be the equivalent of masturbation in normals. To assist us in thinking of meanings inherent in the act of urination, a brief case example involving six normal, six-year-old males may prove helpful.

> It was hot summertime and school had been out for over a month. Six six-year-old males were loafing at a neighborhood pond and were obviously bored with their freedom from school. Near the edge of the pond a log protruded and several turtles were sunning themselves. One boy took notice and said challengingly, "I'll bet I can 'pee' on that turtle way out on the log!" Another boy countered, "You can't even 'pee' off your shoe-tops!" What ensued was a game of target practice and all contestants seemed enthusiastically to take their turns. For our bored contestants, the penis was an active instrument of 'attack' and urine, the 'bullet.'

Male-female anatomical differences, it should be noted, may occasion different approaches to toilet training. Having made these several actions (light-seeking, urinating, etc.) the subject of speculation over their meaning, how can these be employed in toilet training?

Take our light-seeker PMRs. Our first task in training is to get them into the bathroom--whether at home, at school, or in an institution. If light appears strongly reinforcing, use it! If our light-seeking PMRs are institutionalized, and gang, wall-mounted urinals are common, let us place a spotlight above and direct the beam onto the urinal. If there were 5 or 10 urinals in a row, this modification would be employed on only 1 or 2. Teachers or teacher aides would observe to see if the light-seekers (previously identified and catalogued as those for whom light appeared reinforcing) more readily went to the bathroom and, in turn, preferred to stand at the urinal having illumination. As a variation, the light could be placed directly before the urinal (line-of-sight), and urination would break a photoelectric beam and switch on the bright light for, say, two minutes. This would necessitate the desired act actually being accomplished and in the proper place--otherwise, no reward.

In the case of those who appear to urinate using penis and urine as weapons, a different strategy might succeed. In this case we have the urinal respond in a dramatic way to being voided into. For example, when urination breaks a photoelectric beam, release of flushing occurs and colored water pours forth. Thus, the act of urinating gets a visual (blue water) and auditory (flushing sound) reinforcement from the urinal. Also, there is the reward of release of bladder pressure inherent in the act of voiding. If <u>doing</u> something <u>to</u> something to gain stimulation is actually the motivation, we could have a bell or buzzer activated to satisfy the PMRs' need to use penis-urine as active instruments. Again, we would need to observe to ascertain the improvement resulting from use of the "active-doing" urinal versus the ordinary urinal.

Certain precautions are needed in trying out such technological-mechanical teaching aids. A consulting electrical engineer would be invaluable in introducing and developing the "automated urinals." Safety assurances would be mandatory. Concerns about the efficiency of such training also arise and go beyond this consideration to include transfer of toileting skills to other, nontechnical bathrooms.

Other motives of PMRs or perhaps severe autistics may be considered in our efforts to toilet train them. In the group of mass-care setting such as institutions or the public schools, let us examine a <u>possible</u> reason why toilet training of the retarded or autistic child is often unsuccessful or, if it is accomplished, frequent accidents still occur. Reference here is to the human emotion of shyness and the privacy motive--two aspects of humanness rarely considered in relation to very low-functioning persons.

First, an example afforded by observation of normal children and adults in settings where privacy is easily violated and shyness is easy to observe. In the elementary school one ordinarily is expected to relieve one's biological urges during recess but by requesting permission by holding up one's hand and verbally asking to go, exceptions can occur. If a student is overly shy, the discomfort of bowel or bladder pressure might be endured for an entire school day. By having to publicly ask permission the shy ones "blow their cover." At recess, a shy boy might go to the urinal, but because of the incompatible nature of sphincter relaxation and the shyness emotion, fail to void or defecate--the physical closeness of other males serving to thwart a physical need. Again, in the Armed Services during World War II, the restrooms were often very crowded, and the shy men were noted to wait for hours when the restrooms were unlikely to have other occupants, that is, 2 3 or 4 a.m. The men's rooms in a large building of a major university affords yet another example of failure to start urinating or cessation of same when a stranger positions himself at an adjacent urinal. Again, the "invasion" of privacy and activation of the shyness emotion are sufficient to block either urination or defecation in those plagued with shyness.

Although the foregoing examples are noted only among males and normals, females too are not immune from shyness or a need for privacy. Neither, we suspect, are <u>all</u> low-functioning persons immune. J. McVicker Hunt (1960) once remarked, "Multiple mothering is an innoculation against social shyness and fear" and, therefore, we would expect long-term or early institutionalized PMRs or SMRs to be less inhibited in toileting. All of these were very early given multiple mothering as a function of three shifts, high turnover, and so forth. However, for new admissions or those living at home and attending day school, our toileting approaches might need to be tempered with consideration of shyness-privacy needs. To do this, the trainer should be the most familiar and trusted of all teachers or parent surrogates.

Another consideration in toilet training has to do with the symbolism inherent in enuresis. Some authorities (Kessler, 1966; Freud & Dann, 1951) link bed-wetting with release of hostility. To the extent this could be a motive for some, it would appear wise to provide systematically for release of hostility--especially immediately before bedtime. Mom, dad, or surrogate parent might roughhouse or stage a brief sham-battle with the PMR-SMR enuretic and feign losing--getting whipped! This has occasionally served to diminish wetting.

DENTISTRY AND ORAL HYGIENE

Skeletal and dental abnormalities in the mentally retarded are more frequently noted than in the normal population and, as we descend the intellectual ladder to the profoundly retarded, the frequency of these abnormalities increases greatly. Additionally, since a large number of PMRs have convulsive disorders and require medication for seizure control, the problem of oral hygiene is further magnified. Phenobarbital and other anti-convulsants can have the undesirable side effect of causing gum problems. Occasionally a profoundly retarded person has an enormously enlarged tongue. This complicates further the dentist's problem in providing good care. The tongue, a muscle, may become greatly enlarged over time if the PMR is a tongue-sucker. This habit provides continuous exercise and leads to gross enlargement of the tongue and filling of the oral cavity. Pica appetite, discussed elsewhere in this text, as well as coprophagy further challenge dental professionals in their efforts to maintain the PMRs' oral health. Finally (though this list is not exhaustive), PMRs remain relatively fixated at a very early life stage where orality is common behavior. Thumb-sucking is notable and causes the teeth to be in poor alignment. Although the literature on dentistry with PMRs is limited, let's examine some of it to learn something of the problems and the progress that is occurring.

In Chapter 1, several of the author's speculative approaches to differential diagnosis in profound retardation were mentioned. Let's now examine some advances in dentistry that could be of help in diagnostic work. Kraus, Clark, and Oka (1968) proposed, on the basis of studying the dentition of 260 normal and 189 retarded persons (all levels), two new fields of inquiry--odontoglyphics and dentochronology. Odontoglyphics refers to "early detection of the presence of latent damage to the central nervous system by means of dental morphology, and dentochronology--the establishment of the time of insult to the organism" (Kraus, et al., 1968). In their study, the normals had more teeth than the retarded, but the retarded had 29 times (in one sample) or 14 times (in another MR sample) as many dental abnormalities as normals! This line of study appears promising for, as the authors point out, "overt symptoms of damage to the central nervous system may be delayed, but the teeth record the insult instantly and permanently" (p. 916).

Another, more recent study of the dental treatment of the retarded by O'Grady and Talkington (1977) is of interest in spelling out how the profoundly retarded compare with other levels of mental retardation on dental care.

These authors indicate the scarcity of research on dentistry with the PMR. In their survey of 974 residents of the Fairview Training Center, certain patterns of dental care emerged. All mental retardation levels (N = 974) were included in the authors' initial survey, and it was noted that significantly more diagnostic dental services were given to mild, moderate and severely retarded residents than to the profoundly retarded. The profoundly retarded received significantly fewer preventive services as well as fewer restorative services than higher level retardates. Only in number of extractions and sedations given did the PMR equal or excel the higher levels! As the authors point out, PMRs exist largely on soft diets, are often fed by others, and so on. The nonambulatory PMR had significantly more extractions than the ambulatory residents. Overall, as concerns the dental services the PMR appear to need, the authors sum it up nicely: "The PMR are getting the dull end of the needle and the short end of the drill" (p. 43). They suggest a real need to train dental personnel in understanding the PMR better.

As O'Grady and Talkington indicate, PMRs more so than other levels exist on soft diets and are more often fed by others. Other differences exist between PMRs' lifestyle and other mental retardation levels. Of all the institutionalized retarded, the profoundly retarded for various reasons will spend much more time indoors. Thus, the profoundly retarded are subjected to more natural light deprivation than others. In a study by Ott (1973), he replaced cool-white flourescent lighting with "new, full-spectrum tubes that more closely duplicate natural daylight" (p. 192) and found a significant difference in the number of cavities and extent of tooth decay in the new teeth of children in the experimental classrooms. Since the profoundly retarded are so prone to all forms of dental abnormalities, and provision of dental care is so difficult (Bensberg, Barnett & Menius, 1966), much suffering might be prevented if full-spectrum lighting were provided. Although the effects on human physiology and behavior of wide-spectrum lighting are complex and only recently coming under research scrutiny, some investigators in the Soviet Union have reported full-spectrum lighting resulted in improved reaction times and reduction of fatigue in those students exposed to the newer lighting. Students under conventional lighting showed no such improvements (Edelson, 1974). Other behavioral improvements and physiological changes in association with light are reviewed in Cleland, Rago and Case (1977) and interested readers are referred to this source for a more extended discussion.

Another barrier to provision of good dental care is the oft-referred to differential pain thresholds of the profoundly retarded. While most of us, when an abscessed gum or exposed tooth nerve exists, will be given nature's warning or pain, the profoundly retarded may get a different kind of sensation. An example of differential response to pain is supplied by a thirty-year-old, severely retarded male who possessed some speech. Joe approached the author on the school playground and I noticed his visibly-swollen jaw. He laughed and said, "My tooth tickles! For this individual, whose tooth was found to be badly abscessed on dental examination, the pain appeared minimal. For most of us it would have been excruciating. While it is true that pain is a highly subjective and individualistic sensation and is a very complex subject, there are reasons to believe that its function as a warning signal is not as adequate in profoundly retarded persons as in normals. In the first place, an inordinate number of PMRs have some brain damage. Additionally, Cleland and Clark's (1966) review of sensory processes in profound and severely retarded persons revealed that as we descend the intellectual ladder, sensory impairments are more often noted. More recently, O'Grady and Talkington (1976) compared the four levels of retardation on the Behavior Development Survey (Payne, 1968) and found significantly more visual and hearing impairments in the profound level than in any of the three higher levels. Also, some among the profoundly retarded may be congenitally devoid of pain sensitivity. Very little empirical evidence on pain in the retarded exists and few mental retardation textbooks even reference pain. Most of our information is of a clinical-anecdotal nature, but professionals such as dentists and physicians often report that many of the PMRs appear to have high thresholds for pain. Even in the profound level, however, individual differences in pain sensation exist. The point of the foregoing is simply to alert us to the fact that the PMRs may not provide us with the signals (crying, grimacing, screaming) that the normal child or adult would give when in severe pain. Thus, unless dentists are experienced in working with PMR patients, they have considerable difficulty "figuring them out."

Efforts to provide better oral health to profoundly retarded persons is augmented to a certain extent by the fact that institutions are coming, more and more, to be populated mainly with severe and profound levels. Willette and Savage (1978) report on the seriousness of dental problems among retarded individuals and indicate that of a random sample of 100 residents at Fircrest School 39% had periodontal disease, 42% had accretions on teeth, 38% had chronic gingivitis, and 22% acquired absence of teeth! The average age of this sample was only 30! However, these investigators initiated a novel motivational program for their higher-level retarded patients and suggest some guides as to how to improve the profoundly retarded patients' oral health. Among these, the manual guidance teams (working with profoundly retarded) selected the quietest time of the day and indicate that a recreational area proved superior to the bathroom area for conducting their work. These researchers also indicated that patient resistance to treatment was a major concern, but by using two staff members with one cradling the patient's head from behind while the other restrained the resident's hands, success was achieved. Parenthetically, the use of contact comfort (cradling of head) has been suggested elsewhere as a method of quieting the profoundly retarded while shaving them (Cleland & Swartz, 1969), but, fortunately, the electric razor has made this a somewhat easier operation. Willette and Savage also allude to the resistant patients as occasionally biting the toothbrush. As the experienced reader may observe, there are PMRs whose biting constitutes a hazard to the fingers of those who try to serve them--another reason why a degree of wariness is sometimes necessary (Butterworth & Bower, 1958).

In the O'Grady and Talkington study mentioned above as well as in the Willette and Savage study, the profoundly retarded were noted to have more teeth extractions than other levels of the retarded. Historically, institutions have been grossly understaffed and ward densities have been extremely high. On these so-called "back-wards" where the PMRs were crowded together, aggression levels were often high and those who bit others were, not infrequently, rendered harmless by removal of all teeth! So thin were the ranks of the houseparents and so harrassed and desperate were the professionals that radical procedures were often required.

As Arnim, Diercks and Pearson (1963) point out, periodontal disease or pyorrhea and dental caries are real diseases that can make people mentally and physically sick unless action is taken. The public enemies responsible for dental caries are flour and sugar (Armin, et al., 1963). For this reason, operant training programs and the initiators of these programs need to work hard to discover substitute reinforcers for the traditional M & Ms. Furthermore, caution is necessary in the use of candy since certain PMRs are also diabetics. It is important that one therapist does not inadvertently counteract the good work of another! Willette and Savage (1978) provide some examples of reinforcers that are acceptable to dentists, and the references provided should serve to give the non-dentist reader a good grasp of the problems involved in providing for the oral hygiene needs of the profoundly retarded.

Unless the oral hygiene care of the profoundly retarded is diligently provided, things can only get worse for them. A vicious cycle occurs. If tooth decay and gum diseases increase, mouth odors become foul indeed. Elsewhere I have mentioned the HOUND-YAVIS phenomenon--therapists like to work with the young, attractive, verbal, intelligent, and successful. The dentist and dental hygienists can do only so much for their PMR clients, and a great deal of assistance from houseparents or parents is needed. For an excellent overview of dental training programs for attendants in institutional settings, the reader should refer to Bensberg, Barnett and Menius's (1966) survey. Although over a decade has elapsed since their study, many of the problems still exist especially where the profoundly retarded are the focal concern.

Other oral habits exist to frustrate efforts to maintain good healthy teeth and gums. Some profoundly retarded practice bruxism (teeth grinding) both diurnally and nocturnally. Usually, when bruxism is seen in normals it occurs only at night. Over extended periods of time, bruxists' teeth will lose the enamel and flatten considerably. Additionally, bruxism over time will cause the teeth to loosen and bleeding gums are a common sequela of bruxism. Since bruxism is considered to have a neurotic component (Kanner, 1950), our efforts should be directed toward isolating what may be making the individual anxious, fearful, bored, or whatever. Aside from the damage to the bruxists' teeth, some perform so loudly as to disrupt the sleep of others. Of all children seen at the Johns Hopkins University Psychiatric Clinic, Kanner reported about 2% had a history of bruxism.

Enlarged tongues that fill the oral cavity, bruxism, pica and coprophagy, epilepsy, resistance to help (inability to cooperate), plus a greater tendency to feed the PMR soft diets are only a few of the challenges facing dentists and others responsible for the care of the PMRs' oral health. Fortunately, new specialties are evolving in the dental profession in recognition of the special problems of young patients who are grossly mentally or physically handicapped--the pedodontist or pediatric dentist. Specializing in children's dental problems offers promise, since the earlier oral hygiene practices are introduced the more likely that problems will be prevented.

> The mother of a ten-year-old profoundly retarded girl complained to me of a major problem in keeping her daughter at home--getting her teeth fixed. "They (the town's dentists) take one look at my grossly retarded daughter and deny that they can help her--don't have any experiences working with her type, etc. I go shopping for a dentist who can work with the badly retarded and I don't find any."

Where does one turn for help? One possibility might be for institutions to extend dental services to community living profoundly retarded. Since the institutions' population is trending to the severe and profound type of retarded, institutional dentists are becoming more and more specialized in working with these levels of retardation, and some never see a mild or moderate level retardate. So, if one seeks a dentist who is sophisticated in caring for dental problems of the profoundly retarded, the institution would be the logical place to look. The institutional administration would, in conjunction with dental and medical personnel, work out such details as fee schedules. Another avenue of help might be for parents to call the institution nearest them and ask for the name(s) of their dental consultants. Private practice dentists not infrequently also serve as consultants to state or private schools for the retarded and often become rather sophisticated in caring for the oral hygiene needs of the profoundly retarded.

ON BEING LOST AND IDENTIFICATION

The profoundly retarded are notoriously poor in space and time-binding capacity (Cleland, 1962) and should possibly be considered by research and professional people as susceptible to feeling lost. If you will reflect on your own childhood and think of being lost in a crowd, separated from your parents or guardians, it should be easy to establish an empathic set with a situation that conceivably besets the PMR. When one is very young, getting separated from one's parents in a large crowd, such as at a Fourth of July picnic, brings on a catastrophic or near panic reaction. Being adrift in a sea of strangers also heightens one's feelings of helplessness and bewilderment. When we think of a lost PMR, we think of the individual as having wandered away from or being unable to find his or her way. Whether we think of a sheep, or a child, or a PMR adult, being lost means being vulnerable.

When we consider the possibility of the PMR being lost, an unanswerable question arises. Do PMRs even know anything of separation, even in a very rudimentary way? The following actual case illustrates how being lost, how fear of the unknown and darkness, or how simply being uncomfortably cold may interact to create discomfort for the PMRs.

> Huddling close together in a single bed on dormitory X were four, profoundly retarded males of late adolescence. The time was midnight. John Smith, an attendant separated them and returned each to his own bed. On rounds at 2:00 a.m., Smith noted all four had migrated back to the same bed again. After again separating them and returning them to their own beds, Smith wrote in the daybook "Residents __________, __________, __________, and __________ again returned to their own beds." At 4:15 a.m., the same four were again found in the same bed. An identical daybook entry was again registered by Smith. The next night, the same huddling behavior occurred and so on for a week until the four finally "stayed put" in their own beds. The question this brief case generates is "What was it that caused the nightly migration and huddling together?"

Dormitory X housed over 70 residents and in the sleeping area, residents were separated into cubicles containing 12 beds each. Waist high, tile block partitions divided the sleeping area into cubicles so a more homogeneous grouping for sleeping purposes could occur. New construction at the institution allowed dormitory X to reduce their resident population by 12. After the 12 were moved out, the four "migrators" were moved into the cubicle that had been vacated. After the "migrators" were moved (from one end of the sleeping area to the vacated cubicle about 60 feet away), their migration back to their established sleeping area started. The supervisors of dorm X (all 8:00 a.m. to 5:00 p.m. shift workers) thought it would be a good move. What they failed to consider was that even at night, sleeping areas (territories) come to be established and familiarity with one's place can be psychologically comforting. Since attendant Smith's daybook entries did not indicate the huddling to be sexually motivated, are there other reasons for their migration? One possibility could be that in the new and unfamiliar sleeping area, the four were made fearful, and by returning to their traditional and well-known area, fear was diminished. By huddling close together, yet another time-honored fear reduction strategy was employed. Physical closeness is augmented by fear and the fear of darkness is almost universal in young children (Binet, 1895). Still other reasons for huddling close together could be advanced, and it is possible these migrators were simply too cold. One fact stands out, however. Their migratory behavior did not begin <u>until</u> after they had been moved into a part of the ward at considerable distance from their familiar sleeping area. Readers can weigh the case for themselves and relate this migratory behavior to what is known about the developmental level the profoundly retarded typically reach by late adolescence.

Recently, a case was reported in a major Southwestern newspaper of an adult female of severe retardation wandering away from the residential facility where she lived. The caption read, "Search for retarded woman fails." This article appeared three days after her disappearance and helicopters and ground searchers had canvassed a 400-acre area with no success. The woman was reported to have only two words in her vocabulary--"ciagarettes" and "candy." Fortunately, the missing woman was later found in good condition. This actual occurrence forces us to consider the issue of identification when individuals are incapable of telling who they are or where they are from. Diabetics, laryngectomees, heart patients taking anticlotting medication and others having unique problems often carry emergency medical identification in the form of "dog tags" on ankle, neck or wrist. However, with the PMR we are concerned with the need for personal identification in case the person is lost, although they could also have special health problems such as diabetes. How can we develop an effective personal identification when the person is uncooperative? Fingerprints, voice-prints, or a tattoo? Having the name on clothing is not very effective in the case of a profoundly retarded person who may not long remain clothed.

Several years ago a hurricane struck the Corpus Christi State School (Texas) and decommissioned several ward buildings. As an emergency measure, a number of residents were airlifted to several sister institutions until buildings were again ready for occupancy. While the mild and moderate levels could wear ID bands on wrists, severe and profounds were not so cooperative, and "keeping track" was a big problem. (During wartime, you will recall, soldiers' identification was aided by dog tags that included name, rank, serial number and blood type. Thus, the dead could be identified and the wounded could receive the proper type blood, if needed.)

Emergencies can occur in any setting. When a PMR person is lost, it is always an emergency, for their safety is in jeopardy. Having a proper and foolproof identification method should be somewhat reassuring to institution staff as well as to parents or guardians of the PMR. While you may feel this is "Much ado about nothing," it is a real problem, and it may accelerate as PMRs are deinstitutionalized into community settings where surveillance may not be as intense as in institutions.

Identification addresses Maslow's safety needs and I have posed more of a problem than a solution. If you believe a lost PMR is "at risk," then try to develop an ID method that will work and will satisfy parents and guardians as well.

Finally, turnover of attendants and teachers working with the profoundly retarded is notoriously high. For the night shift, it is even higher. The problem is compounded by high absenteeism and the legitimate taking off of 2 days per week. So what? Since one duty customarily performed by the night shift is awakening the residents to take them to the toilet, the likelihood of being awakened by a <u>stranger</u> is enormous. Consider your own reaction to being awakened in your own home by a total stranger, even a friendly stranger. What do you think your reaction would be? Fear, disbelief, terror, or "where am I?" Probably a combination of all. It would hardly be a comforting experience! Thus, reduction of turnover among attendants and other direct-care workers could have benefits far beyond the economic benefits. At the level of the PMR, it might be argued that a bonus or hazard pay differential (like that given for submarine duty in wartime) should be given to direct-care workers to reduce turnover.

Another associated problem, especially for institutionalized PMRs, created by the heavy turnover of direct-care personnel is the misidentification of residents. The problem is exacerbated by the fact that institutions ordinarily have larger numbers of PMRs than private residential schools or community centers. New, and occasionally even some longer tenured employees, don't know their residents by name, and the residents cannot tell, if asked, who they are. What is needed is a rapid method for attendants to learn the names of residents.

Toward this end, 4 x 6 inch color photos could be housed in clear lucite holders and placed on one wall of the attendants' office. Each photo would contain the resident's full name, ID number, and color-coded dots to highlight medical problems such as allergic reactions to certain medications, epilepsy, diabetes, and so on. A track arrangement for these photos would be desirable so that in case of deaths, transfers, or discharges, photos could be easily removed. Also, each resident would have a cloth name plate sewn on his or her clothes to help employees learn "who's who."

Although PMRs are currently placed in smaller groups than the common 100 to 200 bed wards of yesteryear, it is still possible for "greenhorn" houseparents occasionally to send the wrong person for a physical or psychological exam. When we deal with the nonverbal person, every precaution should be taken to insure proper identification.

4

Methods for Subgroup Differentiation

Within the ranks of the profoundly retarded, individual differences are not difficult to detect. Some PMRs are avaricious, assaultive, aggressive, impulsive; others are shy, withdrawn, taciturn--there are "thieves" and "bankers," gluttons and gourmets. In these respects, they mirror all mankind. However, minimal attention has been paid to actually using individual differences and mapping these to use them in placement, program, and research efforts. The entire field of mental retardation, and especially at the level of the PMR, has been handicapped by our failure to recognize retardates as humans, not dieties, and possessed of both good and bad qualities. They are not "Angels Unaware," but people. Our emotional blinders have slowed knowledge production. Lindsley (1964), Miller (1976) and Cleland (1973) have made attempts to utilize individual differences in this very low functioning group to improve our placement, programming, and research strategies, and we will examine some of these in this chapter. Certain of them are empirically based; others suggested by me are hypothetical or speculative. These are given primarily to stimulate discussion and criticism.

MUSIC: AN APPROACH TO A DANCE GROUP

Among the PMRs are there some who would enjoy dancing--either solo or with a partner of the opposite sex? Is there, among them, a frustrated Nureyev? Music and dance are two of the highest art forms, and music is often termed the universal language. Elderly people confined to wheelchairs can, through the medium of the music of their youth, vicariously experience a time of vigor, romance, and ecstasy and, if we add dancing of youngsters (a la Lawrence Welk) to older music, the experience is enhanced (Cleland, 1978). Darwin (1872) says music has other interesting effects. "We know that every strong sensation, emotion, or excitement--extreme pain, rage, terror, joy, or the passion of love--all have a special tendency to cause the muscles to tremble; and the thrill or slight shiver which runs down the backbone and limbs of many persons when they are powerfully affected by music seems to bear the same relation to the above trembling of the body, as a slight suffusion of tears from the power of music does to weeping from any strong and real emotion" (Darwin, 1872, p. 217). My repeated query to certain of my classes, "Do you ever get gooseflesh or goose-pimples when a big band marches onto the field and strikes up a vibrant march?" always confirms Darwin. None have yet denied this visible index to an underlying emotional state of awe or joy. However, when I ask "Do you think PMRs have or display gooseflesh on seeing or hearing a band or viewing something spectacular?" they always shake their heads in puzzlement. But try as hard as we can, we cannot suppress goose-pimples on an emotional arousal.

The above digression introduces us to the question--how can music be used to single out PMRs who might enjoy dancing, music, or both? One approach is through body-rocking. Ordinarily, body-rocking is taken as an index of an unstimulating, monotonous, and sterile environment (Klaber & Butterfield, 1968), but rocking can also be induced by stimulation, by music in particular (Cleland, 1962). In studying volume level preference in the profoundly and severely retarded, I determined it was the "louder the better." The loud music seemed to occasion more smiles. As an ex-musician, I also noticed some were swaying or rocking in accord to the tempo of the music. This being the case, we could take note of those PMRs who have a keen sense of musical timing and who also smile in great delight and consider them as candidates for our dance class. If we determined that some of the candidates we had isolated were also echophraxic (motor mimics), then these would be those most likely to learn dancing rapidly.

Should we tease out the confession from our PMRs that it's listening, rather than dancing, that is the primary appeal, then we could think in terms of providing a class for them in music appreciation. It is not absurd to conceive of some PMRs as capable of enjoying music, even quiet music.

Through the isolation of special subgroups of PMRs with similar interests, and the design of programs to meet these needs, it would be a likely expectation that fighting, screaming, and destructive acts would diminish. To the research-minded person, any program change or environmental alteration should inspire, "Let's wrap a design around that!"

From this brief excursion into the arts, we do not anticipate Nureyevs or Dame Margots; we do anticipate more satisfied PMR recipients of our programs and services.

SELF-AWARENESS IN PMRs: BLUSHING AND OTHER EMOTIONS

Self-awareness involves a "knowledge of one's own traits or qualities; insight into, and understanding of, one's own behavior and motives" (English & English, 1958). Self-recognition, by contrast, means "does one know when confronted by a mirror that the person (image) is indeed himself?" When we raise issues on the several involuntary emotions that humans display, it is interesting to also examine to what extent these emotions are present in the profoundly retarded. For example, _shame_ is a complex emotional state, involving negative self-feeling or a disagreeable feeling of inferiority or defeat and is manifested in such statements as "I'm ashamed of doing that," "I'm ashamed of the way I look in a bathing suit," and the like. Now, according to McDougall, an early social psychologist, shame is incapable of being experienced until a self-sentiment has been developed. In McDougall's views, every primary instinct has its emotional counterpart, for example, the flight instinct generates the emotion of fear (Goldenson, 1970). What are the visible symptoms of shame? Head lowering, gaze-avoidance, and perhaps blushing are common indices of a person experiencing the emotion of shame. In thinking of shame in the PMR, and of McDougall's caveat, what evidence bears on the issue? And, what do others have to say about emotions?

Darwin (1872) maintained that "blushing is the most peculiar and the most human of all expressions" (p. 309). Darwin notes that blushing is involuntary and that the harder one seeks to suppress it, the more blushing is augmented since the wish to restrain blushing serves only to direct attention to oneself. Blushing's onset Darwin puts in normal children at two-and-a-half to three years and suggests it doesn't occur in infancy since mental powers are not sufficiently developed. He further observes that idiots rarely blush and cites Dr. Crichton Browne as having never seen an idiot geniunely blush. Darwin, however, always looked for other evidence and described the case of a microcephalic idiot of 13 years who blushed and turned away when undressed for a medical examination. Other handicapping conditions and blushing were examined, and the congenitally blind and deaf Laura Bridgman blushed as do albinos, the mentally ill, and all races of mankind. Older people blush less than young, and women blush more than men. Darwin's hypothesis relative to blushing "is that attention closely directed to any part of the body tends to interfere with the ordinary and tonic contraction of the small arteries of that part. These vessels, in consequence, become at such times more or less relaxed, and are instantly filled with arterial blood. This tendency will have been much strengthened, if frequent attention has been paid during many generations to the same part, owing to nerve-force readily flowing along accustomed channels, and by the power of inheritance... (and) those of the face will have become eminently susceptible" (p. 337). The mental conditions predisposing one to blush are threefold: shyness, shame, and modesty. Blushing, regardless of the mental state that triggers it, depends on one principle: "this principle being a sensitive regard to the opinion of others" (Darwin, 1872, p. 335).

From the foregoing discussion, we can inquire as to whether our profoundly retarded do have even the dimmest hints of modesty, shyness, shame, and whether or not they ever blush. Spending so much page space on one emotional expression, blushing, may be justified since Darwin considers it the most human of all expressions, and I see blushing as having possibilities for defining functional subgroups within the psychometric range of profound retardation. One fact stands out--seldom, if ever, do professionals or direct-care workers with the PMRs even bother to look for expressions of underlying emotions in this retarded group. Since I first offered my seminar entitled "Profound Mental Retardation" in 1965, I have repeatedly inquired of graduate students, "Have you ever noticed a PMR blush?" and "Have you ever noticed a

PMR sitting alone, in relative solitude, break into a broad grin or laugh?" For, if we had unequivocal affirmatives on both questions, we would have evidence that some among them have the capacity of self or other regard or that a thought crossed their mind and caused them to smile. Conceivably, these PMRs (who display such capabilities) are deserving of additional training along social lines.

However, you may argue, "Why bother to look for subtle emotions in a group whose greatest accomplishment may be to feed and toilet themselves--it's ridiculous!" What is proposed is that natural life events for PMRs be closely observed to see if we can detect blushing, and one such event to observe would be a physical exam. While physicians are usually tuned in on the physical status per se, they are also curious enough to look for blushing if they are simply asked to report any case of it among PMRs. A verified report of a "blusher" could be educationally important--why? Consider Rev. R. H. Blair's report to Darwin that "The blind are not at first (when very young) conscious that they are observed, and it is a most important part of their education...to impress this knowledge on their minds; and the impression thus gained would greatly strengthen the tendency to blush, by increasing the habit of self-attention" (Darwin, 1872, p. 311). Thus, if a PMR does blush, we have isolated one index that some have at least a rudimentary "sensitive regard for the opinion of others."

> In 1973, I received the first affirmative reply to the query, "Have you ever noticed a PMR blush?" Jan Case, a doctoral student, was then working as a ward attendant on a PMR dormitory at Travis State School (Texas) and said, "Yes." When I questioned him about the circumstances, he replied, "I walked into the bathroom and caught __________ doing something he knew he wasn't supposed to be doing--he instantly stopped and turned away blushing."

Returning to McDougall's view that shame cannot be experienced until a self-sentiment has been developed, we may be thwarted in our efforts to employ involuntary emotional expressions as developmental indices in PMRs. For, at a more elementary level, self-recognition precedes the occurrence of sensitive regard for the opinion of others, and knowledge of self is thought basic to all further social interactions (Goldenson, 1970). Self-recognition in normal children as revealed by self-directed behavior toward a mirror appears at about 20 months (Gallup, 1975). What evidence is there when we confront the profoundly retarded with the mirror? Pechacek et al. (1973) conducted two studies on PMRs involving extensive mirror training. In their first study, subjects having a mean Social Quotient of 12.68 and a chronological age mean of 23.0 were exposed to a full length mirror three times daily for a three-day period. A nontoxic dye marker was surreptitiously placed on their foreheads during sleep and on awakening they were individually taken to the mirror. None gave any unequivocal evidence of self-recognition. In study II, subjects' mean Social Quotient was 10.1 and their chronological age was 19.86. All senses, odor included, were involved to enhance attending to the mirror during training and, again, after training, no subject displayed self-recognition. Harris (1977) using subjects having IQs below 19 and a far more extensive training procedure concluded, "PMR subjects do not demonstrate self-recognition" and suggested other procedures or longer training might install self-recognition. Despite these discouraging results, it should be pointed out that all subjects had lengthy institutionalization and had undoubtedly little previous experience with mirrors.

What is suggested from the foregoing is that socialization training must begin very early with PMRs. It must begin with systematic exposure to mirrors if we are to install self-recognition. This kind of evidence, three studies all using adult PMRs and all in agreement that self-recognition is lacking, poses further questions. How is it that they can tell male from female and one attendant from others? Probably because of repeated exposure and by the fact others are <u>acting</u> on the PMR whereas the mirror presents a relatively <u>inert</u> reflection. From this evidence, it appears that adult PMRs who have had prolonged institutionalization and minimal mirror experience are further advanced in their regard of others than they are in self-awareness.

Returning to the issue of blushing in PMRs, I have intensified my search and can report with some assurance that indeed some do blush. My questions have been directed to institutional physicians and attendants. Always the question is the same, "Have you ever noticed any of your profoundly retarded blushing or showing modesty, shame, or shyness?" Those experienced attendants I query invariably seem initially stunned, but then report that some PMRs are good blushers and some are also capable of expressing shyness, shame, and modesty. Also, the attendants usually remark, "I think you're the only person who ever asked me that question."

Although my sample of attendants and physicians is small, numbering only 35 combined, the existence of these emotional states among certain PMRs appears certain. The road to humanization of PMRs must be charted by carefully mapping each individual, for each is unique. To do this, the aid of physicians, nurses, dentists, and houseparents must be sought since their dressing-undressing of residents puts them in a favorable position to report "who blushes." Darwin indicates blushing is the most human of all expressions, and once we learn that 5 out of 70 on a ward are blushers, then we have isolated those who could likely most easily be trained in self-recognition and other social skills as well. It is also evident that those who are shy, modest, and are blushers have revealed to us a very human need for privacy and for these, a grand reinforcer would be a brief period of privacy or solitude. In Chapter 3, privacy and shyness were discussed in relation to toilet training--are there other uses for these emotional states?

We have already progressed considerably in caring for the physiological needs of the PMR. It is hoped that readers exposed to this brief section on blushing will redouble their efforts and consider Maslow's higher order needs and how they can be attained with the profoundly retarded.

ODOR'S ROLE IN DIAGNOSIS AND GROUPING

As long ago as 1955, Adis-Castro and Berger suggested the use of odor discrimination in differentiating between brain-injured and non-brain-injured retardates. Kalmus (1952) had earlier speculated that anosmia (inability to smell) is usually caused by infection or injury as in certain types of brain damage. Adis-Castro and Berger, citing Grinker and Bucy, indicated that cranio-cerebral injuries predispose to olfactory nerve damage and such patients subsequently lose the sense of smell and, not infrequently, the chemical sense of taste as well. Although Adis-Castro and Berger studied only retardates in the IQ range of 40 to 70, they were able to significantly distinguish between the organics and familials--the organics being significantly poorer at distinguishing between olfactory stimuli derived from Henning's classification system.

In differentiating between severe early childhood autistics and organic PMRs, odor might also be used. Rimland (1964) indicates autistic children prefer the chemical senses (odor and taste) over vision and hearing and in adult schizophrenics, Rubert, Hollander and Mehrhof (1961) report 83% of a large sample hallucinated olfactorily. That olfaction could have some diagnostic capability is further supported by Fölling's discovery of phenylketonuria. The mother of the two PKU victims reported an unusual odor in the boys' urine. Maple urine sugar disease and Oasthouse urine disease are also characterized by a unique odor in the victims' urine.

That odor as a possible diagnostic tool has been singularly neglected is dramatized by Nueva-España and Fish's (1976) interesting study of very high risk for death profoundly retarded subjects. In a pilot study, these investigators found "of 80 infirm PMR and 20 comparison group subjects, 22 PMR demonstrated loss of the olfactory sense. It was found that during this six-month period, 20 out of 22 who lost their sense of smell died within a six-week period" (Nueva-España & Fish, 1976, p. 133). Previous investigators, Kalmus and Hubbard (1960), had also noted the relationship between health decline and decline in sense of smell in humans. Nueva-España and Fish in a larger study noted that loss of olfactory capability often preceded any other clinical sign of illness by two or three weeks and concluded, "the Olfactory Assessment Test (is) a good method of determining low viability such that diagnosis, monitoring and treatment can be instituted early enough to prevent at least 65% of the deaths which might otherwise occur" (1976, p. 141). Readers interested in the methodological aspects of this study should consult the original article. Since the PMR as a group are death-prone and fragile people, it is of considerable interest to attending physicians to isolate those who are most "at risk," and olfactory assessment appears a promising diagnostic tool.

Neglect of the sense of smell can perhaps be excused on the grounds of our culture's avoidance of talking of things odorous (a largely acquired aversion) and because of the truth of Allport's (1954) dictum that odors are highly affective and "seldom neutral." The research and potential diagnostic importance of odors should receive increased attention.

PSYCHOMETRICS, Q-SORT, AND TOOL USE AS GROUPING STRATEGIES

Every experienced worker with the profoundly retarded is aware of the fact that even in the very narrow range of intelligence (0-19) that psychometrically defines profound retardation, individual differences abound. Also, it is obvious that some profoundly retarded (not always those having the highest tested intelligence or social quotients) are brighter and more able to cope with problem solving than others. However, such knowledge is often the province of houseparents or teachers in institutional settings and may never be fully utilized in program planning, placement, or research design. This is under-utilized knowledge because turnover among institutional houseparents is very heavy and because houseparents rarely write articles for the professional journals. Further, I suspect, not enough of their opinions and ideas are systematically sought by professionals.

Every aspect of life for the profoundly retarded would be advanced and likely knowledge about them would be fostered if we could delineate subtypes within the PMR level of intelligence. Several efforts to do this have occurred. Miller (1976) studied a group of 648 profoundly retarded that had been administered the Behavior Development Survey--a short version of the AAMD Adaptive Behavior Scales. Miller looked at self-help and physical items plus awareness items (sense of direction or some interaction with others) and found two groups emerged--one that was deficient on all items employed and another that did not manifest severe deficits in expected areas. Put another way, what emerged was one group that might be in a subgroup termed "absolute" profound retardation and the other "relative," since several areas where severe deficits were expected did not occur. Miller's data were on institutionalized subjects, and his more competent subtype were older and many had been diagnosed as nonsomatic, undifferentiated cases. Miller raised the interesting question about his results, "Is this the 'mature' profound, who has attained through maturation his maximum skill level?" (Miller, 1976). The important issue raised here is the issue of readiness. Since his competent profounds had a median age of 24.5 versus 17.5 for his deficient profounds, it could be that for these profounds (now beyond school age) training efforts would be more effective than at earlier ages. Ironically, the 24-year-old profoundly retarded is victimized by the phenomenon of the HOUND-YAVIS tradition. Reference here is to Goldstein and Simonson's (1971) research on psychotherapists' client preferences. The kind of client least preferred was labelled "HOUND" (homely, old, ugly, nonverbal, and dumb) and the preferred client as Schofield's (1964) earlier research revealed was the "YAVIS" (young, attractive, verbal, intelligent, and successful). Successful interventionists with the profoundly retarded must exercise caution and effort to avoid this barrier to progress.

MacAndrew (1973) affords yet another approach to delineation of subgroups within the profoundly retarded range of intelligence. Using an experienced ward supervisor, familiar with every one of his 74 residents, MacAndrew photographed all residents and asked the supervisor to Q-sort residents' photos on the extent to which he saw them as differentially characterized on each of 35 dimensions. These dimensions included food preferences, capabilities on certain tasks, awareness, and so forth. Although MacAndrew employed only one subject, he later acquired the same 35 Q-sorts from 5 other attendants and attained a reliability coefficient of .895. The ordering of the 74 residents (average IQ = 15.4) by these 6 employees was remarkably alike. This strategy of employment of an adapted Q-technique (Stephenson, 1953) definitely holds promise for the extraction of subgroups of profoundly retarded persons, and readers are referred to MacAndrew (1973) for the complete account.

In the United States, the Vineland Training School's research department under the directorship of Edgar A. Doll can be credited with some of the most innovative investigations of the profoundly retarded. Almost 50 years ago, Cecelia Aldrich and Edgar A. Doll undertook a series of studies that dramatically illustrate the key role of incentives on problem-solving behavior of severely and profoundly retarded. Their studies, unfortunately, are not well known to students of mental retardation today, albeit they merit classic status. As Aldrich and Doll indicated, their studies of PMRs were intended to compare the "adaptive behavior of idiots" with chimpanzees, infants, and young, normal children. Difficulties in techniques had, until about 1930, limited the study of mental retardation largely to mild or moderate levels, but Aldrich and Doll quickly saw in Köhler's (1925) problem-solving techniques with chimpanzees a method to trap the profoundly retarded into a confession of their varied adaptive capabilities. Basically, Köhler's apes were caged and a banana was placed outside, well beyond reach, as the incentive. However, a hoe was left in the cage and while handling the hoe, one chimp suddenly "grasped the idea" and secured the desired goodie. In later studies, Köhler made the task more complex by putting in the cage two short sticks that could be joined instead of the longer hoe--again, one grasped the idea and retrieved the banana. In other problem-solving tasks, it was necessary for apes to stack boxes in order to retrieve bananas placed very high in the cage--again, success. Aldrich and Doll, after some preliminary work in 1927-1928, found certain modifications were necessary when PMRs were used. For example, in the box-stacking approach to problem solving, it was found that PMRs were, in some instances, capable of stacking, but fear of falling (alien to Kohler's apes) precluded their actually securing the lure. In any event, modifications were made and the actual studies began. Of their 7 subjects (ages 8½ to 11 years-9 months), only 2 were actually profoundly retarded (IQs 14 and 15) and these are the ones we report on here. Their performance or success on the problems presented (all problems involved the use of sticks as implements to retrieve a lure), were poorer than any of the higher level subjects whose IQs ranged from 20 to 30. However, on the very simplest task, one PMR did attain success. Aldrich and Doll (1931) concluded that Köhler's problem-solving technique used with apes can be used advantageously to study adaptive behavior in PMRs; ability to solve problems is correlated with general level of ability; and stronger incentives facilitate PMRs' problem solving. On the basis of the stick and previous box-stacking studies, they concluded that the "behavior of idiot children in such situations lies between that of apes and that of normal infants" (p. 334).

The importance of the Aldrich-Doll problem-solving studies, practically speaking, is that their approach could be useful in subgroup differentiation within a restricted psychometric range. It also illustrates the value of studying paradigms employed in animal research when our focal interest is the nonverbal human. Problem solving, tool usage, insightful behavior, and the laws of perceptual organization as interests of the Gestaltists gave Doll and Aldrich a springboard for learning more of the behavior of PMRs under various incentive conditions.

Quite recently, Cleland, Rago and Mukherjee (1978) have studied the PMRs for instances of spontaneous tool usage. Unlike the early Vineland studies, these investigators spent over 200 hours in the naturalistic versus the laboratory setting and noted examples of spontaneous tool use by PMRs. It was their conviction that this approach could augment efforts to delineate functional subtypes within the narrow psychometric range characterizing PMR. Adhering to Alcock's (1972) definition of tool use as "manipulation of an inanimate object, not internally manufactured, with the effect of improving the animal's efficiency in altering the position or form of some separate object," these researchers isolated four cases qualifying as tool use. The four subjects' Social Quotients ranged from 10 to 16. Only one example will be given, but it serves to illustrate that this tool-user had capacity-ability, at least in one area, that exceeds usual expectations for a PMR.

Case A: D.O.B.: 1-20-1944; Social Age = 3.7;
Social Quotient = 15

Mas, a short, dwarfed male, approached me with a stick about eight centimeters in length, which he rather vigorously employed in slapping his open-palmed hand. As he did so, a broad smile crossed his face. At about 1.5 meters distance from me he held the stick out for me to take. Once accepted, Mas took my hand in his and proceeded to move my hand up and down to slap his open palm. When I spontaneously continued to slap his palm with the stick, Mas no longer directed my activity but merely smiled in delight. When I added music by humming "Yankee-Doodle" and slapped in keeping with the musical beat, his delight greatly intensified. On ceasing, his facial expression assumed dejection, and he grabbed my hand and again motorically instructed me in the fundamentals of "his game." This activity so amused Mas that he persisted long after I wearied.

On another occasion when a highly desired object was sighted but was beyond Mas's reach, he ran and attempted to drag a heavy steel outdoor bench under the object (the analogy to Köhler's chimpanzees on the box problems is evident). The use of the bench as a tool would credit at the VIII to IX year level on the Vineland Social Maturity Scale (Doll, 1953b)!

The 34-year-old tool-user, totally devoid of any recognizable language, was clearly different in ability from others in his PMR group. Like Aldrich and Doll's PMR subjects of 1930-31, the incentive strength was the key to any problem-solving or tool use. This illustrates the need for workers to religiously catalog each PMR's preferences. In the Cleland et al. (1978) study, all four of their tool-users' preferred incentives were at the level of addiction: one craved coffee (liquid or solid), another tobacco, another cake, while the fourth subject was hooked on television. For a complete account of the tool use study, the reader should consult Cleland et al., 1978.

Before concluding the discussion on tool use as a means of subgroup differentiation, it seems that because tool use is adaptive behavior, whether in man or animal, it could be possible to employ tool-using PMRs in a training role. How? Here is the author's speculative approach to the PMR as a trainer-teacher.

As a first step, through observation and interviewing of attendants, we must isolate a group of tool-users. If it were possible to assemble a group of three to five of like ages and sex, we would then tailor a "classroom" that would maximize the tool-user's skill, that is, use of appropriate incentives in locations forcing use of implements to retrieve the desired goodies. If we are sufficiently ingenious in tailoring the classroom, and their tool-using is further augmented, then what? Next, we could select a PMR who matches our tool-users in all respects except never having been known to use tools. By seeding into the tool-user group a non-tool-user, our question becomes, "Will this subject, as a function of 'confinement' with tool-users, also pick up on this skill?" Aside from peer pressure (we all are tool-users), the heightened opportunity for modeling or imitative learning may help our naive PMR learn a new skill.

Suggested in the above-mentioned method is that those behaviors that reflect a higher order skill than say, feeding oneself, be given greater exposure. If the method is successful to any extent, then we have helped the PMR toward a higher order need and the satisfaction of yet another accomplishment.

THE PLACEBO: ISOLATING SUGGESTIBLE PMRs

In a study of profoundly retarded and hyperactive residents involving the "double-blind" technique, Adamson et al. (1958) found a significant placebo effect. In fact, the inert pills provided as much improvement as the actual medications. Elsewhere in this text mention was made of the curious lack of studies of psychosomatic disorders in PMRs, and I view this omission as due largely to attributing to the PMR too little cognitive ability even to consider psychosomatic problems. However, before we close the door on the possibility that PMRs (at least some of them) can be subject to social and psychological influences, let's look a little further.

Morris (1957) studied the effects of radiant floor heating on enuresis and chilblains in 45 profoundly retarded subjects. Subsequent to installation of the heated floor, both enuresis and chilblains decreased considerably. Placebo effects were noted in the Adamson et al. study of profoundly retarded, and even altruistic behavior in the PMR has been reported (Rago & Cleland, 1978). As Goldenson (1970) points out, the placebo's greatest effect occurs on those conditions having an emotional or psychosomatic component, and DuBois has stated that placebos are more widely employed than any other class of drugs. Other characteristics of patients claiming relief from placebos includes suggestibility and higher anxiety levels (Goldenson, 1970). In Beecher's (1955) study of 1,082 patients, about 1 of 3 reported the placebos gave relief.

What is suggested by the foregoing is that if experimental drug research is undertaken and placebos are employed, it may be of value to isolate those subjects who show relief as a function of the placebo. Why? Because they may be more suggestible and more prone to some psychosomatic disorder. If the readers believe that personality differences exist, even at the PMR level, it is worth the effort to tease them out. For, to the extent that suggestibility is related to social inductions or trainability, the commonly used placebo could be a method of selecting yet another subgroup of PMRs.

SLEEP POSTURES AND RUMINATORS

Cleland, Rago and Case (1977) suggested that sleep-dream percent time could perhaps be employed to distinguish various developmental levels among the profoundly retarded. This possibility exists since it is known that percent of time spent in REM (dream state) sleep declines with age. However, as noted earlier (Cleland & Swartz, 1969), little is known of the night life of the profoundly retarded. Case (1978) undertook a study of the sleep postures of three male and two female (CA range 22-39 years, mean SQ = 12.2) PMRs to increase our knowledge of their sleeping behaviors. In their presleep activity, each subject manifested consistent and unique behaviors. Each slept in his own bedroom and before retiring, three would position their pillows and covers carefully while two others displayed bed rocking for time periods of 1 minute to a full 80 minutes! This latter behavior, as Case observed, is similar to the infant crib-rockers studied by Ribble (1965). The pillow-cover placement by three PMRs conforms to the presleep rituals noted in normals. Regarding sleep activity or movements, Case's PMRs were less active than normal infants of similar mental age or normal adults. The average number of movements per night for the PMRs was only 6.48, while normal infants average 24 and adult normals average about 33. On the basis of earlier sleep research studies, Case suggests that less movement may indicate more dream activity on the part of the PMR. Also, the differential rate of movements in sleep suggests another approach for subgroup differentiation among individuals having a very compressed intellectual range. Developmentally, those showing the most frequent movements during sleep would more closely approximate normals. As serendipitous findings, nightmares and sleep-walking were also observed in two subjects (Case, 1978). From Case's work, another approach to subgrouping arises, and despite the conventional wisdom that night is quiescence on the PMR dormitories, we should remain mindful of Segal's (1974) caveat, "any radical and chronic departure" from one's typical sleep habits may be cause for alarm, because it could communicate illness, anxiety, or other problems.

Turning to another interesting albeit little understood phenomenon that some PMRs exhibit, let's speculate a bit on rumination. Webster (1949) indicates the meaning of rumination is "to chew the cud; to chew again what has been chewed slightly and swallowed. /A second meaning is/ to bring to mind and consider again and again; to muse, ponder." While a number of theories to explain rumination have arisen (Kanner, 1950), it is still a baffling problem, poorly understood. This being so, my speculations can perhaps be excused. The syndrome was first described by Fabricus in 1687 and as Kanner (1950) notes, "intellectual people, notably physicians, supplied the major portion of the patient material" (p. 468), although it is observed to occur at every intellectual level. One could note that rumination occurs in two dimensions, that is, some bring up food (physical mode), some bring up ideas over and over (mental mode), while some engage in both physical and mental rumination. Now, while the content material brought up in mental rumination consists of both pleasant and unpleasant thoughts, Kanner (1950) indicates food rumination is a pleasant thing since "older children (and adults)...show a remarkable selectivity, bringing up only their favorite food while disliked substances are not recognized" (p. 469). As a brief detour, it is interesting to inquire if the PMR ruminator also brings up <u>only</u> liked-preferred foods, could this be one way of determining food preferences for PMRs who ruminate? Food, it would seem, can communicate.

Can sleep states afford any leads when we are concerned with rumination? Although such a question appears odd, there may be some remote connection. Jouvet (1967), a noted sleep researcher, summed up what studies of the deep sleep state revealed: hunting or predatory species (man, felines, and canines) enjoy more deep sleep than the hunted (rabbits and ruminants). The predators spend an average of 20% of their sleep in the deep sleep state, the hunted, only 5 to 10%. One theory of rumination in humans, not widely accepted, is the atavistic analogy to the rumination of herbivorous mammals (Kanner, 1950). Could our PMR ruminators be those who have less deep sleep for the same reason ruminant animals do--namely, they are vigilant because they are hunted? Among the PMRs, as Rago (1976) has noted, there are dominants and subordinates. And, as Cleland et al. (1976) discovered, there are PMRs whom they term "night-stalkers." Among these who seem to be "on-guard" rather than asleep, would we find more than the expected number of ruminators? Since intellectual types appear frequently in the literature on rumination (Kanner, 1950), would the PMR who ruminates be faster intellectually, a better learner, more pedantic? These questions or gross speculations are unanswered at present but they do offer clues as to how we might approach establishing functioning subgroups within the PMR ranks. Earlier, in Chapter 3, coprophagy was discussed in relation to the problem of boredom. Boredom is also one of the competing theories on the cause of rumination in humans and animals alike. Kanner (1950) lists lack of occupation or boredom as one theory of rumination, and those espousing this view see it as analogous to "cage sickness" in animals. This problem was discussed in Chapter 3 in the section on coprophagy. Again, it could be that the occurrence of coprophagy <u>and</u> rumination among institutionalized PMRs could be used as an index as to how PMRs perceive the programs they are subjected to, that is, boring or stimulating. Thus, direct evidence from the PMR consumer might be obtained.

VOICE SPECTROGRAPHY: VISUAL TRANSLATION OF SOUND

Each individual's fingerprints are relatively unique from all others. So too are one's voiceprints. Ostwald (1963) and Pulgram (1959) indicate that spectrographic analysis offers us the most objective and unbiased way to make statements about sound. In 1976, Cleland, McGavern, Case, Grace and Saperston proposed the extension of voice-printing analyses to the profoundly retarded as an aid to diagnosis, to decipherment of underlying motivational and affective states, and to subgroup identification. Cleland et al. (1976b) reviewed some of the extensive spectrographic literature on primate communication and various researchers have learned the functional significance of monkey calls in a variety of settings. For example, distress vocalizations and other affective or motive states have been isolated via spectrographic analysis of the calls of a variety of monkeys. Human infants have also been studied, and Karelitz and Fisichelli (1962) found that brain-damaged infants require more intense stimulation to produce a crying response than normals and that the latency between pain stimulation and crying's onset was different. Ostwald (1960) studied sounds from psychotic patients and speculated that sound-print analyses should "enhance the scientific analysis of how acoustic signals are used and abused for nonverbal communication about hunger, satiation, pain, pleasure, fear and other affective states" (Cleland et al., 1976b, p. 129). From their review these investigators posed the question as to "whether PMR soundmaking is, in fact, an effort to communicate?"

In 1977, Jan C. Case reported on his voice-spectrography study of 11 males whose mean chronological age was 43 years and whose mean Social Quotient was 7.5. Case hypothesized that rate of vocal utterances would be higher in aroused states (Mondays and time before meals) than in nonaroused states (Sundays and after meals), and this was strongly supported. He also found that PMRs while vocalizing under nonaroused conditions showed greater behavioral variability. Interestingly, in Crook's (1967) study of fear in monkeys, stereotypy of calls increased notably as the threat of aggression (high arousal) increased. Also, nocturnal monkeys in contrast to diurnal monkeys display markedly stereotyped calls with variability being the exception (Crooks, 1967). Case's findings suggest that the PMR group under high arousal (before meals) are more vigilant and behavior is constrained whereas after feeding occurs, vigilance is reduced (see also Kaufman & Levitt, 1965; Cleland, McGavern & Case, 1976a). Case concluded that PMR vocalizations are extremely limited but are highly individualized and may reflect "highly specialized displacement-type behaviors which occur regularly in response to motivational conflicts (predicaments) imposed by the environment upon the PMR" (Case, 1977, p. 82).

Ordinarily, spectral analysis has been used mainly by law enforcement officials, biologists, zoologists, and primatologists. However, Case (1977) suggests further research using spectrography with PMRs could be enlightening. Referring to the "night stalkers" isolated in an earlier study by

Cleland, McGavern and Case (1976a), he suggests contrasting nocturnal and diurnal vocalizations of the PMR and the extension of spectrographic study to younger PMRs whose length of institutionalization is short. Clearly, the traditional concept of the physician, psychologist, social worker, and nurse as the "clinical team" is too limited to face the challenge of the PMR. We need to import alien disciplines having different technological skills if we are to decipher the PMR's communicative efforts.

CERTAIN EFFECTS OF LIGHTING

Tropism is a response to a stimulus, such as gravity, light, or touch, that occurs in plants and sedentary animals by growth curvature, and "the direction of curvature is determined by the direction from which the stimulus originates" (Abercrombie, Hackman & Johnson, 1960). Ordinarily, we do not describe humans as possessed of tropisms; it is considered antiscientific and dehumanizing. Yet, in a study of institutional folkwisdom as expressed through cliches (Dingman, Cleland & Swartz, 1970), we find expressions such as "Low grade students are just human vegetables. They can't even feel pain like we do. Custodial care is all they need." How did such cliches as this originate, and, more important, can they be of any benefit? While the body politic of parents and professionals alike is busily engaged in running the vacuum sweeper over the label floor, is it conceivable that old sayings or pejorative labels can communicate anything worthwhile? Most attendants or houseparents in institutional work are educated to about the tenth or eleventh grade level, and their modal age nationwide would be about 48 or so years (Baumeister, 1970; Cleland, 1969; Cleland, 1967). Houseparents thus tend to perceive atypical humans somewhat differently than professionals do and tend to be more literal. Thus, when a neophyte attendant without the benefit (or handicap?) of college degrees initially encounters the PMR who may also be grossly handicapped physically, he may be impressed that all "so-and-so can do is stare into the overhead lights." Since historically many attendants are of rural origin (Cleland, Seitz & Patton, 1967; Cleland & Peck, 1959) and familiar at first hand with plant tropisms, it is easy to speculate on why the term "human vegetable" arose. So much as to origins of institutional folkwisdom--the major concern is can we generate leads or hypotheses from them that could prove beneficial?

On ward rounds with a superintendent of a large western institution, I was shown their new speech pathology and audiology laboratory. Within the impressive building there were numerous anechoic speech training booths. Outside one an 11-year-old boy of severe or profound level was waiting for his session with the speech teacher. The boy was nearly blind, cerebral palsied, and quadriplegic and was strapped upright in his wheelchair. I noticed he was staring at a ceiling light and thought, "I'll bet if he had mobility in his arms, he'd be a hand-waver." I then proceeded to wave my hand before his eyes and thus varied or patterned his light input. The boy instantly smiled and continued until I stopped. When I started up again, his smiling resumed. Obviously, he was gaining satisfaction and delighted in my taking on the hand-waving. I turned to the Superintendent and said, "A rotating color wheel would be a fine thing to get him for Christmas, and it's not far off." This sort of pleasant diversion for others having a similar liking would be one item to include in recreational programming for this subgroup.

Hand-waving by profoundly retarded and some of the blind, as well as staring into light, is not an uncommon occurrence. Ordinarily, it is thought to be motivated by a need for increased sensory input (Cleland & Clark, 1966), but alternative explanations are possible. For example, dentists have used both audio-analgesia (pain suppression by means of auditory stimulation) and photic (light) stimulation in order to minimize or mask pain in their patients. Conceivably, our "light seekers" are, by patterning (hand-waving) light input, avoiding pain from some unknown source.

Scientific concern into the biological effects of electromagnetic radiation and visible sunlight arises out of growing evidence indicating that light in the near ultraviolet and visible ranges does a great deal more for humans than to permit the perception of objects (Frey, 1965). And, since PMRs in institutions spend a greater portion of time indoors behind glass (which filters out most of the near ultraviolet light), it is interesting to see what some light researchers have uncovered. Zacharias and Wurtman (1969) showed the relative absence of light is related to earlier menarche and nonlight perceptive blind were youngest of all at menarche. In a later study by Wurtman (1975), he discovered that sunlight inhibits melatonin synthesis by the pineal gland, and the activity of the pineal in mammals is inhibited as light intensity increases. The hormone melatonin has also been found to reduce sleep. Cleland, Rago and Case (1977) speculated that perhaps a functional relationship may exist between the low intensity artificial ward light and the abnormal nocturnal patterns of some PMRs (Landesman-Dwyer & Sackett, 1975). Another investigator (Ott, 1973) employed new, full-spectrum flourescent tubes in some Florida schools and found within a week a marked improvement in behavior, such as lowered hyperactivity, and irritability and less nervousness. The study which covered a four-month span also revealed significant differences in numbers of cavities and tooth decay. His experimental students exposed to wide spectrum light were markedly better off than those receiving only ordinary light exposure. Another researcher found that elderly males who were deprived of ultraviolet light for three months (living indoors under conventional light) developed an inability to absorb calcium (Neer, 1971).

The foregoing material illustrates that the behavioral or physical effects of light on humans is complex indeed and has only recently become a serious area of inquiry. Light can be an aversive stimulus to nocturnal creatures such as rats, and they will bar-press with gusto to escape into darkness. For those profoundly retarded who give every indication of being attracted by light, it appears timely to consider its use on a systematic basis as a reinforcer or reward. One suggested use is given in the section on oblique approaches to toilet training.

Old sayings, cliches, or labels may, in some obscure manner, help illuminate our efforts to assist these nonverbal people. For the reader interested in the folklore of institutions, Dingman et al. (1970) should be consulted.

SUMMARY

The seven sections outlined in this chapter included both standard psychometric and Q-sort approaches to subgroup identification and several potential or speculative approaches. To the extent that we can successfully isolate and describe unique subgroups among the PMR ranks, our progress in caring for them on a more individualized basis should accelerate. In addition to allowing us to serve them better, the isolation of unique functional subgroups should also have some indirect and perhaps beneficial effect on attendant turnover as well as that of other direct-care personnel. How?

Everyone has "favorite-types" of handicapped he or she enjoy working with, and, if we succeed in subgroup differentiation, attendants or houseparents may then choose the subgroup they prefer, such as tool-users or dancers. Finally, our quest for subgroups could foster improvements in our in-service training for neophyte employees. The reader is challenged to look beyond pathology and to elaborate and improve on the strategies offered in this chapter.

5

Recreation, Play, and Aesthetics: The Good Life

GROUP ACTIVITIES

What is play for a 30-year-old with a mental age of 2? This is not an easily answered question. For that matter, play is not easily defined as reference to Webster indicates. However, without getting involved with definitional problems, let's accept Goldenson's (1970) description of play as "Any activity which is freely sought and pursued for the sake of enjoyment" as a good working definition.

Sullivan (1962, p. 145) maintained that "Observation is the touchstone of psychiatric research," and in determining what play activities the PMR enjoys, we can profit from his advice. Play, for adults or children, serves a variety of functions and promoting growth, releasing energies, and learning social cooperation are only a few of them (Goldenson, 1970). The profoundly retarded, viewed developmentally, may never reach a stage of readiness where they can play <u>cooperatively</u> in groups larger than 3 or 5. For example, Werner (1961) maintains that not until about age 5 or 6 will normal children spontaneously engage in activities of groups of more than 3 members, although the Merrys (1958) indicate that play in groups as large as 6 may begin after age 3.

Thus, whether the profoundly retarded are 10, 20 or 30 years of age, we should always remember their mental age and not attempt to force social groupings beyond their readiness to participate. To do so may only increase aggressiveness, since the Merrys (1958) point out that from 6 months to about 13 months babies tend to view playmates as play material! Another point to remember in tailoring play experiences for the profoundly retarded, especially the young PMR, is that girls mature earlier than boys and can be expected to engage in social activities somewhat sooner than boys (Merry & Merry, 1958). Nearly everyone experienced with the several levels of retardation knows the proclivity of retardates of mild or moderate level to choose playmates who are younger, since it is difficult for them to "boss" age peers of normal intellect (Cleland, 1978). In considering other variables that could influence readiness for social group play, it is somewhat more likely that there are more only children among the PMRs; hence, these children would suffer an added handicap in both play and social development (Merry & Merry, 1958). With these caveats in mind, let's go a bit further with Sullivan's advice.

Sullivan (1962, p. 145) indicated, "The setting of observational situations is a task requiring rather uncommon gifts on the part of the observer, not to mention rather unusual facilities for his work." When we consider Sullivan's statement in relation to the PMR, it calls attention to a related question--"Who is in a position to observe the PMR, and what settings and facilities exist?" Obviously, houseparents, teachers, nurses, and physicians are often in the best observational position, albeit the most frequent setting is a dormitory. So, it is important that inservice training classes include observational strategies. And, settings should be varied as well as toys and playground equipment so as to facilitiate our mapping their play preferences.

Everything imaginable can have an influence on play, weather included. How many readers can recall a spring or summer rain occurring during childhood and the pleading question, "Mom, can I go out and play in the rain?" And, if the summer was drought plagued, "Can I turn the sprinkler on and go play in the water?" Such activities as these just mentioned may not be as common for PMRs as for normals, since health and safety are often overriding concerns. However, natural events such as a good rain seem to occasion playful activities in both humans and chimpanzees. Van Lawick-Goodall (1968) described chimpanzees' behavior and noted, "Often, too, infants and juveniles played wildly when it was raining, jumping and swinging through the trees either alone or with a companion (and) whatever the motivation of the displaying of mature individuals or the playing of youngsters during rain there can be no doubt that they are warmed up by the activity" (p. 172). I have on numerous occasions noted adult PMRs in a private residential school's swimming pool--most were joyously splashing about in babylike fashion, and smiles were abundant. Aggressive behaviors were notably lacking. All that was required to make for a good afternoon of fun was a sufficient number of lifeguards to insure safety.

Another form of play that a group of profoundly retarded can enjoy is the bus ride. Motion appears to have a quieting influence even on some of the most hyperactive profoundly retarded. I learned this about 25 years ago.

> I was substituting for the school's only social worker and interviewing the parents of a profoundly retarded and very hyperactive child who was being admitted to the institution. I asked, "Can you think of any time or times when __________ is not, as you put it, 'in constant motion'?" The parents paused for a few seconds and the wife then said, "Yes, when we take him for a ride in the car he's always quiet and no problem at all. I believe he could ride cross-country if we didn't have to stop for gas--the minute you turn the engine off he starts up!"

Five years have elapsed since the author accompanied a group of PMRs on a bus ride, and my recollection was a nice quiet ride through the countryside. To bolster my own impressions, Mr. Ron Hooks, a staff development employee at the Travis State School (Texas) was asked to seek information from bus drivers and houseparents. In all instances, the response was that the bus ride has a quieting effect on the profoundly retarded and hyperactive resident. My inquiry also gained a little serendipity. The bus ride is a one time per week occurrence for each ward housing the PMR and the attendants spontaneously told Mr. Hooks that they know when it's the bus ride day and become excited an hour or so before the bus appears. Once aboard, they become quiet and when riding along, many smile while looking out the windows.

> During a research project, it was necessary to transport adult PMRs from their dormitory to a research building. I noticed one eagerly attempting to get into his ankle-high, pull-on boots. When the station wagon arrived, we

all boarded and after less than five minutes we reached our destination and unloaded--all except the one with pull-on boots. He not only resisted, he came unglued! Afterward, on returning the men to their dormitory, an attendant told me, "I knew old Billy was gonna blow up. He only gets his boots when he goes out for a weekend three or four times a year, and he was expecting a lot more riding than you guys provided him."

While anecdotal accounts hardly constitute hard data, readers can follow Sullivan's advice and observe firsthand to see if the bus ride is not one favorite among the PMR group. So many persons have now reported on the quieting influence of the bus ride that the author wonders, "Why doesn't someone take a large moving van and equip it as a classroom? Since trying to keep hyperactive children in their seats occupies a great amount of teacher time, just put the whole school in motion."

Socialization of profoundly retarded persons is a major undertaking but a highly desirable objective and, of course, play and recreation are intimately related to the socialization process (Merry & Merry, 1958). It was mentioned earlier that play in groups beyond six, spontaneous play, may well be beyond the PMRs' developmental level regardless of life age. How then can socialization be fostered--is it impossible? Perhaps if we get started quite early in their lives with play that has cooperative effort "built-in," we might enjoy some success. Chapter 4 outlined certain subgroups within the PMR category and thinking along these same lines, let's isolate four PMRs whose body-rocking is legendary. They would also be young, say around 10, and physically reasonably strong. We could then develop a small-scale bullseye type merry-go-round having four hand pumps and teach our rockers to transfer this rocking skill (Cleland & Swartz, 1969). To add to the enjoyment of motion, a player-piano type apparatus would engage only if a given number of revolutions were attained. Perhaps our quartet could learn this operation through modeling. It would, of course, require four PMRs to operate the equipment. Conceivably, some dim awareness that others can help generate pleasure might arise. It is also possible that such an operation might reduce body-rocking.

Another recreational pursuit that is quite suitable for ambulatory PMRs is the largely obsolete means of transportation called walking (Cleland & Swartz, 1969). Physicians hold it to be the safest of all exercises and Nourse, Dubos,

Margenau & Snow (1964) report that the average daily mileage of normals is about eight miles. Among normals, the average speed of walking is about two-and-a-half miles per hour (Spreiregen, 1965). Little is known about whether walking is enjoyed by the profoundly retarded from an empirical standpoint but two studies attest to its great popularity among the mildly retarded (Edgerton, 1967; Cleland & Swartz, 1969). Ross and Sherrill (1977) in reviewing the literature on exercise indicate positive changes occurred in behavior, socialization, and academic achievement in mentally retarded subjects subsequent to exercise programs. Ross and Sherrill studied 22 PMR females randomly placed in an experimental (walking) or control group. The walking PMRs did so for 45 minutes daily, 5 days per week, for 12 consecutive weeks. Changes in body fat did not differ significantly between groups but did favor the walkers, and the distance covered in 45 minutes at the end of the study was considerably increased. Obviously, there is very little information on walking among the profoundly retarded but observation of PMRs' walking attests to its enjoyment. Further information on walking and its possible significance as revealing motivational states in the PMR may be found in Cleland et al. (1976b). According to urban planners, walking is not such a mysterious phenomenon. Spreiregen (1965) maintains "As we walk around, we are completely free to stop, turn around, go faster or slower, go to the left or right, or change our pace--in short, to enjoy the greatest freedom of choice and degree of contact with the people and places we are passing. The maximum contact with a place, so essential to every human settlement, is achieved by walking." The profoundly retarded, if institutionalized, are likely kept indoors to a greater extent than nearly any other people and walks are recreational, healthful, and may, on occasion, elicit some behaviors never before noted. As in other play or recreational activities of a physical nature, physicians' appraisal of fitness to engage should be a routine precaution.

In Chapter 4, we also noted that music could help isolate a group of PMRs who could be good candidates for a dance class. Let's turn now to individual play or recreational outlets for profoundly retarded people.

INDIVIDUAL ACTIVITIES

A good method to follow in selecting activities for specific PMRs is to observe closely what they are trying to tell us they like. For example, let's take the case of a PMR whose sole interest appears to be string-twirling. Ordinarily, such an occupation is considered rather bizarre, especially if the twirler is an adult, but maintaining a developmental perspective, what does it mean to the twirler? Perhaps the string's motion is akin to the little toy celluloid propellers we carried as children and held up in a breeze or out the car window? To the extent that this is a reasonable guess, the thing to do is try out the colored propellers on sticks with our string-twirlers. For safety's sake, the sticks could be shortened but the wind would still do its job. Should the propeller, brightly colored and in motion, evoke smiles of delight, then we've discovered a desirable toy for string-twirlers and, perhaps, string-twirling itself would be reduced.

Another simple game, appealing to a number of profoundly retarded persons, is peek-a-boo. The Merrys (1958) and other child development experts have placed peek-a-boo as one favorite for normal infants in the first year of life. PMRs must be individually tested for preference regardless of their life age. Some adult PMRs will enthusiastically enter into peek-a-boo, and echophraxics (motor mimics) are quite taken by the game. Obviously, child and adult PMRs who engage in peek-a-boo enjoy the game. The major problem in playing is to locate houseparents or volunteer workers who are not afraid to regress a little. More will be said on this issue in a later section on employee training.

Again, in looking for specific things for certain PMRs to do that hold promise of being enjoyed, let's examine the PMR who almost ceaselessly is seen engaged in body-whirling. In equipping a play area outdoors, a firmly anchored swivel chair or a piano stool should compliment their apparent interest in body-whirling. Readers can recall from their own early childhood standing, looking upward and whirling until they fell to the ground. This "labyrinthine play" was quite enjoyable and, of course, the equilibrium mechanism works closely with our kinesthetic or movement sense. Some normals continue body whirling into adult life although, in the context of ballet, its childish aspects are well disguised. Perhaps in the design of equipment to provide for individualizing play outlets, a suitable consultant to engage would be the engineering psychologist or human engineer--those who are sophisticated with man-machine systems in which the human and machine are seen in an interaction (Goldenson, 1970).

The PMR who exhibits stereotyped body-rocking also presents a candidate for an individualized play toy. Namely, a platform rocker. In normal infants when distress or crying occurs, mothers respond almost reflexively by gently rocking baby to and fro. The well-known song "Rock-a-bye Baby" also conveys something of the comforting nature of rocking.

> Recently, I was waiting to meet my class at an institution and noticed a group of adult PMRs in a shaded outdoor play area. One was engaged in body-rocking in a standing position. I noted the time and commenced observing from a distance. Fifteen minutes elapsed when the students arrived and we departed on our tour of the institution; the rocker was still going strong but I had to discontinue my observation. There appeared little doubt that for the rocker, at least, the movement was enjoyable.

There are other stereotypies that are not so innocuous and head-banging or eye-poking are two. What can substitute, if anything, for these sometimes injurious behaviors? Obviously, in the case of eye-gouging or poking, an opthalmologist should be consulted to determine whether some foreign agent or disease is present that could be causing the problem. In both head-banging and eye-poking, behavior modification techniques may prove effective and these procedures are well-covered elsewhere (Thompson & Grabowski, 1972). However, the concern in this chapter is not to view bizarre behaviors as such, but rather to attempt to see something in them that connotes play or adaptive behavior. Let's think of what head-banging might communicate if the person were of normal intelligence--a suicidal intent? A terrible headache? An unusually high pain threshold? Extreme frustration? Or a most likely candidate observers might suggest would be, "He's gone crazy!" For the PMR, also not immune from becoming mentally ill, let's suppose it has as its origin both a high pain threshold and elements of very early childhood behaviors. Some two-year-olds will engage in repetitious head-nodding, either signifying yes or no. This exaggeration and prolongation of head movement reminds us of Miller's (1973) behavioral characteristics of play. He invokes repetition and stresses "the motor activity is often exaggerated or 'uneconomic' in comparison with the form it takes in non-play contexts" (Miller, 1973, p. 89). Admittedly, viewing PMR head-banging as play or amusement is unconventional, but if it sometimes does reflect playfulness, can a substitute be developed?

Once I employed some mildly retarded adolescent males to manufacture giant soap-bubbles for a group of PMRs' amusements. To my astonishment, two who were head-bangers started bursting these multi-colored, giant bubbles with their heads and did so with considerable zeal.

Another strategy that might instill a degree of joy in the head-banger would be to give systematic training in pillow fighting. Employees could serve as models (and we know PMRs are more responsive to houseparents than peers) and stage a pillow fight for their PMR audience. If this "skill" were learned, PMR head-bangers could derive the pleasure of a simple game and simultaneously get their head-banging in sans injuries. This untested approach would require surveillance and monitoring of subsequent aggression in the try-out group, since it could lead to more, rather than less, aggression in other settings as well. Nevertheless, in the PMR where frustration levels may be high and release of aggression outlets low, the pillow fight could prove a satisfactory play activity for the head-banging PMR.

Turning to a harder PMR to reach via play activities, let's examine the problem presented by those who are non-ambulatory. Not always are there enough teachers, aides, or volunteers to individually attend to them. Kamil-Goshgarian, Sackett and Parke (1976) demonstrated that PMRs do manifest visual preferences and they suggest visual fixation time may be useful in determining visual efficiency of such subjects. Fixation time could also be an interest indicator. But, as has been mentioned, we cannot always attend them individually. So, what can we do?

Every living human creates heat and this radiates outward from the body. Richard E. Paige, an inventor, capitalized on this knowledge and developed what he terms a Rotor-Sensor. Very simply, an overhead sign in department stores carrying ads or daily specials rotates on power derived from viewers' heat from below. Such requires no power and it cannot run down. Even a head or hand can operate a rotor two feet across and weighing over a pound. Such would appear to make a nice, interesting mobile for a crib or bedfast PMR. Scenes could be changed to ascertain favorites, and no doubt you could elaborate or improvise further. A cold draft such as air conditioning on the Rotor-Sensor merely reverses the sign's direction. Should the rotor cease entirely, death has likely occurred.

Another possible amusement for the PMR confined to a crib is the judicious use of mirrors. Normal infants between 10 months and a year will often look at a mirror, lean toward it and kiss it or pat the mirror as if playing patty-cake (Merry & Merry, 1958). If the PMR is nonambulatory and young, he too will look, especially if there are no other distractions--just to see the reflection and its movement. If we place such a child in a crib having mirrors on three sides, the attraction is greatly enhanced, much in the fashion clothing stores always provide three-way mirrors so the customer gets the whole picture. If we couple this with a horizontally-slatted crib, climbing is encouraged (our typical vertically-slatted cribs are designed to foil escape). With the type crib described and with a knob for adjusting the height of the three mirrors, we can, very slowly, move the mirrors up to a point where our PMR must raise his head to see the image. An added advantage is that mirrors, for many species including humans, have a social stimulus capacity (Gallup, 1975). There is no unequivocal evidence to date that PMRs are capable of self-recognition (Pechecek et al., 1973; Harris, 1977) but, if they can be taught, early and lengthy exposure appears necessary. In any event, mirrors could be a source of interest, and both the bedfast normal and PMR are subject to a most homogeneous and unstimulating environment (Cleland & Sluyter, 1973).

In the foregoing examples of some stereotypes that are not infrequent in PMRs, the intent was to view them in a nonpathological manner. Doing so is not really absurd. One of Baumeister and Forehand's (1973) conclusions subsequent to their extensive review of stereotyped acts was "that these are essentially normal behaviors that have, through an extensive conditioning process, become abnormally functional to a variety of cues" (p. 92). They point out how even self-destructive acts can become functioning since they give the child a degree of control over the behavior of other people. Readers interested in the theories advanced relative to stereotypy should consult Baumeister and Forehand (1973). These authors also present a number of studies attempting to bring stereotypes under control via behavior modification, drugs, or environmental variations. I have chosen to look on these behaviors as supplying the PMRs with some degree of pleasure, and therefore I have briefly described a few potential substitutions that could be more acceptable and less injurious.

> Over 25 years ago, when wards were enormously overcrowded, understaffed, and vastly oriented to custodial care for the PMR, the mother of a PMR, 13-year-old girl asked me, "What can I get ________ for Christmas?" In relation to the normalization concept, her question was certainly relevant. To provide the answer, I turned to the houseparent for further information and related the question that had been put to me. The houseparent was a rather brusque, no-nonsense woman of 50 or 55 years and reflected only briefly before replying, "Tell her mother to get her a new broom!" I asked, "What made you say that?" Her reply, "Well, I know ________ better than anyone--her mother included. I've had her on this ward for 9 of her 13 years and I've never seen her interested in a blessed thing except to pull straws out of a broom and eat them. She's really sneaky; and short-handed as we always are, we can't keep her from getting to a broom every so often. I'll bet she's had at least 10 fecal impactions removed since she's been here and the culprit is always broom straws--just ask her doctor. Like I say, her first love is a broom!"

The woman informant in the above case was not cruel or unsympathetic to the mother's question--she just reported what she saw repeatedly and concluded, she likes and is interested in brooms. Idiosyncratic behaviors abound in the PMR ranks, and it is obvious that we could not give a broom for this girl's Christmas--it would be life threatening. However, odd as we may view her pica appetite and use of the broom as a "toy," one cannot deny the broom occupies a strategic reinforcer position. We must also conclude that it is unsuitable as a toy in this case.

A toy is "something made for the amusement of a child or for his use in play" (Webster, 1949). And, toys are often found to reduce stereotyped behaviors, and this is generally a desirable objective to attain (Baumeister & Forehand, 1973). In providing toys for this group, several things deserve mention. First, toys need to be age related and appropriately sized for durability and strength. In relation to age-graded toys, consider the following case:

> Five PMRs ranging in age from 19 to 38 were seated at a table where trainers were working with each one on an individual basis. Large, two-piece jigsaw puzzles were

placed before each and efforts were made to show the pupils how to do the puzzles. If correctly assembled, the resultant picture was a rather cartoon-like boy carrying a small basket. In each case of assembly, the trainers' effort was approximately accountable for 95% of the effort, and the PMRs were either incapable or totally disinterested. Two of the five were attempting to masturbate, one repeatedly jumped up and tried to escape the small "classroom" and was returned each time to his chair manifesting a facial expression of absolute dejection. Two questions are posed here: first, from a developmental point of view, why not a picture of some relevance such as the PMR's own face or a good-looking adult female? Secondly, in view of their apparent disinterest in the task and their life age range, why confine them to such a small classroom. Is anything about this scenario congruent with normalization?

Confinement, restraint or isolation can take various forms and in the above case, at least for the escape artist, the class was a form of restraint. In human infants, holding the arms pinned to its sides or other restraining actions usually spawn anger. Thus, individual differences should be respected although as Erickson (1949) points out, there are certain instances when humans actually seek, and are comforted by, limitations placed on their movement.

In relation to the above case, another question arises, "Would sex motivation aid in teaching some PMR males to assemble puzzles?" In a study of profoundly retarded males, De Rudolph (1954) found that masturbation was rather widespread and Gebhard (1973), comparing institutionalized mildly retarded with noninstitutionalized normals, found masturbation was much higher in his retarded group. Observation of the profoundly retarded, as experienced workers can attest, reveals considerable masturbation and symbolic copulatory behaviors. For adult PMRs, this strongly indicates an interest in sexual play. The PMRs can usually detect sex differences and adult males tend to prefer the female voice (Uno, Seitel & Cleland, 1975). For these reasons, would not a _Playboy_ centerfold, cut in half and placed on thin plywood, be a far more desirable jigsaw than a little cartoon boy with a basket? Among humans sexual activity is universal, not characterized by seasonal cycles, (Roe & Simpson, 1958) and in both sexes, sexual excitement may be brought about by stories, pictures, and so on (Bindra, 1959). Zimbardo (1969) cites anecdotal evidence on the negative effects of prolonged sexual deprivation (Arctic and

Antarctic expeditions) and for the monastic PMR, the sexual deprivation could add to their frustration level and increase aggression. Thus, the provision of age-graded materials, such as the Playboy jigsaw puzzle, would appear far more motivational to adult PMRs and could reduce aggression. Exposure to novel and arousing stimuli might also serve to elicit more of their response repertoire.

While the foregoing is not in any way exhaustive of the complex issues involved, nor meant to advocate sexual license among the PMR, I hope it will cause readers to consider some avenues whereby sex motivation could be employed. Maslow's steps to self-actualization include love and belongingness, and the experience of sexual arousal would appear normalizing. An old institutional cliche, "Homosexual activities aren't as upsetting as heterosexual activities" attests to the strength of the sex taboo in institutions--homosexuality won't create pregnancy! Harlow's contact comfort, for many PMRs, is un unmet need. Perhaps large, soft toy animals would satisfy some of this need to love and be loved.

Other toys or amusements for the PMR that have considerable popularity with normal, two-year or three-year-olds include push-pull toys. Here again, for older PMRs, a sturdy wagon that one could pull another one in might be preferred over a little wheeled toy. An attendant model could pull another attendant (this in itself would be novel and attention getting) and observational learning could occur. If PMRs can learn this play skill and learn the joy of being pulled around and the sense of accomplishment of pulling another, then rudimentary cooperative behavior is coming into play. Isolating pairs who seem friendly toward each other should speed the process.

Nonambulatory PMRs, regardless of age, appear to enjoy being taken for rides in a wheelchair and being placed on an undulating air-mattress instills joy in a number of the bedfast. Play with plastic media such as clay or "green slime" ordinarily has appeal also as mental ages of three or less dictate a certain amount of messiness. Some, whose mental ages are around one to two, may even derive pleasure from rattles or pacifiers albeit their life age is advanced. In Tinbergen's (1974) fashion, what we should practice in the early stages of knowledge acquisition is an open-minded observational stance of "watching and wondering." And, when a pleasant sensation is noted, we must hasten to catalog the nature of the stimulus that appeared to cause pleasure. Even compressed music, a la "Chipmunk" talk, may, as Lindsley (1964)suggests, evoke glee in some PMRs.

In the selection of toys, care should be exercised to ascertain whether some toys are fear inducing. While toys are never manufactured with the intent of generating fear on the user's part, some may actually do so. Fear can be indexed by noting if the child or adult flees, breaks out in tears and trembles or shudders, or becomes pale, or simply becomes immobilized (Binet, 1895). Students of primate behavior know well that certain toys are much feared. Hebb and Thompson (1954) indicate chimpanzees fear representations of animals such as toy donkeys, chimpanzees, or a man. A clay model of a chimpanzee's head terrorized the Yerkes colony as did a model of a human head. Harlow, working with Rhesus monkeys, found a small, moving toy bear was an excellent way to generate fear. Among humans, as in lower organisms, defecation and urination are also indices of fear or anxiety and should be noted along with Binet's fear indices.

> A woman having an enormous fear of thunderstorms and lightening was often observed during such occurrences to repeatedly go to the bathroom. She confessed that somehow, voiding or defecation seemed to allay her fear. The fear of storms, at age 84, is still as great as ever.

Fears in primates, while not translatable to humans, either normals or PMRs, do serve to illustrate that when we deal with nonverbals, we can be surprised and certain novel toys can spawn fear. Only by careful observation can we isolate those toys that attract, rather than repel, the PMR. Perhaps another and better method of approach to play activities and toy preferences in the PMR would be to revise the application blanks for admission of PMRs to institutions. Kudlaty (1977) studied the application forms for admission to 79 public institutions for the retarded. None asked for food preferences, and only two asked about the sleep patterns of the proposed resident. Play or toy preferences were scarcely noted as well. It would seem important to learn the food, toy, play preferences as well as uniquely feared situations since most PMRs, once institutionalized, tend to remain so (Eyman & Call, 1977). These bits and pieces of information about everyday life--likes and dislikes--must become known if we are to individualize and humanize their lives.

AESTHETICS

What is beauty to the profoundly retarded? In the main, their aesthetic sense is foreordained since we, not they, create their environment. Art and music, as well as natural phenomena, are aspects of the PMRs' world also, but we know little of their emotional responses to things we consider beautiful or inspiring. Do some PMRs manifest a primitive artistic bent? Over a decade ago, Fantz (1963) tested newborn infants' visual capacities and found they were capable of distinguishing between patterned and plain stimuli and that they preferred the patterned or more complex. We also know that there are developmental stages in children's art from scribbling to the attainment of form concept and naming it (Lowenfeld & Brittain, 1969). If we take a broad definition of art such as Langer's (1953) "Art is the creation of forms symbolic of human feeling," perhaps PMRs do possess a sense of the aesthetic. And, perhaps because we allow them so few materials or resources, they must turn to the resources their own body produces. Consider the following example which I termed "The Data Drain" (Cleland, 1973).

> An interesting phenomenon observed in some PMRs is fecal smearing. Historically, several approaches have been employed in attempting to minimize this practice: physical restraint, seclusion or isolation, and operant conditioning. Dependent upon the seriousness of the practice, its potential effects on behavior of other PMRs, attendants, and other personnel, various tactics are instituted to modify the smearing habit. Invariably, however, the practice is adjudged unsanitary, disgusting, offensive, and a variety of other negative value assignments. Cultural learnings about acceptable and unacceptable behavior, while important for normals, may seriously cloud perception insofar as the <u>meaning</u> of fecal smearing by PMRs is concerned. So strong are these attitudes that many employees "leave the field" in one way or another, turnover being a notable example.
>
> If this practice of fecal smearing (painting) is examined more critically, <u>what</u>, other than "unsanitary-revolting-disgusting," might PMR habitual smearers be telling us? Since our habitual response to smeared walls is to "clean them up" (sanitary and appearance standards are both important), it is evident that this "production" and its meaning as well, is destroyed by zealous employees. To attempt to maintain this "data" and simultaneously uphold

health and sanitation standards, it is proposed that immediately prior to scrubbing down these newly "decorated" walls, color photos of the smeared surfaces be taken. Such slides as are developed can be identified with the date and PMR producer's name. Later, without the odor factor to distort perception, professional staff may examine daily productions to determine whether there are distinctive or changing patterns for individuals or between individual subjects. Do the motions of smearing invariably remain the same or are changes evident? Are there days when an incorrigible smearer fails to smear? Are there diurnal and noctural regularities in this unusual practice? It is conceivable that other questions may arise once this data is systematically examined. What is suggested is the admittedly remote possibility that meaning is attached to such a practice and that smearing may be a symbolic form of communication. Interpretations other than psychoanalytic may be conceivable.

Should the data bank suggested above be entirely beyond credulity or feasibility (or acceptability), some institutionalized PMRs will nevertheless continue their artistry (smearing), and it will continue to alienate personnel and volunteer workers. Granting this, what can be done? One possible approach to modify the practice to one that employees might find unobjectionable would involve behavior shaping. If an incorrigible PMR smearer is placed in a secluded room within a ward (semi-isolation) to prevent contagion of the practice to others or for sanitary practices, a twofold opportunity exists: elimination of the obnoxious aspects so employees may benefit while still permitting the retardate to engage in a seemingly pleasurable practice. It might be desirable to develop a nontoxic paint in a color and consistency approximating fecal matter. If the PMR smearer is subsequently placed in a semi-private room because of smearing, this room might be prearranged with a wall covering similar to the touch of tile or plaster, but removable for later inspection, and preequipped with a conspicuously placed pile of the nontoxic paint. To facilitiate transfer from actual to artificial fecal material, the paint would incorporate a synthetic fecal odor and the employee or experimenter could place the PMR's preferred hand into this material to sensitize the retardate to the availability of a ready supply of "paint." Should this desirable transfer occur, the synthetic fecal "paint" would gradually diverge toward a standard color to ascertain whether color is the dominant attention-sustaining property of the synthetic feces.

It may also be interesting, assuming transfer occurs, to vary the properties of consistency and odor. Ultimately, the objective would be to gain transfer to an acceptable substitute and perhaps even to the subject's smearing of several colors incorporating as many distinctive odors. Would color utilization and varying preferences be indicative of affective states?

Assuming success in transfer, what benefits are foreseeable? For the PMRs, freedom to continue an activity that appears to be enjoyable (an aspect of an evolving recreational program for PMRs?). Employees may harbor fewer aversions, and researchers may be assisted in efforts to understand the needs of this enigmatic group, to establish a reinforcer hierarchy, and perhaps most important, to become more interested in research employing this understudied but important institutionalized subgroup.

If we conceptualize fecal smearers as "frustrated Rembrandts," provide them with a variety of colors and a studio, what else could be learned? If an artistic PMR who consistently paints in yellow, orange, and red abruptly shifts to somber gray, brown, or black colors, it could signal some personality or mood state change. If so, was some desirable program changed or did a favorite houseparent retire? In effect, our Rembrandt's efforts deserve closer scrutiny.

Stockton (1973), in an unpublished study, attempted to check out the author's data drain idea. Studying 14 PMRs, she found that the developmental level of subjects as reflected in Vineland Social Maturity Scale scores corresponded with Lowenfeld and Brittain's (1969) stages of development in children's art. Subjects with social ages of 1.47 or below when presented a crayon attempted to eat it; in the social age range of 1.53 to 2.0 subjects scribbled with the crayon while one subject whose social age was 2.5 had an "ordered circular pattern in his scribbles." In a second study that involved 10 fecal smearers and 11 non-smearers, Stockton presented them with finger paint with the consistency of feces and all smearers readily painted with this medium while only four non-smearers did so. Stockton said of the smearers "They act like artists," and her account deserves notice:

He entered the room and sat down at the table as told. He immediately eyed a small drop of finger paint on the table in front of him, smeared it on his finger, smelled it, and examined it thoroughly, frowning in apparent puzzlement. When offered a crayon, he pushed it aside and continued in deep concentration on the drop of finger paint. He was then presented with an open container of the warm, brown, lumpy substance which he immediately grabbed and emptied (with amazing thoroughness) onto the paper in front of him. Then, with vigorous enthusiasm and busy humming interspersed with knowing laughter, he began his masterpiece. The material was handled with such ease and familiarity, one was reminded of an expert craftsman at one with his medium. The first round of paint and paper soon ran out and a second portion was supplied. The masterpiece continued. It grew onto the table, down the legs, onto the floor, and finally onto the artist's body itself. It ended only when the paint ran out, much to the relief of the author, who was aware of her impending role as the only untouched canvas in the room. He was still humming and laughing when he was led from the room by the participating aide.

While, on the basis of the author's "data drain" and Stockton's (1973) attempt to ascertain its merit, we cannot conclude that PMRs (some at least) are aesthetically inclined, neither does it appear ridiculous to entertain the idea. For, in dealing with the profoundly retarded, we need to keep Kessler's (1966) advice about infants in mind. She suggests, "Because the infant cannot walk, talk, grasp objects, or otherwise show by directed behavior what he perceives and wants, his capacity for response is usually underrated" (p. 19). By giving consideration to art and music for the PMRs, both in the active sense of creating and the passive of viewing or listening, we may, in time, provide them more of the good life--as they define it.

6

Training Employees to Work with PMRs

MAKING PROFESSIONALS/NONPROFESSIONALS PARTNERS

Andrew Carnegie, in a speech published in June 1903 entitled "The secret of business is the management of men," gives us some interesting and perceptive advice on employee-employer relations. To paraphrase Carnegie, we can state that if employees are to give both their loyalty and best effort to the enterprise (regardless of type), employers would make them partners (Bursk, Clark & Hidy, 1962). This is precisely what Carnegie did and he sought young men of genius as his partners early in the Carnegie Steel Company's history--later extending the concept to most employees. There are many arguments to recommend a similar motivational concept for the mental health professions and in the varieties of organizational forms found in this field. However, the vast bulk of the mental health industry is not product oriented and is state or federal government financed. So, how can partnerships be possible in publicly supported organizations?

Economically speaking, it doesn't appear that Carnegie's plan could operate. But from a conceptual-philosophical level, a great deal could occur. Since this text addresses only the profoundly retarded and half or more are in institutional settings, let's look at the possibilities for partnerships between employees and employer in institutions.

IMPROVING CONDITIONS FOR HOUSEPARENTS AND PMRs?

Ordinarily, the heavy turnover of direct-care personnel is considered a negative aspect of institutions. Having little stability of surrogate parentage ordinarily is thought to be damaging insofar as child-rearing is concerned, and turnover is economically costly. The profoundly retarded, as we have seen, are those most likely to be placed in institutions, and they are placed early in their lives. As such, if the effects of turnover are indeed bad, we would expect child-rearing practices to be most damaging to the profoundly retarded. However, let's "look under the rug" and see what one noted psychologist has to say about "multiple mothers."

In an article that deals with a reinterpretation of the drive-reduction position on motivation, J. McVicker Hunt (1960) also addresses the origins of fear. In so doing, he makes a statement having interesting implications for institutional administrators and researchers. "Multiple mothering need not be seen as a traumatizing experience...but rather as an innoculation against social shyness and fear" (Hunt, 1965, p. 8). He cites timidity in overprotected children and the shyness of "rural mountain people" as cases in which his reinterpretations help explain the why or genesis of such phenomena.

In nearly three decades of acquaintance with the institutionalized PMR I have repeatedly observed them rushing to greet strangers--few display fear or shyness when strangers enter their arena. And, perhaps no better subjects could be employed to test Hunt's multiple-mothering hypothesis than the long-term, institutionalized PMR, for the "mothers and fathers" in their lives have been legion. If this hypothesis could be empirically tested <u>and</u> upheld, then an approach to scheduling and morale boosting could be implemented.

Assume that Hunt's hypothesis is valid. If so, let's schedule houseparents' duty shift in a manner insuring even greater amounts of multiple mothering--but mothering of a higher quality. We abandon the old three eight-hour shifts in favor of six four-hour shifts. The aim is to reduce worker fatigue, absenteeism, and turnover. Anyone who has put in an eight-hour day with a ward housing 40, 50 or 100 PMRs knows the strain and fatigue that occurs--and occurs before the shift ends. As employees become fatigued, the likelihood of becoming brusque, harsh, or even abusive to the residents is increased. Importing new surrogate mothers and fathers every four hours should allow the PMRs better "parents," vigorous "playmates" and such would enhance the PMRs' limited time understanding by providing more time anchors. For, as Watson's (1973) mini-meal study and Azrin and Armstrong's (1973) mini-meals demonstrated, the doubling of feedings also doubled the attention and training, improved behaviors and, although not specifically mentioned, it also gave more temporal anchors for their PMRs to build association strength. We already know that PMRs often assemble near windows at times when a new shift is coming on duty (Cleland & Swartz, 1969) and this rudimentary awareness of time appears to build up through repeated associations. Such time signals or anchors as shift changes and feedings appear to offer a ray of hope in disruption of an often boring existence. But, won't six four-hour shifts skyrocket costs?

Over 20 years ago, attendant turnover was estimated to cost over $450 per each departing employee. With escalation, a la 1978, that old estimate would unquestionably exceed a thousand dollars per houseparent. But, you argue, that projected savings in turnover by giving employees a four-hour shift would no wise offset the doubling of staff. Absenteeism and tardiness would also decline, but again not enough to offset the costs of doubling. What can be expected then from such a plan would be improved morale, reduced fatigue, and, we hope, better quality of care for the retarded.

> After every tour of institutions and observing wards housing the four levels of retardation, I ask my classes this question: "Do you think houseparents working with the profoundly retarded should have shorter hours and higher pay (or both) than those who work with the three higher levels?" Almost always the great majority of students favor shorter hours, or if that is not possible, higher pay.

Perhaps some state or private institutions could initiate, on an experimental basis, such a plan to see if benefits to employees and residents alike would accrue. Obviously, it would be easier to implement in a small institution having only PMR residents since jealousy arousal on the part of other houseparents not given the four-hour shift would be a concern.

An alternate plan, not entailing the added expense in the above-given plan, would involve four-hour shifts with the PMR and four hours with either of the three higher levels if the institution is serving all levels. Under such a plan, job enlargement would be one of the plus features and would allow houseparents to broaden their knowledge and experience in working with more than one level of retardation. The initiation of this plan would entail giving the existing work force the option to try it out or to volunteer. Since houseparents are known to want to stay with the type of resident they first gained experience with, newly hired houseparents would be a target group to make the plan work. If instituted successfully, one further advantage might obtain--namely, greater flexibility on the houseparents' part and less rigidity.

The foregoing, briefly outlined plans are alternatives to the standard three eight-hour shifts. Although untried to the writer's knowledge, either plan could improve the quality of child rearing and simultaneously improve the morale and lessen fatigue among direct-care workers.

Making direct-care workers feel more like partners in the institution and reducing the boredom, fatigue, and low morale that too often accompanies their work will require sophisticated and flexible management--flexible enough to encourage houseparents to share in the decision making within the institution. Altman et al. (1978) studied administrators' willingness to allow retarded residents to participate in institutional policy formulation and, on certain categories of policy, administrators were willing to permit resident input. Raynes et al. (1977) studied aides or houseparents' involvement in decision making as this related to quality of care given to residents. They found a strong positive correlation between resident stimulating care and aides' perceiving themselves to be involved in decision making. They concluded that involving aides in decision making is the most "important action that administrators can carry out to develop more individualized and responsive care in residential settings" (Raynes et al., 1977, p. 576). Important policies such as discipline are largely the making of the professional staff as they always have been. Yet, I would argue that were direct-care personnel also represented in the formulation of disciplinary policy, the likelihood of abusiveness to residents might lessen.

Butterfield and Zigler (1965) indicated the length of institutionalization has been the most frequently employed measure of social deprivation. These writers were addressing their remarks toward the residents, but what about the houseparents? If the environment in which residents live is impoverished, programs are poor, and so forth, the houseparents certainly have no immunity from this social or sensory deprivation that influences residents. To counteract deprivation at the houseparent level, Cleland and Peck (1967) presented an employee stimulation paradigm involving sabbatical leaves, role-rotations, consultants as stimulants, a training and observation ward, semi-annual conferences and a Gift-of-the Month. Sabbaticals were recommended for houseparents to minimize over-acculturation to the resident subculture, and since evidence exists that acculturation to another culture occurs following three years (Lorenzo, 1955), these writers recommended sabbaticals be provided subsequent to each two-and-a-half-year service period. There are many ways in which houseparents working with the nonverbal PMR could be stimulated, trained and kept interested, and readers interested in the paradigm mentioned should consult Cleland and Peck (1965). Now let us look at unorthodox training approaches for aides who will work with the profoundly retarded.

HYPNOTIC AGE REGRESSION AND TIME COMPRESSION

Hypnotic age regression, a strategy employed by a number of hypnotists wherein subjects are instructed to behave as they did at various earlier (or later) ages in life may have applicability in the study of the profoundly retarded. Although the results of carefully controlled hypnotic age regression studies are still equivocal as to the extent to which subjects can actually behaviorally duplicate an earlier life age, there is still some potential in such a technique. For example, subjects requested to regress to a specific age, such as six years, usually performed at about a nine-year level (Barber, 1972). Thus, it would appear if we wanted to observe an adult as a two-year-old, the suggestion given by the hypnotist should be to return to the womb state. What foreseeable benefits could the use of hypnosis generate for training people to work with the profoundly retarded? While speculative at best, here are some possibilities.

First, those who enter the field and who are assigned to work with adolescent or adult profoundly retarded are often at a loss when it comes to understanding what their charges want or need. Often too, the profoundly retarded may present an anomalous appearance that serves to undermine the neophyte houseparent or teacher's objectivity. Using normal adults acting under hypnotic age regression in the early stages of in-service training could diminish the initial shock of being surrounded by persons of adult size whose physically deviant appearance and infantile behaviors are so different from any person previously experienced. By substituting normal appearing adults who are now acting *as if* they were two or two-and-one-half years of age, the initial shock could be reduced. Yet, certain needs and wants might be isolated that could have value when the neophytes actually begin work with the profoundly retarded. Thus, neophytes would be gradually introduced over a period of 30 to 60 days experience with age-regressed normals, the ordinary in-service training staff, and gradually make intensified visits to the dorms they ultimately will be assigned to work.

Obviously, this would be an experimental approach to training those who will work with the profoundly retarded. It could be argued that even if it worked and served its purpose, it would be expensive. To this, the counter-argument is simple--the current extremely high turnover among direct-care workers is also very costly. Additionally, neophytes are not likely to last long enough to ever really understand the needs of the profoundly retarded--experience does count. If a worker is to be assigned an adult PMR dorm, then life-age matching of normals to the PMRs and hypnotic age regression might help us more clearly see the PMRs' needs.

Another, perhaps more plausible training approach involves time compression. Under hypnotic suggestion, time's passage can be stepped up or slowed down. When individuals are directed via hypnotic suggestion to slow time's passage, some subjects can memorize material four times as quickly as under ordinary conditions (Goldenson, 1970). At the Foundation for Mind Research in Pomona, New York, studies involving altered states of consciousness, accelerated learning and the creative process are underway. In one interesting case report, a pianist was put into a light trance and instructed to practice a sonata she hand't played for some time but which she would be performing very soon. The hypnotist tells her to take all the time needed to perfect the piece and on emergence from the trance the pianist stated, "After an hour's rehearsal, I'm a lot more confident." The subject then demonstrated her improvement. What actually occurred was that improvement occurred although the subject merely imagined practicing, and subjectively, she had an hour's practice although only one minute had elapsed! However, unless an action practiced in the imagination is known to the body from previous experience, the suggestion won't work. Nevertheless, certain aspects of a houseparent's training such as learning symbols used in medical orders and other rote type learnings would appear to be more swiftly learned under time compression suggestion and for individuals who are susceptible to hypnosis, training time could perhaps be shortened. Several scales have been developed to assist in identifying subjects for hypnosis, for example, Weitzenhoffer and Hilgard's Stanford Hypnotic Susceptibility Scale (1967), and the Harvard Group Scale of Hypnotic Susceptibility by Shor and Orne (1962).

In both instances using hypnosis, employees would obviously have to volunteer and give informed consent. These suggestions, untried and speculative, are offered merely to challenge readers to criticize, elaborate or perhaps even test their merit.

SELECTION OF HANDICAPPED DIRECT-CARE WORKERS

Reducing turnover and increasing our knowledge of the profoundly retarded are high priority administrative goals. A further objective of service-oriented facilities is the rehabilitation of the handicapped. Can selection of direct-care workers become a vehicle to help attain these three goals?

Wards housing profoundly retarded residents, especially in winter time, have been described as "odor factories." And, odors help create turnover and also blemish one's perceptions of the profoundly retarded. However, there are certain persons, otherwise normal, who would be unaffected by odors. Reference here is to the anosmic person or the congenital non-smeller. By hiring such a person the impact of odors on turnover would be negated and their observations of the PMR would, theoretically at least, be less biased.

Another resident variable contributing to heavy turnover is the sometimes bizarre physical appearance and bizarre actions, such as coprophagy, that characterize the PMR. Again, the choice of a congenitally blind but otherwise normal houseparent could be helpful. By not witnessing their charges' appearance or actions, they would have the advantage of lesser prejudice or bias in the impressions they form about the PMR. Also, it is likely their turnover rate may be less a problem than those whose sensory equipment is intact.

A deaf person might be another who would compliment the two types of handicaps mentioned above. Noise, as Glenn et al. (1978) point out, is a major problem on dormitories and can mar communications both of residents and aides. The deaf person, with all other senses intact, would be immunized by nature against the noise problem and free to note more objectively what PMR behaviors mean.

In the foregoing examples, only the potential benefits were mentioned. Obviously, the addition of sensorially handicapped employees would still require the presence of nonhandicapped houseparents to guide or protect the blind or deaf personnel. The greatest benefit to accrue would likely be a different and unique kind of observational input--perhaps new views on the way nonverbal PMRs communicate--little influenced by the factors that cause many direct-care workers to resign after a brief stay. Another potential benefit would be the placement of hard-to-place rehabilitation clients, the sensorially handicapped. The blind person on the night shift might contribute a great deal to our existent knowledge of PMR nocturnal behaviors, etc. The reader can easily counteract what has been cited as increased objectivity of reporting--the blind could still be supersensitive to odors, the deaf to visually disturbing behaviors, etc. And, where would the institution find the anosmic, deaf or blind? The logical place might be the state employment agency, or vocational rehabilitation agencies. The point of the foregoing is to suggest an approach that <u>may</u> augment our knowledge of PMRs via employment, on a try-out or experimental basis, of individuals having a sensory handicap.

SIMULATION OF HANDICAPS

A variation on the foregoing entails simulation training (Swartz & Cleland, 1973). One major advantage such training affords is personal involvement and an enhancing of employees' empathy toward the profoundly retarded. Simulation training also introduces novelty into training and dispels a certain amount of boredom. What kinds of handicaps can be simulated and to what purpose? Since the PMRs are, in a sense, the prototype of the multihandicapped, a number of simulations can be invoked.

One very dramatic and didactic simulation entails being bedfast. In this situation an attendant, nurse or teacher would volunteer to be bedfast. To maximize the reality of the simulation, at least one-half day or four hours should be spent in this condition. Physicians could artificially scissor the trainee's legs via casts or splints and similarly decomission one arm to simulate spastic triplegia. The trainee would be placed on a low, wheeled bed so a "feel" for being looked down at by ambulatory adults could be developed. To further augment the trainees' sense of dependency-helplessness, only one or two occasions of being "looked after" should occur--this, of course, would duplicate dormitory conditions on those days when understaffing due to absentees or weather occurred. Such "sensitivity" training could cause employees to think about ways to help the bedfast PMRs, to think of what happens when unauthorized absenteeism worsens the situation for the bedfast, and to enhance or strengthen the bond between the employee and the PMR. As a means of inaugurating this simulation of bedfastness, it is suggested that the superintendent and perhaps a couple of teachers or physicians "lead the way." This strengthens the partnership between professional and nonprofessional employees and signifies that "top brass" don't ask us to do anything that they themselves won't do!

SHIFT CHANGE TRAINING AND KNOWING ABOUT SHIFTS

Elsewhere, Cleland and Swartz (1969) have addressed the potential for training that exists during employee and resident "down-time." This time occurs when a resident is sitting on the commode or an employee is commuting to and from work.

The author studied 927 attendants' commuting practices and found one-fourth of these institutional employees spent over five hours weekly in travel (Cleland, 1969). Thus, in communities having several residential facilities that operate on the same three-shift basis, considerable "down-time" could be captured for training purposes. One approach would be to involve private business sponsors to broadcast "how-to" training lectures at shift changes. The employees would be rewarded for listening on their way to or from work by salary or promotion for passing exams based on such lectures. Another way to harness commuting "down-time" would be to build an institutional library tape deck of lectures on the profoundly retarded. In this instance, employees' rewards would come by checking out tapes for use in their tape-deck player (auto or home) and obtaining points toward promotion for passing exams over the tape materials. Obviously, these materials or live broadcasts would have to be selected on the basis of proven interest to attendants. Aside from the capturing of down-time of the commuting attendants, what else might such a plan provide? Since the shift change broadcasts would be open to <u>any</u> listener, parents of the retarded, or others, might also benefit. The non-involved lay public might listen and become better informed about the PMR and, possibly the institutional image would benefit.

In a Southern Regional Education Board survey of 26 institutions, one of the things attendants expressed a desire to know more about was "the other duty shifts." Specifically, they wanted a chance to talk to attendants about their duty-shift problems and problems common to all shifts. While most three-shift institutions have 15-minute overlap for this purpose, this does not allow enough time to really exchange much information other than emergency material. As a supplemental training vehicle, can this problem be addressed? If institutions offered attendants who are at retirement age a chance to become listed as substitutes (as in public schools), would some elect to do so? Probably, and if these former attendants were employed for one or two days, every three months, then the three shifts of actives could have their "retreat" on company time. These get-togethers could allow time for more meaningful discourse and could help reduce the between-shift rivalry and jealousy that often occurs. If these surrogate parents can increase their understanding and respect of one another, this improvement will be reflected in improved care and attention for their PMR children.

MISCELLANEOUS THOUGHTS ON ATTENDANT TRAINING

The acculturation to behave in an adult fashion is strongly ingrained in most who become direct-care workers. Childhood and playfulness are in the distant past. Yet, every PMR needs some play, and it is the direct-care worker (parent surrogate) who must supply a good portion of it. For this reason, it could be appropriate to provide as part of in-service training some games and playful activities for the attendants. For example, charades could be of interest since it may serve to enhance one's ability to guess the meaning of a nonverbal behavior and also help isolate those trainees who were the best at decipherment. This training suggestion may sound silly but one of the professionals' biggest gripes towards attendants is "They just want to keep the ward clean and won't play with the kids." It would seem, at least in training the attendants for the PMRs, that some concrete suggestion that "it's all right to play with the children or adults" is needed.

The suggestions for training attendants or others to work with the PMR resident contained in this chapter are admittedly sketchy and in some instances, highly speculative. The intention of the author has been to suggest ways in which a partnership between professionals and nonprofessionals can be strengthened. To the extent this can occur, the PMR should benefit correspondingly and overall morale could be improved.

It should be noted that in the several primate research centers sponsored by the National Institutes of Health, unique missions or objectives for each center foster specialization. For example, one center may focus on reproductive biology, another on mental retardation in primates, etc. Researchers whose interest parallel the mission of a given center thus gravitate there and interact with other scientists from varied disciplinary backgrounds whose interests are shared in common. Further organizational features of merit include the appointment of Visiting Senior Scientists and an opportunity for both graduate and upper-division undergraduates to interact often with senior personnel. Finally, the primate keepers (or attendants) are literally partners with senior investigators, since the conduct of research depends on mutual information exchange and observational data must be obtained from the primates' keepers. Significant advances have been made by primate researchers. In fact, the life span of captive baboons is double that of baboons in the wild (DeVore, 1965). This is not true for the institutionalized PMR human. Indeed, the highest death rate of all PMR new admissions to institutions occurs during the first 90 days (Sabaugh, Dingman, Tarjan & Wright, 1959).

The fact that we know how to keep primate mortality low, whereas we cannot say this where the PMR is concerned, is a reflection of greater research activity with primates than PMRs, and the organization of scientific effort to make partners of students, nonprofessional personnel, and senior scientists alike. The paradigm of the Regional Primate Research Centers may merit the attention of all concerned with the nonverbal, profoundly retarded.

7

Concluding Thoughts and Issues

THE OUTER LIMITS OF NORMALIZATION

In our society there are many phenomena that could be adjudged "normal." But when the retarded are involved, and especially the profoundly retarded, the "dignity of risk" is often overwhelmed by the ingrained idea that these retarded persons are "angels unaware"--or perpetual children or infants. The author has seen a profoundly retarded, 30-year-old male beg and, this failing, steal cigarettes from visitors. By all odds, he enjoys tobacco to the point of addiction, but despite his adult chronological age, he is denied this pleasure. Are his basic rights abrogated? Is this a denial of the "dignity of risk"?

Again, in the realm of appetitive behaviors, no institution ever gives the adult profoundly retarded any whiskey, wine, or beer, to my knowledge. Undoubtedly some would enjoy spirits, but, again, the perpetual infant is the overriding consideration. Yet, our conventional wisdom in this respect seems to generate (but does not condone) the development of oral behaviors such as pica, coprophagy, and the eating of lead-based paint. Among normals in our society, heterogeneity of food and drink is evident in eating of snails, rattlesnake steaks, and a variety of whiskies and liquors. Perhaps a similarly heterogeneous diet, at least for adult PMRs, could be no more harmful than some of their bizarre intake? Given the fact that they live a very short time compared to normals, is it right on our part to deny them a few of life's pleasures during their abbreviated stay?

Take another phenomenon of modern day America--the Uniform Anatomical Gift Act that has gone into effect in all 50 states. Could the PMR who has, at death, certain intact organs be a donor or, conversely, might a PMR be a recipient? Obviously, surgical implants to PMRs are rarely considered since PMRs are so resistant to help and are thought to be "too dumb" to even consider receiving an implant. Is the idea of this too ludicrous to even debate?

In a study by Cleland, Rago, Case, Jones & McGavern (1977), the normalization principle was investigated in relation to the burial practices of institutions for their indigent and no-next-of-kin retardates. A comparison was made with a community cemetery and a large military base cemetery. For the institution's deceased who are sans identity, there is a simple 6" x 6", ground-level bronze marker engraved with the deceased person's case number as the sole identification provided. By contrast, in the military and community cemeteries, graves were replete with identification, birth and death dates, and, often, an epitaph of some length.

Of interest, in view of the fact that HEW guidelines do not mention anything about the conduct of research on human subjects if deceased, permission had to be secured merely to observe within the institution's cemetery. I emphathize with the institution's exercise of caution in obtaining legal clearance. However, it appears that certain kinds of behavioral research, such as surveys, observational, or records research, that involve no risk and insure anonymity could be expedited. In certain inter-agency kinds of research in which both agencies operate under HEW regulations in regard to research on human subjects, up to five committes must pass on the proposed research--even if it is only observational in nature. Such duplication of effort by committees of two agencies of state government, both bound by the same HEW regulations, is slowing research and is a waste of time for some committee members whose salaries may be relatively high.

While I do not advocate "license for researchers to hunt," it is evident that the profoundly retarded, those about whom we know least, are likely to have little research participation. It might even be argued that, of the rights of the PMR, the right to be researched would rank high. Why? Because while it is emotionally appealing to speak of mainstreaming or deinstitutionalization for the PMR, the architects who designed "deinstitutionalize the PMR" have not provided the public schools and their personnel with any "how-to-do-it" formula. The principal reason, as readers should be aware of by now, is a knowledge vacuum as concerns the PMR. Ellis' (1975) caveat is especially relevant--"the current popular view of retardation suggests that we know how to train, educate and habilitate retarded people and that political action will rid us of the problem. Nothing could be further from the truth. Neither governmental action programs, nor court orders, nor public conscience will wipe out this problem, nor will it disappear with the re-labeling of retarded persons. While 'normalization' is a worthy goal, it may blind us to a child's need for special help" (Ellis, 1975, p. 2). Research holds the key--especially of the profoundly mentally retarded. Knowing the fragility of the PMR and the hazards of relocating them (Cleland & Swartz, 1969; Miller, 1975 & 1976), deinstitutionalization zealots could be consigning them to an early death. Popularity of a concept does not equal validity, and such brush-fire issues as mentioned above deserve close scrutiny when the retardate is of profound level.

Normalization "means making available to the mentally retarded patterns and conditions of everyday life which are as close as possible to the norms and patterns of the mainstream of society" (Nirje, 1969). As concerns the implementation of normalization for the profoundly retarded and the maintenance and upholding of their rights, P.L. 94-142, "Education for All Handicapped Children," is designed to insure educational opportunity (PCMR, 1977). The President's Committee also acknowledged that "Unless basic and applied research is continued and adequately supported, it will hardly be possible to meet projected educational goals" (PCMR, 1977, p. 239). It is ironic, indeed, in view of the HEW Guidelines for the Conduct of Research on Human Subjects, to note that the Massachusetts Supreme Court ruled on July 13, 1976 that "Life prolonging treatments may be withheld from a severely retarded patient who is incapable of making such a decision himself" (Hospital Week, 1976). Truly, it stretches one's credulity to see the sanctioning of "mercy killing" while innocuous research involving only observation of subjects requires one or several research boards' approval! Or, legal approval to study an institutional cemetery! In my opinion, we have attained in respect to research "encouragement" and subsequent knowledge production as concerns the most neglected and least understood human--the PMR--a reductio ad absurdum. The regular classroom teacher and the public schools are instructed to implement "zero-reject," the President's Committee on Mental Retardation simultaneously acknowledges our woeful lack of knowledge of "what" and "how" to teach the PMR, and researchers are considerably slowed by "informed consent," "debriefing," and so on. In the case of the legal ruling regarding withholding of life prolonging treatment, we cannot but wonder if "informed consent," even from an advocate or guardian, was sought? The outer limits of normalization are poorly defined as concerns our nonverbal, profoundly retarded, and encouragement of research appears the most promising avenue by which the parameters of the concept can be mapped. We do not advocate turning PMRs into Guinea pigs, but we seek to allow them to assist in bettering their own training and treatment by being participants in no-risk research.

Denial of tobacco or booze, on grounds that the PMR adult would be harmed, are debatable rights issues. There are many things we don't know. For example, in normals from chicken to man, the appetite or food intake is augmented by the presence of others--the so-called social facilitation effect. In the PMR, where sociability is considerably less than in normals, would the social facilitation effect on appetite hold, or would appetite increase under private conditions? Again, the PMR currently has balanced caloric and vitamin intake in institutional settings, courtesy of dieticians and nutritionists. In 1878, the institutionalized PMR had no such dietary balance. Are PMRs of 1978 taller and heavier than their 1878 intellectual peers? We know normals are larger than their grandfathers--do PMRs parallel this trend?

Normalization and mainstream America encompasses many phenomena that we consider not atypical--they are "normal." Examples include model agencies to supply beautiful people, athletic greats, old people, or tall or short people. These people barter their uniqueness or fame to sell various products, and in return they are given handsome monetary rewards. Among PMRs, some are clinical types and rare as Farrah-Fawcetts, for example, they are Hurler's disease or gargoylism. Would it be absurd to think of a model agency that would take and sell pictures of these rare PMRs to medical or behavioral textbook publishers? Naturally, the parent or guardian would need to give permission and, in turn, would receive money for the PMR model. When the author proposed this idea to his graduate seminar on PMR, students were initially somewhat dumbfounded. I inquired, "Is this idea exploiting the PMR, or is it providing them money and making textbooks in medicine or behavioral sciences more realistic and didactic?" And, "albeit Farrah-Fawcett can give informed consent to permit use of her pictures to promote sales of clothes, and the PMR adult cannot, is selling clothing more critical to societal well-being than instruction or teaching in the sciences?"

> One student went home after class and called her parents to get their opinion. Her brother was Down's Syndrome. At the next class meeting she told me her brother was Down's Syndrome and that she'd asked her parents' opinion on my "model agency" proposal. Her mother was adamantly against the idea but her father, after pondering the issue, indicated he thought it would be O.K. His reasoning, my student told me, was that the income would help to give brother more of the things he liked and that it could be helpful in teaching scientists in training. If guaranteed that his son's picture would <u>only</u> be used educationally, he would have no objections. She further told me that her father sort of equated this use of pictures with a physician's request to perform an autopsy on his father. There is something inherently strange in either instance, but "if it will help someone a generation off, then it is probably worthwhile."

The issue here is that of exploitation of the PMR versus the idea that model agencies in our society are "normal" aspects of everyday life. To help chart the outer limits of normalization, it may be worthwhile to convene a panel of parents of PMR children and adults, some experienced physicians, psychologists, and lawyers and discuss the model agency relative to attitudes of those most concerned with the welfare of the PMR. Parents of the PMR do have rights, and they harbor deep-seated hurts, aspirations and protective wishes for their child or children--it would be beneficial to learn more about their desires and attitudes.

Another everyday occurrence in the mainstream of society is going to bed. Normal adults usually exercise freedom of choice as to when they retire, but institutionalized PMR adults are put to bed earlier than any level retarded person in the institution. While true that the PMR is also the most fragile of humans, there are some whose behavior suggests they would enjoy staying up later. Can bedtime be normalized-individualized?

In the dialectic relative to normalizing the profoundly retarded, it becomes apparent that there are degrees or a hierarchy of possibilities for normalization of this most difficult group. It is equally obvious that our knowledge base is inadequate. We have a great many more legal caveats related to resident-client and parental rights than we have "know-how" to implement the court's rulings. The expanded nature of parent rights is exemplified in the following paragraphs.

Public Law 94-142, the Education for All Handicapped Children Act, is designed to insure a free and appropriate education for every handicapped child. The profoundly retarded, under this law, are thus accorded the right to be in a public school setting. Parents of such children are, under the act, entitled to considerably more information about their child's school program than ever before. Their right to participate in conferences at the school when their child's program (Individualized Education Program) is being considered is insured, by law. Prior to enactment of P.L. 94-142, diagnostic staffings in institutional settings or staff conferences in public school were primarily the province of professionals. Although exceptions occurred and an occasional parent was invited to such conferences, the decisions reached were exclusively the <u>decision</u> of professionally trained individuals. Among the expanded rights of parents of handicapped persons, the following are among the more significant.

1. You must receive notice in writing before the school system takes (or recommends) any action that may change your child's school program. Notice in writing is also required if a school refuses to take action to change your child's program.
2. You have the right to give--or withhold--permission for your child to be: tested to determine whether or not he requires special education services (identification); evaluated by specialists to determine what his educational needs are (evaluation); placed in a specific school program to meet his needs (placement).
3. You have the right to see and examine all school records related to the identification, evaluation, and placement of your child. If you find that certain records are inaccurate or misleading, you have the

right to ask that they be removed from your child's file. Once removed, they may not be used in planning for your child's placement.

4. If you do not agree with the school's course of action at any point along the way, you have the right to request an impartial due process hearing. This means that you can initiate a hearing to protest any decision related to identification, evaluation, or placement of your child.
5. If you fail to win your case, you have the right to appeal the results of the due process hearing to the State Department of Education; and you can appeal to the courts if you lose your case at the state level. (from Closer Look, 1977)

The rights of the retarded, all levels, relative to discriminatory testing, to treatment, to due process, and so forth, are more fully covered in standard texts such as MacMillan (1977) and Cleland (1978). One of the rights concerns Individualized Education Plans (IEP) and these are to be updated annually for each child. A considerable emphasis on ways to individualized programs or plans has been given in this text. We hope that readers will expand on or alter the suggestions offered so the neglected retarded (PMRs) can enjoy a quality of life that transcends its present level, which is based on our past and current "expertise" in tailoring training, recreation, and other programmatic elements to their needs. We do have "a ways to go."

Appendix A
Excerpts from a Ward Daybook

Seventy profoundly retarded males having an average chronological age of 42 years, an average social quotient of 9.3 (mental age $\bar{X} = 2.32$), and an average length of institutionalization of over 28 years are the actors in this drama.

Unless you have an institutional background, it is unlikely that the rich data of the ward daybook has ever been revealed to you. The daybook is very much like a ship's log--all significant events are here recorded. These excerpts from the daybook are unedited except for deletion of the residents' names and the sign-off watch names of the attendants. From reading these brief excerpts from the three duty shifts, you can vicariously step into the attendant's role and gain a knowledge of how the duties of each shift differ from the others. Also, you may ponder what certain behaviors may be telling us about the residents' needs for the daybook allows us another window into the mental life of the PMR.

These reports, drawn from entries made around Christmas, highlight a rare occurrence for a few PMR residents--a few may go home for a short visit. The institution shifts are 6:00 a.m. to 2:00 p.m., 2:00 p.m. to 10:00 p.m., and 10:00 p.m. to 6:00 a.m. Over half of all the United States' PMRs are in institutional settings and the excerpts provided are not atypical of the adult PMRs' everyday life.

First Shift

9:00	12/12/1974 All of the resident stay inside because the weather was too cold.
10:00	Water and Hi Cal was given out and __________ drink 2 glasses of water.
Note:	The following was D.C. on these medications: __________ DC on Synalar Creame; __________ DC on Otabiotic Otic; __________ DC on Otabiotic Otic; __________ on Pyrocidin Opth.; __________ DC on Pheno ½ gr. tid.
12 Noon	Medication set up and given out per doctor orders.
10:00 a.m.	__________ Both feet treated. __________ L hand treated & bandaged. Wyanoid Suppository inserted--have medication counted by both shift med. key, 6 dorm key given 2-10 charge @ 1:45 p.m. Cap 70, on roll 70, on dorm 69, 1 in hospital-- __________.
12/15/75	6 a.m. to 2:00 p.m.
	Medication counted by both shifts med. key 6 dorm keys given to charge (602) @ 5:45, dorm 69, 1 in hosp. Dorm was in good order.
7:00 a.m.	Medication set up and given out per Drs. order.
7:50	__________ had mild seizure lasting about 3 minutes and clinic was notified.
9:00	All of residents stay inside because the weather was too cold.
10:00	Water and Hi Cal was given out and __________ drink 2 glasses of water.
12 Noon	Medication set up & given out per Dr. orders. Medication counted by both shifts med. key, 6 dorm keys given 2-10 charge @ 1:45. Cap. 70 on Roll, 69 on dorm, 1 in hosp.--__________.
1:40	__________ got choked off some bread.

12/16/75 — 6 to 2 p.m.
Morning Shift

Med. counted by both shifts med. key 6 dorm keys given to 6-2 charge @ 5:45. Cap 70, on Roll 70, on dorm 69, 1 in hosp. Dorm was in good order.

7:00 a.m. — Medications set up and given out per Dr. orders.

Note: — Any employee who would like to participate in singing X-Mas carol from dorm call recreation this evening before 7:00 o'clock.

9:00 — All the residents stay inside because the weather was too cold.

10:00 — Water & Hi Cal was given out & __________ drink 3 glasses of water.

10:20 — __________ - Valium 5 mg. was given for behavior this AM.

10:30 — Treatments done on __________'s left hand & __________ - nose & neck. Treatments also done on __________, __________, __________ and __________.

12 Noon — Med. set up and given out per Dr. order.

1:15 — __________ was put on Mellaric Concentrate 25 mg. TID change all B$\bar{c}$C to Homerelirm 1 tap P.O. daily. Med. counted by both shifts, med key 6 dorm keys given to 2-10 charge @ 1:45. Cap 70, on Roll 70, on Dorm 69 - 1 in hosp. - __________.

12/18/1974 — 6 - 2 Shift

5:45 a.m. — Same as above 70-70 & 69. Dorm good order.

7:00 a.m. — Medication set up & given out per Drs. order.

9:00 — All residents stay in because the weather was too cold.

10:00 — Water and Hi Cal was given out and __________ drink 2 glasses of water and also __________.

10:30 — __________ got 33 cc of Kaopectate $\bar{c}$ paragoric for loose stool.

12 N	Med. set up & given out per Dr. order.

1:45 p.m.	Med. counted by both shifts - keys given 70 on roll, 69 on dorm, 1 hosp. __________. Ward, keys, med accepted.

2:00 p	Notice All Employees
Residents are to no longer pull laundry in or out, mop, or do any housekeeping jobs.
By order __________ and __________

Note! Soil (feces) has been found in jump suits, 2 shirts, and underwear of residents, also pillow cases have been used to wipe off & up soil, the pillow cases are to go out with the laundry. Each shift charge is to check all things to be washed on the dorm at the end of each shift. If soil is found by the people who washes the clothes please leave me a note on this.

Thank you,

Mrs. __________

10:30 a.m.	__________ was given 30 cc's of Kaopectate c̄ paragoric.

12/22/74

5:45 a.m.	Dorm ✓ 5 keys rec'd - Note the 6th key was found on South Wing by Mrs. __________. 70, 69 & 1 hosp.

7:00 a.m.	Med. given per Dr. orders. All residents ate breakfast except __________. He refuse to get out of bed. Teeth were brushed.

7:30 a.m.	__________ Temp 100° clinic notified - has been drinking lots of water.

9:45 a.m.	__________ was checked - Temp 101° clinic notified, was checked for IMPACTION.

10:00 a.m.	__________ to clinic to be ✓ by doctor.

10:30 a.m.	__________ admitted to hospital.

10:00 a.m.	Water & Hi Cal given to residents. __________ drank 2 glasses of water. Residents were trained

	on dorm because of weather.
12 N	Med. given per Dr. orders. All residents ate lunch, teeth brushed.
1:15 p.m.	Medication - __________, __________ - __________ to go to recreation.
1:45 p.m.	__________ on off-campus visit with his mother.
1:45 p.m.	Dorm √'ed, 70, 69 & 1 hosp.
12/23/74	
5:45	Dorm √'ed - OK.
7:00 a.m.	Med. given per Dr. orders.
7:50	__________ had a seizure lasting 3 minutes.
8:30	__________, __________, __________ didn't eat their breakfast.
9:30 a.m.	Valium 10 mg. given to __________ for continuous seizures.
Note!	__________ to go to minor surgical clinic on Friday Dec. 27, 1974 @ 8:45 a.m.
8:10	__________ had a bad seizure lasting 3 minutes.
8:45 a.m.	__________ had seizure lasted 5 min.
9:35 a.m.	__________ went home for a week will be back on Dec. 30, 1974.
10:00 a.m.	Hi Cal & water given out & __________ drank 3 glasses of water.
1:10 p.m.	__________ hit __________ up against the gate in Group I area & cut his lip.
Note:	The boys on Lithomath are to go to the lab early Monday morning Dec 30, 1974.
1:45 p.m.	Dorm √'ed 70, 2 hosp, 2 furlough.

12/25/74 Merry X'mas

5:28 a.m. Med. counted cap 70, roll 70, dorm 66, 2 furlough, 2 in hosp.

7:00 a.m. Med. set up & given per Dr. orders, all ate their breakfast.

10:30 a.m. __________ home on leave with father. Temperature taken 99/R.

12 Noon Med. given per Dr. orders. All ate their lunch. Teeth brushed.

1:45 p.m. Med. counted, dorm checked
Cap 70, Roll, 70, Dorm 65 - 2 hosp. __________ & __________. 2 furlough __________, __________. 1 LOA __________.

1:30 Injury made on __________ - large cut on back of head - nurse & clinic notified.

1:55 Relieved by attendant __________.

12/26/74

5:45 a.m. Med. counted, dorm √'ed - cap = 70, Dorm 65, 2 hosp., 2 furlough, 1 LOA.

7 a.m. Med. given out per Dr. orders. All ate breakfast except __________. He refused to get out of bed to eat. Temp taken 99°.

9:45 a.m. We pick up 2 fruit baskets for __________ from his parents to give to residents. We gave to central kitchen.

10:00 a.m. Hi cal was given to residents.

12 Noon Med. given out per Dr. orders - all residents ate lunch - teeth brushed.

12:35 Injury on __________. __________ was fighting with __________ and __________ scratches him on right ear. Treated on dorm by Mrs. __________ and sent to clinic @ 1:00.

1:15 p.m. Injury on attendant, scratches on upper left arm. Clinic notified. __________ pinched & scratched her.

1:45 p.m. Shift change - Cap 70, on roll 70, dorm 65, 2 hosp. __________, __________; 2 furlough __________ & __________; 1 LOA __________. __________ relieved by __________

Second Shift

12/12/74 2 to 10 Shift Start

Medication counted on dorm checked by both shifts, med. key, 6 dorm keys rec. from __________ @ 1:45 p.m. Dorm was in good order 69 boys on dorm 1 in hospital.

2:00 p.m. 32 residents went on bus ride.

2:15 p.m. __________ to clinic for shot.

5:00 p.m. Medication set up & given out per Dr. orders.

9:00 p.m. Medication set up & given out per Dr. orders. Injury report made on __________ cut on head. Medication counted & dorm checked by both shifts. Medicine key and 6 dorm keys given to 10-6 charge. Cap 70 on roll, 70 on dorm, 69 - 1 in hospital __________.

12/15/74 Medication counted and dorm checked by both shifts. Med. key, 6 dorm keys rec. from 6-2 charge @ 1:45 p.m. Dorm was in fair order. 69 boys on dorm, 1 in hospital.

5:00 p.m. Medication set up and given out per Dr. orders.

5:30 p.m. __________ had a seizure lasting 4 minutes - it was a hard seizure.

5:20 p.m. __________ in time out for fighting residents and employee.

4:30 p.m. Injury report made on __________ kicked by __________.

7:45 p.m. __________ had a seizure lasting 2 minutes - hard seizure.

9:00 p.m. Medication set up & given out per Dr. orders. Medication counted & dorm checked by both shifts. Med key, 6 dorm keys given to 10-6 charge @ 1:45 p.m. Cap 70, on roll 70, on dorm 69, 1 in hosp. - __________.

<u>12/16/74</u> Med. counted & dorm checked by both shifts. Med key, 6 dorm keys rec. from 6-2 charge @ 1:45 p.m. Dorm was in good order, 69 residents on dorm, 1 in hospital.
Note: __________ change to regular tray.
__________ - put on Valium 5 mg. TID.

2:00 p.m. Residents outside for a parade.

3:30 __________ to clinic for shot.

5:00 Medication set up and given out per Drs. orders.

9:00 Med. set up & given out per Drs. orders. Med. counted & dorm checked by both shifts, med. key, 6 dorm keys given to 10-6 charge @ 9:20 p.m. Cap 70 on Roll 70, on dorm 69, 1 in hospital.

<u>12/18/74</u>

1:45 Dorm checked, both shifts - In good order. 70 roll, 69 on dorm, 1 hosp.

2:25 p.m. Injury report made on __________ cut over right eye.

<u>Note!</u>
8:30 a.m. on 12-19-74 These residents are to go to X-ray - let them eat early & be sure to give their 7 a.m. medication.
__________, __________, __________, __________, and __________.

5:00 p.m. Medication set up & given out per Drs. orders.

9:00 p.m. Med. set up & given out per Drs. orders.

9:50 p.m. Med. counted, dorm √'ed, roll 70, on dorm 69, 1 hospital.

12/19/74

1:45 Dorm ✓ by both shifts - dorms OK. All panels & curtains up, 1 panel (overhead, i.e.,) loose on north wing.

3:30 p.m. __________ to clinic for shot.

3:30 p.m. Hi Cal & juice given to residents.

3:30 p.m. 39 residents returned to dorm from Barber Shop. 1 resident didn't return. He ran off from Barber Shop & went to the Butler Bldg. Mrs. __________ went after him. It was __________. Attendants __________, __________, __________ & __________.

4:25 p.m. 29 more residents returned with attendant __________ & __________.

5:00 p.m. Med. given per Dr. orders.

9:00 p.m. Med, given per Dr. orders. 70 roll, 69 on dorm, 1 hospital.

12/24/74

1:45 p.m. Dorm ✓'ed - dorm in good order.

2:00 p.m. Residents inside, bad weather.

4:30 p.m. Med. given per Dr. orders.

8:30 p.m. Med. given per Dr. orders.

9:30 p.m. Head count 70 capacity, 67 in dorm, 2 in hospital, __________ & __________.

12/26/74

1:50 p.m. Dorm in good order.

3:15 p.m. __________ returned from leave.

5:35 p.m. Injury report on __________. Cut on back of head.

5:00 p.m. Med. given per Dr. orders.

9:00 p.m. Med. given per Dr. orders.

9:50 p.m. Dorm checked 70, 66 2 hosp., (__________ & __________) 2 furlough (__________ & __________).

12/29/74

1:45 Dorm checked.

2:00 p.m. All residents inside because of weather.

2:30 p.m. Injury report on __________ fell in shower hurting both knees, one bruised, clinic notified. Have Dr. check in a.m.

3:30 p.m. Injury report made on __________ sore under left foot.

4:30 p.m. Med. given per Dr. orders.

8:30 p.m. Med. given per Dr. orders. __________ admitted to hospital.

9:30 p.m. Cap. 70, on dorm 65, 3 in hosp., 2 on furlough (__________ & __________).

12/30/74

1:45 p.m. Dorm check, in good order.

3:25 p.m. Injury report made on __________ cut over left eye.

5:00 p.m. Med. given per Dr. orders.
Note __________ didn't eat any of his supper and __________ didn't eat supper.

9:00 p.m. Med. given per Dr. orders.
70, 70, 66, 3 hosp. (__________, __________, __________) 1 furlough __________. 144 tennis shoes to laundry.

1/2/75

1:45 p.m. Dorm in good order.

2:15 p.m. 19 residents went on bus ride.

3:15 p.m. Injury report on __________ cut over left eye & left side of forehead. __________ hit him.

3:20 p.m. Injury report on __________. Skinned left knee, he fell down.

5:00 p.m. Med. given per Dr. orders.

7:30 p.m. __________ returned from hospital.

9:00 p.m. Med. given out per Dr. orders.

9:45 p.m. Dorm checked. Cap. 70, on dorm 67, 2 in hosp, __________, __________ 1 on furlough, __________.

<u>Third Shift</u>

<u>1-20-75</u> 10 - 6 Shift

<u>Night Report:</u> Medication & dorm ck'd by both shifts, med. key & 6 dorm keys rec'd from __________ @ 9:45 p.m.

Dorm was in good order.

At shift change there were 68 residents present, 1 in hosp.

Laundry - loads washed - 6.

All residents slept well during night, with exception of __________ knocking over benches, climbing up tables, pulling sheets off residents, keeping them up.

__________ did not want to stay in bed. He was put back to bed several times & would sit there but he just wanted to stay by the door.

__________ did not want to stay in bed. He just wanted to keep up the noise so the other residents would wake up.

__________ had loose stool. In counting medication at 9:45 p.m. there was 1 Pheno over in __________ & 1 Valium 5 mg. in __________. Supervisor was called over for correction. Medication counted by both shifts. Med. key & 6 dorm keys given to morning charge at 5:45 a.m.

Cap 70, on roll 70, on dorm 68, 1 __________, 1 __________.

1/22/75 Med. counted by both shifts. Med. key & 6 dorm keys rec'd from Mrs. __________ at 9:45 p.m. Dorm was in good order. Cap 70, on roll 70, on dorm 68, 1 __________, 1 __________.

Residents had a good night with exception of:

1) __________ was very upset the first part of the night from 10 p.m. until 1:30 - he finally settled down.
2) __________ was awake all night, changing pillows on beds.
3) __________ was awake all night - had to keep a close eye on him to keep him out of other residents' beds.
4) __________ walked until 3:30 a.m., then he finally decided to go to bed.

Med. & dorm ck'd by both shifts. Med. key & 6 dorm keys given to morning charge at 5:45 a.m. Cap 70, on roll 70, on dorm 68, 1 __________, 1 __________.

1/23/75 Med. Info.

Dorm was in good order. On dorm 68 1 __________, 1 __________.

Laundry - loads washed.

All shoes laced.

The following residents were disturbed:

__________ - disturbed from shift change last night. Went to sleep at 12:30 a.m. but awoke at 1:45 a.m. and has been talking since.

__________ - walked until 1 a.m. when he went to sleep.

__________ was up until 12:45 a.m. when he went to bed but has not slept. He got out of bed @ 1:30 a.m. and started turning over benches. Attendants put him back in bed, where he stayed for awhile but returned to the benches.

_________ awoke at 2:45 a.m. & has been turning on lights inside rooms & turning on bathroom pipes. Attendants had to sit and watch him most of the night.

1/26/75 Dorm in good order.

Key broken.

Same dorm count.

Laundry - 7 loads washed.

All shoes laced.

All residents slept very well tonight with exception of:

1) _________ walked all night. He didn't want to stay in bed - just wanted to wake other residents up by making loud noises.
2) _________ was jumping from bed to bed turning over benches, mop bucket, turning water on & off in bathroom, pulling sheets off residents. He settled down awhile at 5:40 a.m. when an attendant had to constantly watch him all night carefully.

- Medical info. same.

1/27/75 Dorm was in good order.

68 residents present.

7 loads washed @ laundry.

All residents slept well except:

- _________ was up about 1:30 turning off lights, turning on & off water faucets, jumping from bed to bed clapping hands.
- _________ did not want to stay in bed - wanted to walk & look out door - he was closely watched by attendants.
- _________ jumped from bed to bed.
- _________ had an upset stomach - his supper didn't agree with him.

1/29/75 68 on dorm.

__________'s eye has been bleeding quite a bit tonight.

__________ fell out of bed while sleeping but no injury.

__________ had soiled on the floor but no one on 2-10 p.m. shift had cleaned it up - so we had to.

1/30/75 Dorm was in good order. W/exception of ________, who was up and about for a short while, all residents had a quiet night.

2/2/75 Dorm was in good order.

68 residents present.

__________ had a seizure - mild in nature (3 mins.). Hosp. & night supervisor notified.

__________ didn't sleep last night - has been sitting up in bed most of the night, laughing & clapping his hands - got out of bed twice.

4 a.m. - had a BM - very loose stools (black and offensive).

__________ was up at 2:00 a.m.; has not slept since. Has been turning lights on over sleeping residents in side rooms & also turning on bathroom faucets.

__________ - also didn't sleep; has been making noise & frequent trips to bathroom.

__________ awoke at 2:30 a.m. & has been walking the hall since.

Other residents had a restful night.

2/3/75 Dorm was in good order.

67 present, 3 in __________.

All residents slept well with the exception of: __________ who has been awake all night.

__________ had a good night also.

__________ was admitted to hospital (2-3-75 at 4:45 p.m.).

2/5/75 Dorm was in good order.

67 on dorm, 3 in __________.

All residents slept well during night.

__________ awake all night.

__________ awake all night.

4:30 __________ had a mild seizure lasting 3 min. - hosp. & supervisor notified.

4:45 Injury report made on __________ - scratches found on stomach & rt. leg - hosp. & supervisor notified.

2/6/75 Dorm was in good order.

Med. count on __________ was incorrect - total should be 88 - 1 over pheno gr. 1 - supervisor notified.

All residents had a good night with the exception of:

__________ - woke at 2:30 a.m., up & about, singing, clapping, turning on lights inside rooms, turning on water - will not stay in bed.

__________ was awake until 1 a.m.

__________ has been up & about all night, wouldn't stay in bed, has been turning off lights & pushing other residents' beds to the wall.

2/9/75 Dorm was in good order.

The following residents did not have a good night:

__________ - awake til 3 a.m., has been laughing and clapping his hands.

__________ - awake since 3 a.m.

__________ - slept til 3 a.m., walked around, then back to bed.

Other residents slept well.

Dorm Temp. @ 10 p.m. - NW 69° - SW 72°
Dorm Temp. @ 4 a.m. - NW 69° - SW 69°

2/10/75 Dorm was in good order.

All residents had restful night except:

__________ - awake til 2:30, has been laughing, talking, & clapping hands.

__________ awoke at 3 a.m. & stayed awake.

__________ had a very good night, slept all through.

Dorm Temp @ 10 p.m. NW 72 - SW 72
Dorm Temp @ 4 a.m. NW 70 - SW 70

2/12/75 Dorm was in good order.

__________ was highly upset - he was given water very slowly & watched very carefully - he kept residents on north wing awake for quite a while.

__________ was upset on S wing - up til 10:15, pulling sheets off residents, shouting.

All other residents slept well.

2/13/75 Dorm was in good order.

Still 67 present.

__________ was very upset, running & pulling off his clothes, trying to fight residents & employees - awake until 4:30 a.m. getting into residents' beds.

__________ was highly upset - he wanted to run & jump in other residents' beds, settled down finally at 3:15.

__________ was very upset - because __________ kept jumping into his bed.

__________ was very upset - awake all night, jumping into beds - an employee had to sit with him all night.

2/16/75 Dorm was in good order.

Please have Dr. look at __________'s nose as the cut on it seemed a bit too open and runny.

__________ had a good night - up at 2:45 a.m. - was changed, went back to sleep - awake again at 4:15 a.m.

__________ slept until 2 a.m. & has been awake since, clapping & making noise.

__________ did not sleep most of the night - wanted to walk & make noise - climbs into other residents' beds when sent to lie.

__________ awoke at 3 a.m. and has been walking since.

Other residents had a restful night.

__________ had 2 bowel movements during night.

Second, at 5 a.m. was pinkish in color - mucous & water (specimen saved)

2/17/75 Dorm was in good order.

__________'s med. (Pheno Gr 1) was incorrect - night supervisor notified - 55 in container - total of 56 on training record.

All residents had a good night with exception of:

__________ slept til 2:45 a.m., awake since then, making noise & trying to get out of bed.

__________ did not sleep well, awakened by __________ at 12:30 - __________ was pushing his bed up to the wall - slept for short periods - sitting up in bed most of night.

_________ has been awake all night - turning off lights & pushing beds into wall, finally settled down at 4:45 a.m.

2/19/75 Dorm was in good order.

Dorm temp @ 10 p.m. - S: 70 - N: 70
Dorm temp @ 4 a.m. - S: 70 - N: 70

All residents slept well except:

_________ was up at 12:30, walking & clapping & turning off lights, finally fell asleep at 5:30 a.m.

_________ was a bit restless, he walked until 3:30, wanted to be in others' beds.

_________ was noisy - settled down at 3:15 a.m.

2/20/75 All residents acct'd for.

All ceiling panels & window curtains are up.

There weren't any behavior charts for Grp I or Grp II areas.

Everyone is sleeping well tonight, so far.

2/23/75 Dorm was in good order.

All residents had a very good night except:

_________ who awoke at 1:30 a.m. and started turning over benches - had to be watched to keep him in bed.

2/24/75 Dorm was in good order.

All residents had good night except:

_________ was highly disturbed - got very noisy, waking others, night supervisor informed, to put in Grp. I play area where he settled down and slept at 12:30 - he was watched all night.

_________ up for awhile - slept for short periods.

2/26/75 __________ stayed up for last 2 nights - have doctor check him - keeps turning over benches & climbing on tables.

2/27/75 __________ didn't sleep well - he was upset, didn't want to stay in bed - wanted to sleep on __________'s bed which made __________ very, very upset.

__________ wanted to throw __________ onto floor.

__________ settled down at 2:30 a.m., riding his horses.

__________ settled down at 1:15.

__________ was up all night, running around.

__________ was up most of night slipping benches, turning over tables - to sleep at 4:20 a.m.

3/2/75 Dorm was in good order.

All residents had restful night except:

__________ - slept for short periods & threw over benches.

__________ was very noisy in early night, wanted to walk, after upset, so we had to watch all 3 very carefully.

__________ up at 4 a.m. - clapping hands & walking - finally settled down & back to bed.

Appendix B The Biography of James

MacAndrew and Edgerton (1964b) have indicated the profoundly retarded leave no artifacts and sustain little culture. For this reason, Swartz, Cleland and Altman (1971) proposed that time capsules housing PMR videotapes, voiceprints and medical information be established in institutional settings for researchers a century or more into the future to utilize.

Another type of artifact the profoundly retarded never leave behind is their life history or biography. The famous leave us a rich legacy of either autobiography, biography, or both. To partially rectify this lack of biographical material on PMR subjects, I suggested to my graduate seminar that volunteers having a flair for writing might, with parental or guardian permission, develop several PMR biographies. Then, during the final class meeting, I gave 9 of 12 students enrolled (3 cuts that day) this assignment.

> James, the subject of our biography, was 19 years and 7 months old at his death. He never spoke and his mental age was given as "below 2" and his IQ was estimated as "below 19." He was born in 1958 and diagnosed as "anoxia at birth." In 1963. at age 5, James was admitted to the __________ State School. He had two older sisters and

one older brother, all normal.

Each student was given one arbitrarily selected stage of James's life to cover--these were as follows:

Birth to 1½ years--every family member unhappy
1½ to 3 years--unhappiness mounts
3 to 5 years--things worsen
5 to 7--father abandons and James institutionalized
7 to 9--early institutional life
9 to 11--James's adjustment improves
11 to 13--there is some joy and unhappiness for James
13 to 15--James's first illness and hospitalization
15 to 17--James has two good years; institution changes
17 to Death--a bad time

Students were given 20 minutes to write and the author wrote the tenth stage. The resultant hypothetical biography is the product of our joint effort.

A new life started at 11:13 p.m. when Mrs. __________ gave birth to a 4.8 pound baby boy whom the parents named James. The physician in attendance shortly thereafter informed the parents that their son suffered from anoxia during the protracted birth and that this would result in severe mental retardation. Both Mr. and Mrs. __________ were extremely shocked since their older children were normal and healthy and they were unable to understand why this happened to them. Especially did Mrs. __________ experience great emotional shock and she felt she had failed her husband. Mr. __________, in turn, felt great anger toward Mrs. __________ and the doctors as well. The other children, aged from 16 months to four years, sensed something was wrong but were too young to comprehend. The __________ family income was marginal with the father being employed as a truck driver, and Mrs. __________ was unemployed.

Both parents were confused as to how to cope with James but the physician's advice was to institutionalize James as soon as possible. Instead, Mr. and Mrs. __________ took James home.

James's contribution to the __________ family consisted, in large measure, of crying and whining and disturbing the entire family. He was in and out of the physician's office many times during the first year and a half of life compounding the family's problems.

James's social stimulation during the first 18 months was supplied by his mother and siblings. Initially, Mrs. _________ spent a great amount of time with James and she tried real hard to get him quiet by the time Mr. _________ got home from work. Within about four to six months, Mrs. _________ was forced to pay James less attention since she was becoming physically exhausted. For James's first 18 months of life, he was confined to a small crib--ambulation skills were some time ahead.

By the time his oldest sister was five, she had become a little baby-sitter to James. She tried to teach him to crawl and, although not due to her teachings, James did manage this skill by 16 months. James required hand feeding because he was extremely messy and could not use even a spoon.

James did possess some interest in his environment. Near his crib was an electric outlet in which a small red night light was located. Mrs. _________ noticed that James would position himself in his crib so he could watch the light and he often stared intently at this for several hours before falling asleep.

By the eighteenth month of life, James had created an enormous burden--his extremely delayed development, the attention required and the doctor bills made Mrs. and Mrs. _________ seriously discuss institutional placement.

By the time James had reached 18 months, the entire family began to manifest outward signs of frustration and emotional upheaval, often evident in friction between the parents and between parents and other siblings. Family arguments became frequent and almost physically violent. Both the father and James's sisters and brother came to resent the attention given James by his mother.

As James approached two years of age, James's mother decided it was time to attempt to toilet train him as she had other children to consider. Conventional methods were utilized which only resulted in frustrating his mother even more in that not only were they unsuccessful, but they also were met with temper tantrums on James's part. As his third birthday rolled around, his mother resigned herself to the fact that "he will never be toilet trained."

Resentment of James on the part of his siblings continued to grow. This resentment was fed by the teasing of his sisters and brother by other children in the neighborhood.

After numerous neighborhood fights, the siblings began to stay inside their own family for companionship more and more as James grew older. Due to this, the older children asked for and needed a larger portion of their mother's time and emotional support which she was unable to give as the largest part of her time, attention, and energy was given to James.

Efforts to teach James basic self-help skills resulted in little success. James was taught to finger feed and to assist in dressing by such things as holding out an arm when putting on his shirt or stepping into his pants when held for him. It was still necessary for him to be fed.

The "terrible two" period in James's life encompassed more than the life of a so-called normal child. This was a time truly terrible for all. The father felt that the mother's love for him had diminished, the children had guilt feelings because they could not care for their brother, and the mother was both physically and emotionally exhausted.

At three years of age, James had shown no real signs of learning. His mother was in a constant state of exhaustion. Her day consisted of trying to keep James's diapers clean so that he didn't constantly engage in the annoying habit of removing feces from the diaper and smearing it on his bed, floor, face or body. His main entertainment now consisted of banging his head against the wooden slats of the playpen where he spent most of the day. James also liked to put anything he could find, including dirt, hair, toys, shoestrings, etc., in his mouth, and a great battle occurred with screaming and kicking when these items were removed. Seldom did his mother get a decent night's sleep because she woke to hear him banging and rocking the bed and wondered what he had managed to get into. She often pleaded with James's father to go and check on him but to no avail. Her husband's revulsion seemed only to increase with time as James continued to engage in such disgusting practices. After a long night during which she got up to check on James two or three times, Mrs. __________ began anew with the struggle to feed and clean James up while getting the older children off to school. James's brother and sisters seldom attempted to play with him anymore and complained loudly if they were asked to feed or change him. He was a constant source of embarrassment to them so they never had their friends or playmates over, because of James's loud blood-curdling vocalizations and his bizarre banging behavior. They spent most of their time outside. So, the mother received very little assistance. Her physical and mental condition seemed to be deteriorating from exhaustion and from being cooped up in the house with James. Since she couldn't find anyone to babysit James and didn't trust the other children to care for him, she never went out except to the grocery store while the oldest daughter watched him. Her husband came home later all the time, spending two or three hours after work at the local beer joint. He arrived in a foul mood, demanded dinner and then slammed the door to the den, blocking out James and the activity that centered around him.

James's mother got very little emotional satisfaction from caring for him because he still hadn't smiled at her and showed no shame or sense of guilt when she scolded him for his constant misdeeds which included making messes, more dirty clothes and sheets, and biting his arm until it bled.

James was seldom taken out of the house because of his offensive and embarrassing behavior. His mother had taken him to the doctor for various reasons and found it to be a very trying experience. Even the doctor seemed apprehensive to touch and examine him and made comments about how she should do something about all the tooth decay already rotting his uneven, malformed teeth. James's mother thought, "How does he expect me to do anything about it when James bites me or chews on the toothbrush when I attempt to brush his teeth? And, his advice about solid foods to clear up diarrhea! The only thing I can get down him is pureed food, and that's a real struggle!"

"If only James hadn't learned to walk! He's beginning to get out of the playpen and now I'll never be able to keep him out of things! Yesterday he chewed the cord all the way off the venetian blinds and I had to pull it out of him--half was already down his throat! And, he was trying to bite me the whole time. I just don't think I can take it!"

As the mother got more and more exhausted each day, James's father became more and more abusive. He slapped and hit the other children and screamed at James to shut up all the time. Every night James's parents engaged in a new battle.

At age five, James had progressed to the point that he deviated from the norm to such an extent that institutionalization was being discussed by his family. James's mother was against institutionalizing James. She felt she could care for him at home. James's father wanted him institutionalized. James was a disgrace to him. He threatened his male ego for having conceived a child like James. There was a constant argument between mother and father. Finally, the father, guilt ridden, left.

Now the mother was left to care for James alone. It was hard for her to understand James's needs, since he was non-verbal. James was also very hyperactive which made his mother's job even more difficult. There was no one for James to play with, so this left him with mother constantly. Also, she couldn't get anyone to stay with James.

As hard as she had tried, she couldn't toilet train James. This was very frustrating for her. She also fed James, which took a lot of her time.

Now, money was running out. James's mother knew she must get a job, but what would happen to James? She couldn't leave him with anyone. She felt she was the only one who could understand him and his needs. James's older sisters and brothers believed, as their father did, that he should be institutionalized. James was a constant embarrassment for them. They tried to pretend he didn't exist, but this was impossible with all the banging around and noise he made.

Finally, the pressure was too much. James's mother couldn't take the pressure any longer. His behavior was so deviant now that she had trouble controlling him and with outside pressures to have him "put away," she finally gave in. She contacted __________ State School and discussed placement for James. He was accepted. There was a short waiting period before he was actually admitted.

The guilt the mother felt during this time was tremendous. Had she done the right thing? She loved James, but she also hated him for what he had done to her life. She had given up on the hope that he would improve.

Now it was time for James to be placed at __________ State School. She thought back. She knew she tried to get help from many different sources. Even the doctors were hesitant to examine James. No one really understood.

James's early institutional life was a very traumatic time. His familiar mother, father, and sisters were suddenly replaced by ever changing attendants. James had previously appeared to enjoy people but now came a sudden change in behavior. In response to overwhelming changes, e.g., caretakers, James could usually be found sitting in a corner with his head buried in his lap.

James was, however, more active at night and was soon termed a "night-stalker." His activity level was so high at night that finally the attendants resorted to mechanical restraints. So, alas, this one time of the day when James felt safe to explore his environment without assaults from other residents was taken away from him. As a result of the mechanical restraints, James's frustration level was too high to allow him to get much sleep at night. This took a toll on his physical condition and made him more susceptible to colds, flu, stomach viruses, etc.

Being a nondominant, James suffered much physical abuse at the hands of dominant peers in the institution. It took almost the entire two years for James's presence to be somewhat accepted by other residents.

James suddenly took to ruminating and by 9 years of age, ruminations were up to 30 a day! Perhaps this method of cutting boredom was chosen over coprophagia or fecal smearing because of successful toilet training that was begun immediately on admission to the institution.

At the end of his ninth year, James was beginning to show signs of a desire to come out from his corner and participate in activities. Predictions were made by his teachers that after he adjusted to the new life setting, they would be more successful in getting him to interact with others. Predictions were also made that this increased participation would cut down on or extinguish his ruminating behaviors.

After James's ninth birthday party on the dorm, he walked over to his favorite chair and began rocking. While rocking he enjoyed his cake again through his ruminating behavior. James seemed more content in the dayroom today, due to the fact that Martha, his favorite trainer, had come back to visit on his birthday. He blushed when she gave him a big birthday kiss and hug. This kiss and hug lingered in his mind the rest of the day.

At the age of 9½, James resumed roaming at night. He loved to seek out the best lighted area of the dorm and examine his hands. It soon became a game with him to outwit the trainer and escape his dark bed.

James became more aggressive after he reached the age of 10. He would shove the other clients out of the way and would throw shoes at the trainers. After being aggressive he would go to his favorite chair and giggle. James loved his new game. He received more attention for throwing shoes than sneaking out of bed. When James's aggressive acts started to cause him to serve a period of time in isolation, he sought out a new game to play with the trainers. He began to eat anything he could get in his hands. This pica appetite not only brought attention, but it stimulated his mouth.

Just before reaching 11, James became attached to a shoe-string. He soon became overspecialized in twirling the string and twisting it around his little finger. If the string were taken from him, he would begin to slap his head.

James entered adolescence in the state institution. He had been in the institution for seven years by this time, but visits from his family ceased five years previously. In all intents and purposes, James had no family now.

On James's thirteenth birthday, a new attendant began working on the PMR ward where James lived. Previously, James had formed only one strong attachment to any institutional worker or other patient. He was considered a "loner" who was never great trouble. But the new attendant on the ward seemed interested in establishing a relationship with all the patients.

The attendant's name was Alice. She was a rather tall woman, with a deep husky voice and bright red hair. She was not content to let James sit and stare at his fingers, even though he was causing no harm. Every day when she began her shift, the residents were in the day room and James would always be sitting on the bench next to the window. She would speak to each resident and then she would come to James. She would hold out her hand to shake hands and then hold James's face so that they made eye contact, and then she would say, "Hello, James."

After Alice had been on the ward about 10 months, she came in one morning and began her familiar routine of greeting the residents. When she came to James, before she could speak he held up his head, smiled and held out his hand. James began following Alice around during the day and going through the handshake routine several times. When Alice left to go home after her shift, James resumed his usual behaviors.

One day Alice didn't return to work. James became restless and often paced the floor. Like so many other teenagers, James's first crush ended with disappointment.

When James was first institutionalized, he demonstrated instances of pica appetite but this condition did not become overly serious until he reached age 13. On the dormitory, he initially began picking up small pieces of broom straws. After playing with them for a while he would ingest them. Later on he added pieces of string (i.e., shoe laces, elastic from waist of state pants), pieces of paper, plus yard grass and soil to the list of delicacies.

When he was 14, the effect of this eating habit became physically obvious. His complexion was very pale, the color of his lips and nails turned to a purplish shade. He was not responsive to training. He would not eat regular food, and became very thin.

At the time he was in a feeding program, and the immediate objective was for him to bring the spoon to his mouth after the trainer had assisted in dipping. Due to the loss of weight, this program had to be abandoned and James was fed by force.

At times James accepted the food if he didn't have to do anything himself, but most of the time he refused even to open his mouth. Physical restraint and forceful opening of his mouth became the only effective methods for feeding James. This method did not really work because James vomited unpleasant odorous bile immediately afterwards.

This condition caused hospitalization. James was hospitalized for three months. When he came back it was noted that his appetite for regular food had been restored, but that if not supervised, his pica appetite would manifest itself.

When the medical staff was questioned about James's hospitalization, it was reported that his stomach was pumped, and that whole pieces of string and broom sticks were found.

Three weeks following James's fifteenth birthday, the first of several institutional changes occurred. Apparently, the first of three program changes which occurred between James's fifteenth and seventeenth birthdays was the direct result of numerous administrative changes adopted by the new superintendent who was hired approximately six months before the first program change. This change coupled with changes in attendants, attendant shifts, diet, etc., had a marked negative effect on several of James's ward companions. Insomnia, self-abuse, aggression appeared to increase markedly on his ward.

But it appeared to have the opposite effect on James; at least superficially in the beginning. According to an attendant who had served on James's ward for seven years, and I quote, "It seemed to be the happiest time of his life." She went on to discuss changes in his interest toward other patients. Prior to his fifteenth birthday, James was reportedly a solitary being. But the attendant reported that after the first program change, James began to display curious behavior regarding other patients. He would often reach out to others and gesture frequently. This was unlike his earlier behavior when he seemed to display behavior resembling total avoidance of others.

Although James's personality changed to a more extroverted nature, his body weight did suffer during this two-year period. James had never been a heavy eater before 15, but he at least maintained a fairly constant weight for the five years preceding his fifteenth birthday. During the two-year period between 15 and 17, he gradually lost 23 pounds. The physician for his dorm even placed him on supplementary liquids shortly after his sixteenth birthday because the weight loss had become such an apparent problem.

Apparently, this resulted in lowering his resistance to disease because he was hospitalized 13 times for various problems ranging from the common cold to acute pneumonia during this two-year period.

By 17, James had endured three program changes, frequent changes in attendants, almost complete loss of appetite, and a body weight reduction of 23 pounds, all in a two-year period. He appeared frail and pale but the paradox was that he had "come out of his shell" during this same period of time.

This proved to be quite a paradox. On the one hand, there was marked evidence of increased emotional stability and happiness; on the other hand, an apparent degenerative health situation. But in retrospect, such is the existence of the institutionalized PMR. So many questions and contradictions, yet so few answers and explanations.

Winter of 1977 was harsh for everyone but especially for James. An upper respiratory viral infection had created quarantine conditions on several dorms housing moderately retarded males. By late January, it had spread to ward 9 and James was the first to contract it. Unlike the moderately retarded who recovered ordinarily within a week, James was transferred to the institution's hospital for intensive care.

Once hospitalized, James's bewilderment and sense of loss of the familiar geometrically increased his discomfort. His fever soared to 103° and his mouth was bone dry. Although in intensive care and reasonably well cared for, he couldn't get enough water to assuage his mounting thirst. Low moans replaced his usual gutteral vocalizations and one orderly remarked, "He won't last long, he's picking the covers."

The attending physician, Dr. Smith, requested next of kin be notified of James's perilous physical condition. Even though James's mother was notified, no one came. His father, who had abandoned the family when James was only five, was unable to be located.

On the third day of hospitalization, James's fever hit 104° and life was playing out rapidly. Dr. Smith ordered IV feeding which, of course, necessitated restraints. He also ordered levine suctioning to prevent James's choking to death on mucous. These support systems plus the "heat of Hades" occasioned by the fever made James extremely uncomfortable. His greatest comfort was given by a sensitive and kindly orderly, Mrs. Jackson, who would bathe his fevered brow, smile and talk comfortingly to him. James managed to smile back between gasps and moans.

On the fourth day, in the early morning, Mrs. Jackson called Dr. Smith and said "I think James is gone." Dr. Smith checked and told Mrs. Jackson, "No, but his pulse is very weak. Keep close watch and try to make his passage as comfortable as possible."

That night, at precisely midnight, James joined countless generations of humans who had gone before--geniuses, ordinary people and special ones like himself.

Burial was at the State School Cemetery the day after his death. Two people attended, Mrs. Jackson, who recalled James's intense and pleasant brown eyes fondly, and the institutional chaplain. Father O'Malley said of James, "His odyssey is over. He left little but his life inspired others. We will miss him." The casket was lowered and the brass marker was set. On it was James's ID, No. 32,975.

The readers may rightly inquire, "Of what value is such a hypothetical biographical exercise?" First of all, as we noted in Chapter 2, Maslow's motivational approach grew out of his study in normality as opposed to theorists whose focal interest was the pathological. In the theorizing of the self-actualization camp, personal documents such as diaries, letters, or biographical or autobiographical materials are admissible data for the study of human behavior. Since such data are not provided by the profoundly retarded, this writer argues that volunteers in residential settings could provide us with such historical accounts of the noncommunicating PMR. It, biography, also serves to sensitize readers or workers to the fact that we are dealing with a human life. Even the fictional account given above, the joint product of a graduate seminar on profound retardation, occasioned a universal empathetic set among the students--they all felt involved in the task I gave them.

Is it so incongruous during a period of time when normalization and humanization of the retarded are Zietgiest terms to suggest biographical material as a strategy to help the profoundly retarded? Their lives, like normals' or geniuses', are worthy of note. Finally, the hypothetical assignment provided this instructor with a rather good estimate of students' knowledge of PMRs. And, when each student read aloud his/her contribution, it was evident to each that so-and-so is really an excellent writer.

It is with pleasure that I acknowledge the contributions of my students Carolyn C. Behne, Bari L. Brower, Sue Bunney, Tria N. Fink, Herbert Howard, Kathy Hutto, Melanie Jephson, Consuelo Medina, and Margaret A. Roberson to the "Biography of James."

Appendix C Incomplete Research Proposal for Class Criticism

A. Title of Proposed Research

"Menstrual Synchrony in the Profoundly, Severely, Moderately, and Mildly Retarded"

B. Proposed Research and Use of Data

The proposed research seeks to elucidate the mechanism(s) involved in menstrual synchrony among females living in communal settings which McClintock (1971) detected in a study of college women. A corollary objective is to determine if menstrual synchrony occurs among profoundly retarded women--if the data support this research question, then another regularity of uniformity between the lowest functioning human and normals will have been established. Additionally, by studying several levels of retardates (profound, severe, moderate and mild), it may be possible to determine (should synchrony not occur among the profoundly retarded) at what intellectual level menstrual cycling does occur.

C. Statement of Research Problem

Previous research with a variety of species has demonstrated the effect of the social group on the endocrine system of the group's members. McClintock (1971) has recently investigated the effect of living together on the synchrony of menstrual cycles in a college student population. She found a reciprocal relationship between time spent together and synchrony of menstruation. Women who spent more time together found that the difference in time between menstrual onsets was reduced and approached simultaneity when contrasted to those dormitory residents who spent less time together. This proposed research intends to investigate menstrual synchronization in a population of profoundly mentally retarded women and through an extension of the research into the moderate and mild areas of retardation to assess the effect of varying degrees of mental retardation on the synchrony of menstrual onset. Thus, a profile of menstrual synchrony will be obtained that leads directly into McClintock's work with normals.

D. Method

Subjects: The universe of women at the __________ State School who are between the ages of 10 to 40 years and who represent the four levels of mental retardation (Grossman, 1977) will be employed in this study. No actual subjects (clients) will be physically involved since this research involves only inspection of existent records.

Procedure: The medical charts maintained on each dormitory will be examined and dates of menstruation for each client will be recorded. Anonymity will be assured by coding each client's name and this raw data will, subsequent to data analyses, be turned over to __________ State School authorities. The intent is to collate the dates of Ss' menses across time.

Data Analysis: The data will be divided according to Ss' dormitory group membership and analyzed intragroup, intergroup, and interbuilding by means of the Wilcoxon matched-pairs, signed-ranks test, a nonparametric test of significance. Since data will be grouped, complete confidentiality will be maintained.

Necessary Personnel and Equipment: No equipment will be needed. A small room will be needed to review the data. Once the appropriate institutional records have been provided, no institutional personnel time will be required.

E. Time Considerations

1. Proposed Starting Date: September 15
2. Estimated Duration of Proposed Study: Two full 8-hour days with the 3 experimenters recording data.

F. Risk to Subjects

This research is viewed as records research, and as such there is no risk to subjects. All data will be coded and then analyzed as group data thereby providing maximum subject confidentiality.

G. Value of Proposed Research

This investigation of menstrual synchrony in mentally retarded women seeks to demonstrate the possible existence of another uniformity between normals and the mentally retarded. This research could represent an addition to the existing knowledge on the menstrual behavior of the mentally retarded. Also, it is conceivable that if synchrony does occur among PMR women, it may have implications for socialization and/or grouping strategies.

Appendix D Class Exercises and/or Test Questions

1. On educational television mankind and an endless variety of animals have been shown in natural and unnatural settings (man in space, animals in captivity, etc.). "Nova" programs have focused on the life of Einstein and other famous men and women of genius intelligence, and National Geographic Films have covered Van-Lawick Goodall's life among chimpanzees. Nature specials by Jacques Cousteau and others such as "Wild Kingdom" have generated interest and spread information on all manner of species to TV viewers. Aboriginal man has also been the subject matter of TV specials, and developmental psychologists' studies of babies have been documented. The mentally ill or mentally retarded have also received some popular and scientific attention on specials for the tube. A few exposé-type or sensationals have also appeared for political and/or humanitarian purposes on TV but transmittal of knowledge of PMRs as humans has been minimal.

   Write a grant proposal to do a documentary on the everyday life of the profoundly retarded. This proposal would go to The National Geographic Society, and its aims would include:

   1. Present the known facts about PMRs,

2. Generate interest in this rare human,
3. Avoid the expose or spectacular--"sell steak, not sizzle," and
4. Avoid the angel unaware tactic.

Since half or more are in institutions, this will be your filming arena. Prepare your grant request to include a rationale for the study (film), a description of the subjects, clearance or release of film rights from parents-guardians, use of consultants, if any, and what accomplishments you hope to achieve.

Your paper will be graded on these criteria:

1. Originality
2. Persuasion or appeal
3. Adherence to facts
4. Appropriate referencing
5. Coverage of 24 hours
6. Flow and style of writing
7. Title appropriateness for audience appeal

2. Normalization and deinstitutionalization of all the retarded are accepted by most authorities in mental retardation. Considering <u>only</u> the profoundly retarded, defend the thesis that <u>both</u> normalization and deinstitutionalization are premature, inapplicable and perhaps even cruel at the present state of knowledge. In a word, you are saying that both concepts are hollow and merely reflective of "selling sizzle" instead of steak. Prepare your response as a lawyer advocate attempting to influence a jury.

   Your response will be judged on the basis of:

   1. Definition of terms
   2. Citation of relevant references
   3. Elaboration of the major issues

3. The overwhelming problem in profound retardation is, at least from the author's viewpoint, the mutual communication barrier. This implies that the PMR's nonverbal behaviors, at least certain of them, reflect some drive or motivation on the PMR's part to "reach us, to ask for

something." From your reading and lecture notes, criticize this assumption and bring in support for your argument. Next, support this view or assumption and cite relevant material to uphold your view.

4. Many authorities in mental retardation hold the retarded are more anxious than normals. By far, most evidence is derived from research with mildly retarded persons. Describe an approach that could extend anxiety research to the profoundly retarded and that would include several techniques so as to make a battery.

5. Defend or criticize the author's focus on darkness as opposed to daylight research with PMRs. If you agree that night behaviors are critical to understanding PMRs, isolate those reasons you feel are crucial to your _pro_ position. If you take the _con_ position, do likewise.

6. The _Pennsylvania_ decision mandates public school education cannot be denied _any_ child despite the severity of mental or physical handicap. A further influence in our modern approach to training-educating the handicapped is seen in the deinstitutionalization, normalization, and mainstreaming movements. Since over half of the profoundly mentally retarded (IQs below 19; nonverbal and often possessed of other physical or sensory impairments, etc.) are in public or private institutions and, hence, subject to deinstitutionalization efforts (nursing home placement, public school settings, etc.), discuss the pros and cons of alternative placements. Cite the literature supportive of institutional vs. alternative placements and vice versa. Finally, in considering _only_ the profoundly retarded, give your views on the relevance-soundness of the _Pennsylvania_ decision and how the public schools may implement or "skirt" this mandate for this special subgroup of retardates.

   Criteria for grading:

   1. Grasp of and appropriate employment of literature.
   2. Clarity of writing style.

7. The quantification of resident satisfaction with the institution has received little research attention. From

readings and experience, list some of the ways in which we can develop an index of resident satisfaction for PMRs.

Appendix E Research Proposal for Class Discussion

The proposal that follows was initially submitted in 1966 to a Federal Funding Agency. It was, in 1970, revised and submitted to a Private Foundation for review. A further submittal in 1974 to a Federal Agency was, as in previous efforts, rejected.

As a class exercise, review the proposal and discuss some of the reasons why it did not get funded. As an additional class project, think of ways to improve the proposal.

Names and references have been deleted and no budget is attached. In your opinion, would such a proposal have any better or worse chance of funding currently?

A Proposal for a Center for the Study of Minimal Communicators

This proposal seeks to establish "A Center for the Study of Minimal Communicators" at The University of __________. As envisioned, the target groups to be studied and served would include the profoundly mentally retarded, severely autistic children, aphasics and others who comprise the <u>neglected</u> sector of the handicapped population. As some indicated, these groups have been largely denied any public education, but the option to deny public education is rapidly being closed as a result of recent court decisions. However, when such principles are considered relative to nonverbal humans, our knowledge of their real needs is so limited that it precludes application.

In our society's desire to assist these profoundly handicapped persons, it seems apparent that the key to providing training, services, and preparation of individuals to render services is communication, broadly conceived. Humanization and normalization are intimately linked to the process of language--the single most defining characteristic of humans. Language enables man to express not only his basic needs but also to express emotions such as love, compassion, rage, joy, etc. When profoundly retarded and severely autistic are the concern, it is obvious at the onset that we need to understand whatever meanings inhere in their nonverbal behaviors, that is, postures, grunts, gestures, screams, squeals, eye-gaze, and even illness. It is on what can be learned of the meaning of their nonverbal communications that we may be able to attend their actual needs, rather than foisting our own needs on them, perhaps prematurely. In many respects, our success in providing services to all handicapped, young or old, hinges on deciphering their needs as expressed in various nonspeech modes. Our research strategies involve decipherment efforts of the several nonverbal groups' rudimentary communicative efforts. Thus, while much of the research will be basic in nature, it could as well be termed "market research" since it is the isolation and description of the profoundly retarded and autistics' desires, needs, and so forth, as consumers or customers that is the ultimate objective.

In primates below man, our nation has already benefited from medical advances and knowledge of their behavior via the establishment of the NIH Primate Research Centers. These centers, each specializing in restricted types of research, have made important contributions to the physical and mental health of man. It is somewhat ironic that our knowledge of the communications of nonverbal humans is less advanced than is true of our knowledge of subhuman primates. From our understanding of the profoundly retarded, it is known that institutionalized (captive) profoundly retarded have the highest death rate of all new admittees, while the life span of captive baboons, in contrast to those living in natural settings, is nearly doubled.

As is true of the several Primate Research Centers, the proposed center for the study of minimal communicators will also specialize. The major thrust will be to elucidate the meanings inhering in these neglected humans' communicative behaviors. As these meanings are revealed, clinical populations in adjacent residential or out-patient settings may more speedily be served and trained.

SUPPORTING FACILITIES AND PERSONNEL

__________, with its splendid array of both residential and out-patient facilities for the handicapped, plus the __________ Public School's classes for the handicapped, makes this one of the "natural" health-care and educational centers of the Nation. As Akron, Ohio, is to the rubber industry, __________ is to the education of the handicapped. In a very real sense, __________ has over a period of many years developed a heavy specialization in caring for the many types of handicapped and as long ago as 1958, Masland recognized __________'s potential for such a center.

With both professional and subprofessional personnel experienced in working with the several types of nonverbal humans, __________ has a highly skilled and trained manpower pool. Excellent libraries include the __________ Medical Association plus those of the University of __________. The support of major involved facilities for such a proposed center is assured.

As is true of the NIH Primate Centers, the proposed center would complement both the research and training components with visiting scientists. For example, there are only a scattered few researchers in the U.S. whose work is directly related to the profoundly retarded or the severely autistic child. Certain of these individuals, having interests relevant to the center's mission, could be attracted as visiting scientists for a semester or year's work at the center. The addition of visiting scientists would, again as in the NIH Primate Research Center's program, also encourage the participation of advanced graduate students whose theses or dissertation problems were relevant to the center's objectives. Thus, an ongoing training component would be built in to the structure of the center at levels ranging from undergraduates through postdoctorates to those with multidisciplinary academic backgrounds.

In brief, this proposal seeks to establish under _________ auspices an experimental or prototype center. Training activities and service to our most severely handicapped citizens cannot be separated from a strong research program since knowledge is so lacking at these levels of handicap. As such, the envisioned center could provide _________ with a model or prototype which may grow in number to equal the scope and knowledge productivity of the very successful NIH Regional Primate Research Centers.

COMPLETED STUDIES AT _________

Thirty-seven studies of the profoundly retarded have been completed at _________ by _________ and co-workers. These include theory-guided studies as well as replications of the work of others. In addition to studies completed and relevant to the proposal, _________ has, for the past 12 years, offered a graduate level seminar on the nonverbal human and a number of PhD dissertations by _________'s students have addressed the nonverbal human.

REPRESENTATIVE STUDIES OF PROPOSED CENTER

The investigation and translation of the behavior of the profoundly handicapped as communicative attempts requires the consideration of all activities including readily observable behavior such as verbal utterances and bodily movements as well as neural and chemical changes which are not overtly manifested. The lack of normal communication capacity and skill in the profoundly handicapped limits their means of communication within and outside of their unique society. It is therefore necessary not only to recognize and understand the significance of their behavior but also to train/educate them to react more meaningfully to other individuals.

However, the general lack of information does not permit the initiation of educational procedures with the profoundly handicapped. A close examination of the literature on mental deficiency, for example, will show that a significant proportion of the published research is basically anecdotal in nature and often lacks methodological sophistication. Also evident is the relative neglect of research on the profoundly retarded with most studies using severe or mild level retardates as target subjects. The difficulty in discussing the entire spectrum of mental deficiency, much less the behavior of the profoundly retarded, is apparent. Research into the behavioral (communicative) significance of the profoundly retarded must be accelerated in order to provide a sound database for future training, education, and therapeutic work with predictable success.

A. Projected Studies

Much of the research to date has been attempts to compare the behavior of the profoundly handicapped with normal individuals and in some cases with primates and other animals. This approach is logistically sound when one of the primary interests is the intelligence-behavior relationship and when confronted with questions which are pragmatically based and designed for direct and immediate application to the welfare of the profoundly handicapped. Researchers have also usually recognized that although retardates, for example, sometimes function at the same level as normal humans and subhumans, the processes involved may not be the same. At any rate, the transference of research methodology from the study of normal organisms is a productive approach providing us with comparative data and information about the effectiveness of experimental procedures.

In attempting to elucidate the meaning in the nonverbal handicapped persons' efforts, however strange they may seem to us, all nonverbal communicative modalities will be studied from several directions. Among the nonverbal communications we will study, several styles are apparent. For example, paralanguage (voice qualities, speech nonfluencies, yawns, etc.), proxemics (utilization of personal and social space), body motion or kinesthetic behaviors (facial expressions, eye movements in both awake and sleep conditions, gestures, postures, etc.), olfaction as a possible communicative mode, are all potentially revealing of underlying needs or affective states. Prior theorizing on facial expressions, e.g., smiling as an appeasement gesture, holds such behaviors to be cross-cultural and species-specific and __________ adduced some cross-cultural evidence supportive of the universality of the affective component in facial expressions. A knowledge of underlying emotions is important as one index of what stimuli are held to be pleasant or unpleasant as well as a potentially important signal that a new program or change in schedule is, or is not, a disruption rather than a benefit.

Some of the projected studies will continue to rely on hypotheses and results derived from ethological, comparative, and developmental studies. Others will be based on respondent and operant conditioning principles using response measures ranging from autonomic nervous system activity to gross motor movements. When appropriate, comparisons with normals will be made. Theoretical models (e.g., learning, developmental, and perceptual) will be used to evaluate the performance of the profoundly handicapped.

1. Sociobehavioral studies. Research strategies with a sociobehavioral orientation can be broadly categorized into those relying primarily on (1) behavioral observations and documentation of results and (2) behavioral observations followed by the manipulation of variables. Observations and manipulations will be dictated by comparative norms established by normal organisms, theoretical position, and behavioral consistency exhibited by target populations. Some of the initial research questions, based in part on anecdotal and serendipitous observations, will give way to systematic experimental manipulation with an emphasis on successive serial studies as compared to single-study "shotgun" affairs. Described below are areas of proposed study relying on the authors' serendipitous observations, hunches, and theoretically based hypotheses.

The research and educational literature in mental retardation is relatively consistent as concerns one of the retardates' major problems, attention--retardates being generally deficient in this process. Stimulus intensity and novelty would appear one manner of "riveting attention" upon relevant stimulus parameters. Theoretically, one line of studies would depart along lines suggested by Festinger--cognitive dissonance. In institutionalized populations of retardates or autistics, these subjects come, over time, to crystallize in their expectancies-cognitions. Hence, in our prolonged study series, various of these expectancies would be challenged in an effort to establish which cognitive domains are susceptible to "easiest-hardest" alteration. In effect, these theory-guided studies on the PMRs' cognition would aid in establishing less fragile attentive behavior and could assist in the mapping of their "normal" communicative modes--a first step in the direction of decipherment of the meaning of their nonverbal communicative styles.

Another theoretical approach that has demonstrated utility in working with profoundly retarded persons is that of ethological motivation theory. In previous work by _________, enuretic and encopretic profoundly retarded males were studied in relation to territorial enlargement and cessation of admissions into their ward. Since scent-marking by means of urine or feces to stake out a "territory" is mostly a behavior of males of species below man, it was hypothesized that for nonverbal humans, the enuretic-encopretic behavior could have been a form of territorial defense. When a 64% spatial enlargement occurred in their sleeping area, both wetting and soiling declined dramatically. Thus, this study suggests that the PMRs were telling the experimenters (nonverbally, i.e.) that spatial enlargement was a pleasing state of affairs. Not only was this study a partial confirmation of ethological theory, it could as easily be termed market research in that a space need was identified.

Thus, two primary motivation theories will serve to guide research systematically in the sociobehavioral studies series--one, instinct-based, the other, cognitively-based. These theory-based studies then will complement certain of the studies generated by more anecdotal and serendipitous observations made by the authors of this proposal. It is notable that in previous work with the profoundly retarded, serendipitous findings were ubiquitous.

2. Psychophysiological studies. The second proposed research area will focus on the autonomic response characteristics of the profoundly handicapped. The basic assumption of this research approach is that autonomic nervous system arousal or activation accompanies all psychological processes such as perception, motivation, emotion, and mentation. Due to deficiencies in normal communication modes, autonomic response measures in the profoundly handicapped could be used as response indices in many learning and nonlearning situations. This is especially obvious in situations where there is no overt indication (verbally, physically, or otherwise) of perception of mild forms of stimulation. Autonomic and other physiological measures can therefore provide another avenue of communication with the profoundly handicapped. Several proposed studies of the psychophysiology of the profoundly retarded are described below.

Study 1: Communication withdrawal in an unfamiliar setting.
Study 2: Communication withdrawal in a familiar setting.
Study 3: Stimulus disparity on the orientation reaction.
Study 4: Tactile and social interaction effects.
Study 5: Biorhythms of the profoundly retarded.

3. Conditioning studies. This class of studies will center around the concept of respondent and operant learning as they apply to theory testing and behavioral management and training. The research literature on the profoundly handicapped, especially the profoundly retarded, is characterized by two notable features. One is the scarcity of studies which have investigated the respondent and operant parameters of learning, and the second is the widespread use of behavior modification techniques which have been adopted from the behavior of nonretardates. At the same time, it is realized that we must use whatever method is most effective regardless of its empirical base. Although it appears that the conditioning procedures found to be effective with normals and nonprofound retardates are also often effective when applied to the profoundly retarded, higher success probability may be achieved if behavior modification procedures applied to the profoundly retarded were based on the study of the profoundly retarded. The first group of studies will be directed toward the study of profoundly retarded subjects in standard respondent and operant conditioning situations.

The second group of studies has an applied orientation. Eventually, laboratory-based behavioral principles must be extended into the real world of behavior management, training, and education. Studies will be designed to determine the extent to which certain types of behavior can be brought under respondent and operant control.

Respondent Conditioning

Study 1: Delay conditioning
Study 2: Temporal conditioning
Study 3: Anticipatory responding and CR topography
Study 4: Compound to component transfer

Operant Conditioning

Study 1: Crespi effect
Study 2: Secondary reinforcement effect
Study 3: CR retention over several days
Study 4: Activational peaking
Study 5: Perceptual vigilance

SUMMARY

Nowhere in the United States do we find, for nonverbal humans, the counterpart of the NIH Regional Primate Centers. The courts, as __________ et al. point out, have mandated service and care to all handicapped including educational privileges. The only flaw in the court mandates, when the nonverbal handicapped are the focal population, is that our knowledge base is inadequate to permit instant compliance. The parameters of the nonverbal person's educational-training capabilities must be mapped. This would be a primary objective of the proposed center. As mentioned, __________ is possessed of a large subject pool of nonverbal children and adults. Its varied library resources are the South's largest and a considerable specialization with the neglected nonverbal handicapped has already occurred. As envisioned, the proposed center, as growth occurs, can recruit interested and known specialists on a visiting scholar or professorship basis. Thus, as a model center, __________ could become operational in the shortest possible time and begin dissemination via trained researchers and publications to other concentration areas where interests and subjects are exceptional. On many fronts, the courts, the parents, the legislatures, and so on, the call for help to the aforementioned neglected groups are becoming more stridulant. It remains an inescapable conclusion that such a center as the one herein proposed could help operationalize the call for help to all handicapped, not solely for those who can articulate their needs.

Appendix F
Case Study: Training Nonprofessional Employees

The following case of an actual occurrence illustrates certain complexities that inhere in training nonprofessional employees to work with the profoundly retarded. It also demonstrates that actual occurrences, in school or institutional settings, when properly disguised to insure anonymity of the actors, can be developed into case histories. The case-study method as employed in the Harvard Business School and in legal training can be quite effective in training classes as well. As a class exercise, develop a case study based upon your own experience in working with the mentally retarded.

Newcomers assigned to work with the profoundly retarded have a challenging job. Their duties demand the ability to work with large groups of people who may never speak, may never show gratitude, may never show improvement. Their job will include exposure to extremely deviant behavior such as self-destruction, eating unusual substances, rocking, biting, banging, screaming, and the like. Cleaning up after physical grownups may be a part of the work, and all of this must take place with the frequently added demands of professionals, parents and/or interested others.

John Happy, newly hired to work on a PMR ward, was a friendly, easy-going person who had no previous experience in this field. John wanted to do a good job and on his first day asked many questions of the charge attendant. Bill Johnson, the charge, had worked ward 23 for 13 years and prided himself on knowing his residents, but in replying to John he said, "Best way I can tell you is just learn like I did." Following this, Bill told John, "Give the shower room a good cleaning today."

During John's first day at work he saw many things that were new in his experience. The following incidents were shocking to him: (1) A very retarded person about 35 years of age ran into the bathroom and before John realized what was going on, took a drink from a commode. (2) Two other PMRs sat facing the walls all during John's shift. Bill told him, "They always sit that way. Best just leave them be." (3) One smaller man was slapped quite hard by a burly peer for no apparent reason. (4) While out in the recreation-play yard with the residents, John saw for the first time grown men playing in the dirt like little children. What really bothered John was seeing one eating sticks and rocks.

At home, following his first day of duty, John told his wife about all these strange and sometimes disgusting occurrences. While relating these events, "John thought, "She's listening with more attention to what I've got to say than she ever did before." The next day John saw many other strange behaviors, and again that evening he told his wife and also some friends who had dropped in from a neighboring town for a brief visit. Not only did John discover that his wife was still interested, but the friends listened attentively and asked many questions about the work at the school. It seemed to him that he had suddenly gained a great deal of importance and he felt very good about his job for the first time.

By the end of John's third week of work he had stopped asking Bill's advice about the job, because Bill never gave any assistance. John still felt good about his job but worried a little about the lack of supervision given him as a new employee.

John usually spent his off-duty time at a neighborhood cafe, and his friends there, having learned of John's new work, asked him about it. As with his other friends, John soon learned that he now possessed a powerful weapon; when he spoke, people listened. Not only did they seem enthralled by John's stories about the PMRs but they questioned him further about training of employees, hospital policies, and the like, and even urged him, "Tell us more about old so-and-so, that one you said...." John obliged at all times because he felt they were interested and because he loved the attention. In short, John felt that he understood the patients, and now his friends respected him. At last he could see a career at the institution.

About three months after John was hired, the superintendent called him to his office. John felt good and even thought, "I may be going to get a raise. After all, the residents like me and I think I am doing a good job." The superintendent asked John to be seated and a stinging reprimand ensued. He charged John with violating institutional policies in that he discussed residents outside the hospital, was telling lies about rules and had mailed residents' letters for them. The superintendent went on to say that there was no reason nor any excuse for such conduct and that a recurrence would mean dismissal. John remarked that he had never been told and did not receive any instructions on being hired other than the supervisor telling him, "Just ask anybody where ward 23 is. Most any of them can tell you where to report." The superintendent concluded the discussion by telling John, "Remember, one more report on you and you're through!"

Some three weeks later, John resigned and took a job in a downtown bakery.

Questions

1. What could have prevented John's resignation?
2. What do you suppose John's attitude will be toward the school? Toward all institutions?
3. Under the circumstances, do you feel that John's talk about the residents was justified? What does this represent?
4. What do you think about the school's administration, personnel department, supervisor, and charge attendants?
5. Is "talk" necessarily bad and is this practice limited to any particular work group?
6. Why do attendants talk about their residents and the institution? Is it only the new attendants who talk in this way?

Appendix G
Play Activities: Normal versus Profoundly Retarded

Normal: Paul G., an 18-month toddler, dearly enjoyed the visits of his grandmother and grandfather. On their arrival, Paul ran to them as fast as his short, fat legs would carry him. When granny held him on her lap, Paul explored her every facial feature. Her eyeglasses were a magnetic attraction and Paul would attempt to grab them. Finding granny "too quick," Paul moved his hands to her purse which he often was allowed to explore. Some items he'd grab and attempt to retain, others he threw away.

When his grandpa took Paul in his lap, Paul's exploration narrowed. His grandpa's bulbous nose was the attraction, and its being somewhat red in color made it even more appealing as a target for Paul's grasping hands. Although grandpa defended his nose, his guard could not be constantly maintained and at such moments, Paul's eager hand grasped it firmly! Such was Paul's 18-month favored entertainment, and his face mirrored pure delight when grandpa's "guard" was down.

Profoundly Retarded: Ray was about 29 years of age and he had been institutionalized since he was four. He, like Paul G. in the above case, liked company. He was like Paul G. in another way--Ray's mental age was identical to Paul's life age.

When visitors from a nearby university arrived on Ray's dormitory, Ray was usually at the vanguard of "greeters." Since Ray was physically adult and rather quick in his movements, he invariably had a good time with the visitors. He would approach a female visitor with a broad smile and in an instant, her purse had been snatched. Attempts to retrieve it by the victim and one or more houseparents was Ray's greatest enjoyment as he held onto the purse for dear life and laughed vigorously. Ray also delighted in "lifting" eyeglasses and for male visitors, their pockets were eyed for <u>any</u> telltale bulge. If the male to be victimized carried cigarettes in his shirt pocket, these Ray seized quickly to the astonishment of the victim. The delight registered on Ray's face clearly conveyed pleasure in "a job well done."

The foregoing examples illustrate the parallels in playful or gamelike activities that exist between an 18-month-old normal and an adult profoundly retarded person. It also suggests how play activities can be tailored to the individual PMR's preferences. Two examples should suffice: since "stealing," grabbing of women's purses, is such a treat, perhaps visitors should deposit their real purses in a dormitory "safety deposit box" on entry and be issued substitute purses (paper sacks or canvas tote bags) so PMRs like Ray could seize them and have their fun. Alternatively, since visitors are not an everyday occurrence, one could use volunteers instead. If nose grabbing is a favorite activity, a large Cyrano-type false nose could be worn by our volunteer(s). Similar to the breakaway Jersey used in football, such "noses" could provide harmless fun to PMRs who are big enough to be dangerous, yet infants enough to enjoy their game of grabbing. The point is that development is arrested at a very early age but it is also evident that pleasures or playful actions are quite well camouflaged by their adult size.

<u>Normal</u>: In the first year and on into the second, normal children are often enthusiastic participants in peek-a-boo or patty-cake. Some people continue to delight in these games throughout their lives and some of the PMRs are such people. The reader needs no example of peek-a-booing or patty-caking normal 1- or 2-year-olds--memory will serve this purpose. However, two examples of these fun activities involving PMR adults may help us understand their needs better.

<u>Profoundly Retarded</u>: Mary was 32 years of age and had spent 24 of her years in the institution. She had a mental

age of 15 months, was ambulatory and had no marked sensory impairment.

During an observation period on Mary's dormitory prior to a research study, I dropped my clipboard from a counter that was about waist high--the noise attracted the attention of a few of the PMR women. I bent over to retrieve the clipboard and momentarily disappeared behind the counter. On becoming visible again, Mary shielded her eyes, then peeked out. I countered by doing her trick and the peek-a-boo went on for some minutes. Delight was evident in Mary's face and eyes.

Profoundly Retarded: Jack, a classic or textbook example of microcephaly, was 29 years of age, ambulatory, and a favorite on his dormitory due, in large part, to his echophraxic skill. I held my hand over my head, Jack mimicked me. I then held my hands before me palms up--waving them up and down. When he placed his hands on mine and I moved them, patty-cake style, he started patting and smiled in delight. I stopped and patty-caked by myself and Jack did the same. In each case of imitation, Jack was thoroughly enjoying himself--although 29 years old, his delights in play are much like those of a two-and-a-half-year-old normal child.

Normal: Another winner in the ranks of normals of ages one to three is "trot-a-little-horsie." Everyone of us has witnessed a child in an adult's lap being "trotted" and have heard the squeals of delight when "Don't fall down" was followed by the drop. Let's see how this game translates when the one being "trotted" is an adult PMR weighing 156 pounds.

Profoundly Retarded: Jay was about 18 at the time and when I arrived for a tour of his dormitory he was sitting dejectedly on a bench. I walked over to him and held my hand out and smiled. After about a minute and a half, my patience was rewarded as Jack shook hands. Next, he stood up, put out both hands for me to grasp and I moved his hands up and down. As I moved his hands up and down, Jay jumped up and down in obvious delight. Next, Jay turned around and put his back to my front. Not knowing what to expect, I clasped my arms around his chest tightly. To my surprise, Jay abruptly extended his legs straight out leaving me holding him as the stick figures illustrate.

My class, as well as the houseparents who witnessed this, were astonished but Jay was elated and "insisted," in his way, that the game be continued. After about five occurrences, I had had enough so one of the male students took over. Actually, Jay's game was more of a reverse trot-a-little horsie.

Jay's example shows that one must be prepared for surprises when the PMR is involved. It also should alert readers to the need for design and development of suitable toys and fun equipment for these "giant babies." Some greatly enjoy being rocked, so think in giant cradle terms. Two-year-olds who are normal often enjoy turning lights on and off to the dismay of their parents. So too do some PMRs--they, like everyone else, enjoy causing something to happen, to create effects. And whenever we can tailor activities that safely allow them to act on something to create an effect, we should do so. These few examples are provided to show readers a few of the pleasures some PMRs seek. It is true, however, that we must pay attention to individual differences, and for each PMR in our class or dormitory we must let their spontaneous activities guide us in developing a catalog of preferred play and recreation. It should also be mentioned that if we are alert in our observations of play, we may on occasion isolate a profoundly retarded person whose level of play is advanced beyond his designated level of intelligence. Play offers us another opportunity to isolate subgroups within the ranks of the PMR.

Insofar as play objects are concerned and the meaning PMRs attach to them, our best guide is systematic observation. We know very little about perception in PMRs but certain theoretical guides may arise from the work of developmental psychologists such as Heinz Werner. Werner posits physiognomic perception as more characteristic of children than adults and this perception is the inclination to endow <u>things</u> and people with motor and emotional qualities. As such, very young children bestow sticks, stones, and other inanimate objects with feelings and although similar to anthropomorphism, Werner maintains physiognomic perception predates anthropomorphism. That very young normal children do assign emotions and actions to things is evident in daily experience. If the profoundly retarded person of adolescent or adult status also does this and remains fixated at the level of physiognomic perception, it would conceivably help explain the strong attachments to sticks, rocks, or strings that some PMRs display. For, to them, inanimate and animate may be more alike than we, in our adult sophistication, know. Sticks, rocks, and string we think of as dirty or soon to become so and, when we remove such objects from the PMR, we could be divesting them of a "playmate." Some do put up quite a struggle to retain their stick or rock. This line of thinking is admittedly highly speculative and is offered only to develop readers' empathic set and to assist in seeing some "bizarre" behaviors as being developmentally normal.

Finally, another speculative approach or method to get a handle on improving play and recreation for PMRs involves time distortion and age regression under hypnosis. As normal adults, our recall of the pleasures of the first three years of life is dimmed considerably by the socialization process. However, under hypnotic age regression those readers who are susceptible to hypnosis could be freed of adulthood and actually be instructed to practice two- or three-year-old play activities. And, if combined with the suggestion that an hour's practice of play were to occur (actually 10 minutes of time), others in in-service training could get some ideas as to how to play with PMRs. As mentioned in Chapter Six, to be repeatable in time compression hypnosis, an action must have been known to the body in previous experience, and <u>play</u> is an experience we have all enjoyed.

References

Abercrombie, M., Hickman, C., & Johnson, M. L. _A dictionary of biology_. Baltimore: Penguin Books, 1970.

Adamson, W., Runge, E., Killian, E., & Cleland, C. C. Use of tranquilizers for mentally deficient patients. _AMA Journal of Diseases of Children_, 1958, _159_, n.p.

Adis-Castro, G., & Berger, A. Olfactory discrimination of three etiological groups of mental defectives. _Training School Bulletin_, 1955, _52_, 24-30.

Albin, J. B. The treatment of pica (scavenging) behavior. _Mental Retardation_, 1977, _15_, 14-17.

Alcock, J. The evolution of the use of tools by feeding animals. _Evolution_, 1972, _26_, 464-473.

Aldrich, C., & Doll, E. A. Problem solving among idiots: The use of implements. _Journal of Social Psychology_, 1931, _2_, 306-334.

Allport, G. W. _The nature of prejudice_. Garden City, N.Y.: Doubleday, 1954.

Altman, R., Cleland, C. C., & Swartz, J. D. Social responsivity in the profoundly mentally retarded. Perceptual and Motor Skills, 1972, 34, 101-102.

Altman, R., Zucker, A., Talkington, L., & Cleland, C. C. Resident participation in institutional policy. Exceptional Children, 1978, 44, 619-621.

Ardrey, R. The social contract. New York: Atheneum, 1970.

Arnim, S. S., Diercks, C. C., & Pearson, E. A. What you need to know and do to prevent dental caries and periodontal disease. Journal of the North Carolina Dental Society, 1963, 46, n.p.

Azrin, N., & Armstrong, P. M. The "mini-meal"--A method for teaching eating skills to the profoundly retarded. Mental Retardation, 1973, 11, 9-13.

Barber, T. X. Suggested ("hypnotic") behavior: The trance paradigm versus an alternative paradigm. In E. Fromm & R. E. Shor (Eds.), Hypnosis. Chicago: Aldine, 1972.

Baumeister, A. A., & Kellas, G. Reaction time and mental retardation. In N. R. Ellis (Ed.), International review of research in mental retardation (Vol. 3). New York: Academic Press, 1968.

Baumeister, A. A. The American residential institution: Its history and character. In A. A. Baumeister & E. Butterfield (Eds.), Residential facilities for the mentally retarded. Chicago: Aldine, 1970.

Baumeister, A. A., & Forehand, R. Stereotyped acts. In N. R. Ellis (Ed.), International review of research in mental retardation (Vol. VI). New York: Academic Press, 1973.

Beecher, H. K. The powerful placebo. The Journal of the American Medical Association, 1955, (n.v.), 1602-1606.

Bensberg, G. J., Barnett, C. D., & Menius, J. A. A survey: Dental services in state residential facilities. Mental Retardation, 1966, 4, n.p.

Berkson, G., & Mason, W. A. Stereotyped movements of mental defectives: III. Situation effects. American Journal of Mental Deficiency, 1963, 68, 409-412.

Berkson, G., & Landesman-Dwyer, S. Behavioral research on severe and profound mental retardation. American Journal of Mental Deficiency, 1977, 81, 428-454.

Berlyne, D. E. Laughter, humor and play. In G. Lindzey & E. Aronson (Eds.), Handbook of social psychology (Vol. 3). Reading, Mass.: Addison-Wesley, 1969.

Bindra, D. Motivation: A systematic reinterpretation. New York: Ronald Press, 1959.

Binet, A. Fear in children. In R. H. Pollack & M. J. Brenner (Eds.), The experimental psychology of Alfred Binet. New York: Springer Publishing Co., 1969 (1895).

Bowman, P. Neglect of the profoundly retarded. PCMR Message, 1968, 11, 2.

Bursk, E. C., Clark, D. T., & Hidy, R. W. The world of business (Vol. 3). New York: Simon & Schuster, 1962.

Bush, S. A change of scene can be fatal. Psychology Today, 1977, 10, 32.

Butterfield, E., & Zigler, E. The influence of differing institutional social climates on the effectiveness of social reinforcement. American Journal of Mental Deficiency, 1965, 70, 48-56.

Butterworth, T., & Bower, J. R. Self-biting among feeble-minded persons. Pennsylvania Medical Journal, 1959, 62, 201-204.

Case, J. C., Harris, L. P., Sarma, N., & Lance, T. Eating behaviors in profoundly retarded males. (Unpublished manuscript, University of Texas at Austin, 1975)

Case, J. C. Vocal utterances of the PMR. In L. W. Talkington, C. C. Cleland, & R. O'Grady (Eds.), Research with the profoundly retarded, Vol. III. Austin, TX: Western Research Conference, 1977.

Case, J. C. Sleep postures and pre-sleep activity of the PMR. In J. D. Swartz, R. Eyman, C. C. Cleland, & R. O'Grady (Eds.), The profoundly mentally retarded, Vol. IV. Austin, TX: Western Research Conference, 1978.

Chaney, R. H. Respiratory complications in the profoundly retarded compared to those in the less retarded. In J. D. Swartz, R. Eyman, C. C. Cleland, & R. O'Grady (Eds.), _The profoundly mentally retarded_, Vol. IV. Austin, TX: Western Research Conference, 1978.

Chapman, T., & Foot, H. _Humor and laughter: Theory, research, and applications_. London: John Wiley & Sons, 1976.

Cleland, C. C. Severe retardation: Program suggestions. _Training School Bulletin_, 1962, _59_, 31-37.

Cleland, C. C. Intra-institutional problems IV: Communications. _Training School Bulletin_, 1967, _64_, 81-92.

Cleland, C. C. Commuting practices and labor transfer potential. _Training School Bulletin_, 1969, _66_, 115-126.

Cleland, C. C. Possibilities for social research among profoundly retarded? In R. Eyman, C. Meyers, & G. Tarjan (Eds.), _Sociobehavioral studies in mental retardation_. Washington, D.C.: American Association on Mental Deficiency, 1973.

Cleland, C. C. _Mental retardation: A developmental approach_. Englewood Cliffs, N.J.: Prentice-Hall, 1978.

Cleland, C. C., & Altman, R. Dissonance, arousal and anxiety: A taxonomic model for idiots' communications. _Psychological Reports_, 1969, _25_, 835-842.

Cleland, C. C., Altman, R., & Swartz, J. D. Dominance and submission in the profoundly retarded under conditions of strong motivation. _Journal of Psychology_, 1971, _78_, 185-191.

Cleland, C. C., Case, J. C., & Ford, B. L. Multiple births and pathology: A territorial perspective. _The Journal of Biological Psychology_, 1977, _19_, 10-15.

Cleland, C. C., & Clark, C. M. Sensory deprivation and aberrant behavior among idiots. _American Journal of Mental Deficiency_, 1966, _71_, 213-225.

Cleland, C. C., Manaster, G., & Case, J. C. IQs and etiologies. Unpublished manuscript, University of Texas, 1977.

Cleland, C. C., McGavern, M. L., & Case, J. C. Daybook analysis of disruptive behaviors of the profoundly retarded. Mental Retardation, 1976, 14, 33-35. (a)

Cleland, C. C., McGavern, M. L., Case, J. C., Grace, M., & Saperston, B. Approaches to decipherment of PMRs' communications. In C. C. Cleland, L. W. Talkington, & J. D. Swartz (Eds.), The profoundly mentally retarded, Vol. II. Austin, TX: Western Research Conference, 1976. (b)

Cleland, C. C., & Patton, W. F. Idiocy and longevity: A brief note. Psychological Reports, 1965, 17, 649-650.

Cleland, C. C., & Peck, R. F. Psychological determinants of tenure in institutional personnel. American Journal of Mental Deficiency, 1959, 63, 876-888.

Cleland, C. C., & Peck, R. F. Intra-institutional administrative problems: A paradigm for employee stimulation. Mental Retardation, 1967, 5, 2-8.

Cleland, C. C., Powell, H., & Talkington, L. W. Death in the profoundly retarded. Mental Retardation, 1971, 9, 36.

Cleland, C. C., Rago, W. V., Case, J. C., Jones, J., & McGavern, M. The institutional graveyard: A disappearing phenomenon. Texas Psychologist, 1977, 29, 4-6.

Cleland, C. C., Rago, W. V., & Case, J. C. Programming and decipherment approaches with the PMR. In L. Talkington, C. C. Cleland, & R. O'Grady (Eds.), Research with the profoundly retarded, Vol. III. Austin, TX: Western Research Conference, 1977.

Cleland, C. C., & Rago, W. V. Replication: A methodological note. Mental Retardation, 1978, 16, 273.

Cleland, C. C., Rago, W. V., & Jones, J. Coprophagy and boredom in the profoundly retarded. In J. D. Swartz, R. Eyman, C. C. Cleland, & R. O'Grady (Eds.), Research with the profoundly retarded, Vol. IV. Austin, TX: Western Research Conference, 1978.

Cleland, C. C., Rago, W. V., & Mukherjee, A. Tool use in profoundly retarded humans: A method of subgrouping. Bulletin of the Psychonomic Society, 1978, 12, 86-88.

Cleland, C. C., Seitz, S., & Patton, W. F. Birth order and ruralism as potential determinants of attendant tenure. *American Journal of Mental Deficiency*, 1967, *72*, 428-434.

Cleland, C. C., & Sluyter, G. V. The heterobedfast ward: A model for translating "normalization" into practice. *Mental Retardation*, 1973, *11*, 44-46.

Cleland, C. C., Sluyter, G. V., & Rago, W. V. De-institutionalization of the mentally retarded: Considerations for preventing future shock. *Journal of Applied Rehabilitation Counseling*, 1977, *7*, 249-255.

Cleland, C. C., & Swartz, J. D. *Mental retardation: Approaches to institutional change*. New York: Grune & Stratton, 1969.

Cofer, C. N., & Appley, M. H. *Motivation: Theory and research*. New York: Wiley, 1964.

Conolly, J. *The construction and government of lunatic asylums*. London: Dawsons of Pall Mall, 1968. (orig. publ. 1847)

Cooke, W. R., & Weaver, J. D. Gynecologic investigation of patients in state eleemosynary institutions. *Texas Medical Journal*, 1948, *43*, 765-767.

Crook, J. L. Observational learning of fear in monkeys. Unpublished manuscript, University of Pennsylvania, 1967.

Darwin, C. *The expression of emotion in man and animals*. Chicago: University of Chicago Press, 1965. (orig. publ. 1872)

Davenport, R. K., & Berkson, G. Stereotyped movements of mental defectives: II. Effects of novel objects. *American Journal of Mental Deficiency*, 1963, *67*, 879-882.

Deacon, K. F. An experiment in the cottage training of low-grade defectives. *American Journal of Mental Deficiency*, 1954, *58*, 644-649.

Deane, W., & Ansbacher, H. L. Attendant-patient commonality as a psychotherapeutic factor. *Journal of Individual Psychology*, 1962, *18*, 157-167.

Delaney, J., Lupton, M. J., & Toth, E. *The curse: A cultural history of menstruation*. New York: Dutton, 1976.

DeRudolph, G. An experiment in the treatment of masturbation in oligophrenia. *American Journal of Mental Deficiency*, 1954, *58*, 644-649.

DeVore, I. *Primate behavior*. New York: Holt, Rinehart & Winston, 1965.

Dingman, H. F., Cleland, C. C., & Swartz, J. D. Institutional "wisdom" as expressed through folklore. *Mental Retardation*, 1970, *6*, 2-8.

Doll, E. A. Growth studies in social competence. *American Journal of Mental Deficiency*, 1939, *44*, 90-96.

Doll, E. A. *Measurement of social competence*. Princeton, N.J.: Educational Test Bureau, 1953. (a)

Doll, E. A. *The measurement of social competence: A manual for the Vineland Social Maturity Scale*. Minneapolis: Educational Testing Bureau, 1953. (b)

Dollard, J., Doob, L. W., Mowrer, O. H., & Sears, R. R. *Frustration and aggression*. New Haven: Yale University Press, 1939.

Dorland, W. A. N. (Ed.) *The American Illustrated Medical Dictionary*, 22nd Ed. Philadelphia: W. B. Saunders, 1951.

Edelson, E. Let there be natural light. *Family Health*, 1974, June, 18-19.

Edgerton, R. B. *The cloak of competence*. Berkeley: University of California Press, 1967.

Ellis, N. R. Toilet training the severely defective patient: An S-R reinforcement analysis. *American Journal of Mental Deficiency*, 1963, *68*, 98-103.

Ellis, N. R. Current issues in mental retardation. *Division 33 Newsletter, American Psychological Associates*, 1975, *2*, 1-2.

English, H. B., & English, A. C. *A comprehensive dictionary of psychological and psychoanalytic terms*. New York: Longmans, Green & Co., 1958.

Erickson, M. H. Psychological significance of physical restraint to mental patients. American Journal of Psychiatry, 1949, 105, 612-614.

Erikson, E. H. Childhood and society (2nd Ed.). New York: W. W. Norton & Co., Inc., 1963.

Eyman, R., & Call, T. The effects of behavior problems on the placement of the profoundly retarded. In L. W. Talkington, C. C. Cleland, & R. S. O'Grady (Eds.), Research with the profoundly retarded, Vol. III. Austin, TX: Western Research Conference, 1977.

Fantz, R. L. Pattern vision in newborn infants. Science, 1963, 140, 296-298.

Fenichel, O. The psychoanalytic theory of neurosis. New York: W. W. Norton & Co., 1945.

Freud, A., & Dann, S. An experiment in group upbringing. Psychoanalytic Study of the Child, 1951, 6, 127-168.

Frey, A. H. Behavioral biophysics. Psychological Bulletin, 1965, 63, 322-337.

Fromm, E., & Shor, R. E. Hypnosis. Chicago: Aldine, 1972.

Fuller, P. R. Operant conditioning of a vegetative human organism. American Journal of Psychology, 1949, 62, 587-590.

Gagnon, F. Contribution to the etiology and prevention of cancer of the cervix of the uterus. American Journal of Obstetrics and Gynecology, 1950, 60, 516-522.

Gallup, G. G. Towards an operational definition of self-awareness. In R. H. Tuttle (Ed.), Socio-ecology and psychology of primates. The Hague, Netherlands: Mouton, 1975.

Gebhard, P. H. Sexual behavior of the mentally retarded. In F. de la Cruz & G. LaVeck (Eds.), Human sexuality and the mentally retarded. New York: Brunner/Mazel, 1973.

Glenn, L. E., Nerbonne, G. P., & Tolhurst, G. C. Environmental noise in a residential institution for mentally retarded persons. American Journal of Mental Deficiency, 1978, 82, 594-597.

Goldenson, R. M. The encyclopedia of human behavior, Vols. I & II. Garden City, N.Y.: Doubleday, 1970.

Goldstein, A. P., & Simonson, N. R. Social psychological approaches to psychotherapy research. In A. E. Bergin & S. L. Garfield (Eds.), Handbook of psychotherapy and behavior change. New York: John Wiley, 1971.

Gorman, W. Flavor, taste and the psychology of smell. Springfield, Ill.: Charles C Thomas, 1964.

Grossman, H. J. (Ed.) Manual on terminology and classification in mental retardation. Washington, D.C.: American Association on Mental Deficiency, Special Publication Series, 1977 (Revised).

Hackerman, N. Ignorance as the driving force. Science, 1974, 183 (editor-page).

Harris, L. P. Self-recognition among institutionalized profoundly retarded males: A replication. Bulletin of the Psychonomic Society, 1977, 9, 43-44.

Hebb, D. O., & Thompson, W. R. The social significance of animal studies. In G. Lindzey (Ed.), Handbook of social psychology, Vol. I. Cambridge: Addison, Wesley, 1954.

Hereford, S. M., Cleland, C. C., & Fellner, M. Territoriality and scent-marking: A study of profoundly retarded enuretics and encopretics. American Journal of Mental Deficiency, 1973, 77, 426-430.

Hinde, R. A. Animal behavior (2nd Ed.). New York: McGraw-Hill, 1970.

Hinsie, L., & Shatzky, J. Psychiatric dictionary. New York: Oxford University Press, 1953.

Holt, L. E., & McIntosh, R. Diseases of infancy and childhood. New York: Appleton-Century, 1933.

Hospital Week. Life prolonging treatments may be withheld. 1976, 12, 1.

Hunt, J. McV. Experience and the development of motivation: Some reinterpretations. Child Development, 1960, 31, 489-504.

Hutt, M. L., & Gibby, R. G. The mentally retarded child, 2nd Ed. Boston: Allyn & Bacon, 1965.

Jackson, G. M., Johnson, C. R., & Ackron, G. S. Food satiation as a procedure to decelerate vomiting. American Journal of Mental Deficiency, 1975, 80, 223-227.

Jones, J., & Shirley, J. Naturalistic studies of PMR humor. In J. D. Swartz, R. K. Eyman, C. C. Cleland, & R. O'Grady (Eds.), The profoundly mentally retarded, Vol. IV. Austin, TX: Western Research Conference, 1978.

Jouvet, M. The states of sleep. Scientific American, 1967, 216, 62-72.

Kalmus, H. Inherited sense defects. Scientific American, Reprint No. 406, San Francisco: W. H. Freeman and Company, Publishers, 1952.

Kalmus, H., & Hubbard, H. The chemical senses in health and disease. Springfield, Ill.: Charles C Thomas, 1960.

Kamil-Goshgarian, N., Sackett, G., & Parke, R. D. Looking at pictures: Nonsocial and social preference tests in "untestable" children. In C. C. Cleland, J. D. Swartz, & L. W. Talkington (Eds.), Research in profound retardation, Vol. II. Austin, TX: Western Research Conference, 1976.

Kanner, L. Exoneration of the feebleminded. American Journal of Psychiatry, 1942, 99, 17-22.

Kanner, L. Child psychiatry (2nd Ed.). Springfield, Ill.: Charles C Thomas, 1950.

Karelitz, S., & Fisichelli, V. R. The cry thresholds of normal infants and those with brain damage. Journal of Pediatrics, 1962, 61, 679-685.

Kaufman, M., & Levitt, H. A study of three stereotyped behaviors in institutionalized mental defectives. American Journal of Mental Deficiency, 1965, 69, 467-473.

Kennedy, F. The problem of social control of a congenital defective: Education, sterilization, euthanasia. American Journal of Psychiatry, 1942, 98, 13-16.

Kessler, J. Psychopathology of childhood. Englewood Cliffs, N.J.: Prentice-Hall, 1966.

Keys, A. B., Brozek, J., Heuschel, A., Mickelson, O., & Taylor, H. L. The biology of human starvation. Minneapolis: University of Minnesota Press, 1950.

Keyes, J. B. Pilot program lowers patient aggression. Feelings, 1978, 3, 2.

Klaber, M. M., & Butterfield, E. C. Stereotyped rocking--a measure of institution and ward effectiveness. American Journal of Mental Deficiency, 1968, 73, 13-20.

Kleitman, N. Patterns of dreaming. In T. J. Teyler (Ed.), Altered states of awareness. San Francisco: W. H. Freeman and Company, Publishers, 1972.

Knobloch, H., & Lilienfeld, A. M. Neuropsychiatric sequelae of prematurity: A longitudinal study. Journal of the American Medical Association, 1956, 161, 581-585.

Kohler, W. The mentality of apes. New York: Harcourt, Brace, Jovanovich, 1925.

Kraus, B. S., Clark, G. R., & Oka, S. W. Mental retardation and abnormalities of the dentition. American Journal of Mental Deficiency, 1968, 72, 905-917.

Kudlaty, B. M. Comparative study of social case histories from public institutions for mentally retarded in the United States. Unpublished study, University of Texas at Austin, 1977.

Landesman-Dwyer, S., & Sackett, G. A research strategy for studying non-ambulatory profoundly mentally retarded individuals. In C. C. Cleland & L. W. Talkington (Eds.), Research with the profoundly retarded. Austin, TX: Western Research Conference, 1975.

Langer, S. Feeling and form. New York: Charles Scribner's Sons, 1953.

Lawick-Goodall, J. V. The behavior of free-living chimpanzees in the Gombe Stream Reserve. Animal Behavior Monographs, 1968, 9(3), 161-311.

Lee, J. M. Gynecology of the profoundly retarded. Unpublished doctoral dissertation, University of Texas at Austin, 1971.

Levine, J. Motivation in humor. New York: Atherton Press, 1969.

Libb, J. W. Fixed-interval frustrative nonreward in profound retardates. Psychonomic Science, 1970, 19, 219-220.

Libby, D. G., & Phillips, E. Eliminating rumination behavior in a profoundly retarded adolescent: An exploratory study. Mental Retardation, 1978, 16, 57.

Lindsley, O. R. Direct measurement and prothesis of retarded behavior. Journal of Education, 1964, 157, 62-81.

Lindsley, O. R. Can deficiency produce specific superiority--The challenge of the idiot savant. Exceptional Children, 1965, 31, 225-232.

Lorenz, K. King Solomon's ring. New York: Harper & Row, 1952.

Lorenzo, J. M. Acculturation as a function of time. Unpublished doctoral dissertation, University of Texas at Austin, 1955.

Lowenfeld, V., & Brittain, L. Creative and mental growth. London: Macmillan Co., 1969.

MacAndrew, C. The role of "knowledge at hand" in the practical management of institutionalized "idiots." In R. Eyman, C. E. Meyers, & G. Tarjan (Eds.), Sociobehavioral studies in mental retardation, Monograph No. 1. Washington, D.C.: American Association on Mental Deficiency, 1973.

MacAndrew, C., & Edgerton, R. The everyday life of institutionalized "idiots." Human Organization, 1964, 23, 312-318. (a)

MacAndrew, C., & Edgerton, R. IQ and the social competence of the profoundly retarded. American Journal of Mental Deficiency, 1964, 69, 385-390. (b)

MacAndrew, C., & Edgerton, R. B. On the possibility of friendship. American Journal of Mental Deficiency, 1966, 70, 612-621.

McClintock, M. K. Scents: What they reveal. Family Health, 1971, 3, 14.

McGavern, M. L., Cleland, C. C., & Swartz, J. D. Locating the profoundly retarded. Mental Retardation, 1974, 12, 49-50.

MacMillan, D. L. Mental retardation in school and society. Boston: Little, Brown & Co., 1977.

Maslow, A. H. Motivation and personality. New York: Harper & Row, 1954.

Melzack, R., & Scott, T. H. The effects of early experience on the response to pain. Journal of Comparative and Physiological Psychology, 1957, 50, 155-161.

Mental retardation: Past and present. Washington, D.C.: President's Committee on Mental Retardation, 1977.

Mercer, J. The myth of 3% prevalence. In R. Eyman, C. Meyers, & G. Tarjan (Eds.), Sociobehavioral studies in mental retardation. Washington, D.C.: American Association on Mental Deficiency, Monograph No. 1, 1973.

Merry, F. K., & Merry, R. V. The first two decades of life (2nd Ed.). New York: Harper, 1958.

Metzler, R. K. The use of music as a reinforcer to increase imitative behavior in severely and profoundly retarded female residents. Journal of Music Therapy, 1974, 8, 67-73.

Miller, C. R. Deinstitutionalization and mortality trends for the profoundly mentally retarded. In C. C. Cleland & L. W. Talkington (Eds.), Research with the profoundly retarded, Vol. I. Austin, TX: Western Research Conference, 1975.

Miller, C. R. Subtypes of the PMR: Implications for placement and progress. In C. C. Cleland, J. D. Swartz, & L. W. Talkington (Eds.), The profoundly mentally retarded, Vol. II. Austin, TX: Western Research Conference, 1976.

Miller, S. R., Miller, T., & Repp, A. Are profoundly and severely retarded people given access to the least restrictive environment? Mental Retardation, 1978, 16, 123-126.

Mitchell, G. Abnormal behavior in primates. In L. A. Rosenblum (Ed.), Primate behavior. New York: Academic Press, 1970.

Mitchell, L., Doctor, R. M., & Butler, D. C. Attitudes of caretakers toward the sexual behavior of mentally retarded persons. American Journal of Mental Deficiency, 1978, 83, 289-296.

Morales, N. The social competence of idiots. American Journal of Mental Deficiency, 1942, 47, 209-214.

Morris, J. V. The habit training of severely retarded defectives. American Journal of Mental Deficiency, 1957, 61, 474-477.

Müller-Schwarze, D. Scents of monkeys and deer. American Psychologist, 1971, 26, 209-210.

Murphy, A. T. Speech pathology and mental subnormality: A personal conception. Journal of Education, 1964, 147, 25-44.

Neer, R. M. Stimulation by artificial lighting of calcium absorption in elderly human subjects. Nature, 1971, 229, 255-257.

Nirje, B. The normalization princple and its human management implications. In R. B. Kugel & W. Wolfensberger (Eds.), Changing patterns in residential services for the mentally retarded. Washington, D.C.: President's Committee on Mental Retardation, 1969.

Nourse, A. E., Dubos, R., Margenau, M., & Snow, C. P. (Eds.) The body. New York: Time, Inc., 1964.

Nueva-España, D. S., & Fish, C. H. Olfactory assessment related to diagnosis and prognosis of human viability. In C. C. Cleland, J. D. Swartz, & L. W. Talkington (Eds.), The profoundly mentally retarded, Vol. II. Western Research Conference, 1976.

O'Grady, R., & Talkington, L. W. Selected behavioral concomitants of profound retardation. In C. C. Cleland, J. D. Swartz, & L. W. Talkington (Eds.), The profoundly mentally retarded, Vol. II. Austin, TX: Western Research Conference, 1977.

Ostwald, P. F. Visual denotation of human sounds. Archives of General Psychiatry, 1960, 3, 117-121.

Ostwald, P. F. Soundmaking: The acoustic communication of emotion. Springfield, Ill.: Charles C Thomas, 1963.

Ott, J. N. Health and light. New York: Pocket Books, 1973.

Overbeck, D. Elimination of rumination in a profoundly retarded adult through an in vivo satiation procedure. In L. W. Talkington, C. C. Cleland, & R. S. O'Grady (Eds.), Research with the profoundly retarded, Vol. III. Austin, TX: Western Research Conference, 1977.

Paluck, R. J., Esser, A. H. Territorial behavior as an indicator of changes in clinical behavioral conditions of severely retarded boys. American Journal of Mental Deficiency, 1971, 76, 284-290.

Pattullo, A. A., & Barnard, K. E. Teaching menstrual hygiene to the mentally retarded. American Journal of Neurology, 1968, 68, 2572-2577.

Payne, D. Regional cooperation in mental retardation data collection. Mental Retardation, 1968, 6, 52-53.

Pechacek, T., Cleland, C. C., & Bell, K. Self-recognition in profoundly retarded males. Bulletin of the Psychonomic Society, 1973, 1, 327-330.

Platt, J. J., Sutker, L. W., & James, W. T. Social facilitation of eating behavior in young opossums: II. The effects of isolation. Psychonomic Science, 1968, 10, 267-268.

Pratt, C. L., & Sackett, G. P. Selection of social partners as a function of peer contact during rearing. Science, 1967, 155, 1133-1135.

Pulgram, E. Introduction to the spectography of speech. The Hague, Netherlands: Mouton & Co., 1959.

Rago, W. V. Territoriality in the profoundly mentally retarded. In C. C. Cleland, L. W. Talkington, & J. D. Swartz (Eds.), Second annual proceedings of the Western Research Conference. San Antonio, TX: 1976.

Rago, W. V., & Cleland, C. C. Altruistic behavior in a profoundly retarded male. _Sensory World_, 1978, _3_, 16-17.

Ralls, K. Mammalian scent-marking. _Science_, 1971, _171_, 443-449.

Rank, O. _The trauma of birth_. New York: Harcourt Brace & Jovanovich, 1929.

Raynes, N. V., Pratt, M. W., & Roses, S. Aides' involvement in decision-making and the quality of care in institutional settings. _American Journal of Mental Deficiency_, 1977, _81_, 570-577.

Rheingold, H. L., Stanley, W. C., & Cooley, J. A. Method of studying exploratory behavior in infants. _Science_, 1962, _136_, 1054-1055.

Ribble, M. A. _The rights of infants_. New York: Columbia University Press, 1965.

Rice, H. K., McDaniel, M., Stallings, V., & Gatz, M. J. Operant behavior in vegetative patients, II. _Psychological Record_, 1967, _17_, 449-460.

Rimland, B. _Infantile autism_. Englewood Cliffs, N.J.: Prentice-Hall, 1964.

Robinson, H. B., & Robinson, N. M. _The mentally retarded child_. New York: McGraw-Hill, 1965.

Robinson, N., & Robinson, H. B. _The mentally retarded child_ (2nd Ed.). New York: McGraw-Hill, 1976.

Roe, A., & Simpson, G. G. (Eds.) _Behavior and evolution_. New Haven: Yale University Press, 1958.

Romig, D., & Cleland, C. C. Educational applications of humanistic psychology. _Journal of School Psychology_, 1972, _10_, 289-298.

Rosenhan, D. L. On being sane in insane places. _Science_, 1973, _179_, 250-258.

Ross, B. K., & Sherrill, C. Changes in profoundly retarded adult females during a walking program. In L. W. Talkington, C. C. Cleland, & R. S. O'Grady (Eds.), _Research with the profoundly retarded_, Vol. III. Austin, TX: Western Research Conference, 1977.

Rubert, S. L., Hollander, M. H., & Mehrhoff, E. G. Olfactory hallucinations. *Archives of General Psychiatry*, 1961, *5*, 313-318.

Sabagh, G., Dingman, H. F., Tarjan, G., & Wright, S. W. Social class and ethnic status of patients admitted to a state hospital for the retarded. *Pacific Sociological Review*, 1959, *2*, 76-80.

Scott, J. P. *Aggression*. Chicago: University of Chicago Press, 1958.

Segal, J. How much sleep do you need? In *Annual editions: Readings in Psychology '74 and '75*. Sluice Dockict: Duskin Publ., 1974.

Selye, H. The general adaptation syndrome and the diseases of adaptation. *Journal of Clinical Endocrinology*, 1946, *6*, 117.

Shaller, G. B. *The mountain gorilla, ecology and behavior*. Chicago: University of Chicago Press, 1963.

Shor, R. E., & Orne, E. C. *The Harvard group scale of hypnotic susceptibility*, Form A. Palo Alto, Calif.: Consulting Psychologists Press, 1962.

Southwick, C. H. Experimental studies in intratroop aggression in rhesus monkeys. *American Zoologist*, 1966, *6*, 3-10.

Southwick, C. H. An experimental study of intratroop agonistic behavior in rhesus monkeys. *Behavior*, 1967, *28*, 182-209.

Spreiregen, P. D. *Urban design: The architecture of towns and cities*. New York: McGraw-Hill, 1965.

Stephenson, W. *The study of behavior: Q-technique and its methodology*. Chicago: University of Chicago Press, 1953.

Stockton, C. Artistic expressions in the profoundly retarded. Unpublished study, University of Texas at Austin, 1973.

Sullivan, H. S. *Schizophrenia as a human process*. New York: W. W. Norton & Co., Inc., 1962.

Swartz, J. D., Cleland, C. C., & Altman, R. Time capsules for research in profound retardation. Mental Retardation, 1971, 9, 29-30.

Swartz, J. D., & Cleland, C. C. Multihandicapped mentally retarded. Austin, TX: The Hogg Foundation for Mental Health, University of Texas 1973.

Takooshian, H., Haber, S., & Lucido, D. J. Who wouldn't help a lost child? You, maybe. Psychology Today, 1977, 10, 67-88.

Talkington, L. W., Hall, S., & Cleland, C. C. Behavioral correlates of noncommunicators. Psychological Record, 1971, 21, 213-217.

Talkington, L. W., & Riley, J. Reduction diets and aggression in institutionalized mentally retarded. American Journal of Mental Deficiency, 1971, 76, 370-372.

Thompson, T., & Grabowski, J. Behavior modification of the mentally retarded. New York: Oxford University Press, 1972.

Thorpe, L. P. Child psychology and development (2nd Ed.). New York: Ronald Press, 1955.

Tillman, P., Grot, J., & Steinke, J. Blood lead levels in an institutionalized developmentally disabled population. Mental Retardation, 1978, 16, 265-266.

Tinbergen, N. Ethology and stress diseases. Science, 1974, 185, 20-27.

Tredgold, A. A textbook of mental deficiency, Baltimore: Williams & Wilkens, 1937.

Tucker, J. An investigation into the relationship between personal space and various stress indices in educational environments. Unpublished doctoral dissertation, University of Texas at Austin, 1972.

Uno, T., Seitel, A., & Cleland, C. C. Operant preferences for male and female voices by profoundly retarded males. Psychological Reports, 1975, 36, 891-894.

Van Lawick-Goodall, J. The behavior of free-living chimpanzees in the Gombe Stream Reserve. Animal Behavior Monographs, 1968, 1, 161-311.

Wald, G. Determinancy, individuality, and the problem of free will. In J. R. Platt (Ed.), _New views of the nature of man_. Chicago: The University of Chicago Press, 1965.

Watson, C. The effects of feeding schedule alterations on behavior and weight of profoundly retarded humans. Unpublished doctoral dissertation, University of Texas at Austin, 1973.

Webster's new collegiate dictionary. Springfield, Mass.: G. & C. Merriam, 1949.

Weitzenhoffer, A. M., & Hilgard, E. R. _Revised Stanford Profile Scales of Hypnotic Susceptibility, Forms I and II_. Palo Alto, Calif.: Consulting Psychologists Press, 1967.

Werner, H. _Comparative psychology of mental development_. New York: Science Editions, 1961.

Willette, J. C., & Savage, J. A. Positive motivation: A method for promoting oral health among mentally retarded people. _Mental Retardation_, 1978, _16_, 233-235.

Wurtman, R. J. The effect of light on the human body. _Scientific American_, 1975, _233_, 68-77.

Zaharia, E. S., & Baumeister, A. A. Estimated position replacement costs for technician personnel in a state's public facilities. _Mental Retardation_, 1978, _16_, 131-134.

Zimbardo, P. G. _The cognitive control of motivation_. Glenview, Ill.: Scott, Foresman & Co., 1969.

Index